Promoting Workplace Well-Being

Also by Neil Thompson

COMMUNICATION AND LANGUAGE (*Palgrave Macmillan*)

LOSS AND GRIEF (*Palgrave Macmillan*)

PROMOTING EQUALITY, second edition (*Palgrave Macmillan*)

PEOPLE PROBLEMS (*Palgrave Macmillan*)

PROMOTING WORKPLACE LEARNING (*The Policy Press*)

POWER AND EMPOWERMENT (*Russell House Publishing*)

THE CRITICALLY REFLECTIVE PRACTITIONER, with Sue Thompson (*Palgrave Macmillan*)

LOSS, GRIEF AND TRAUMA IN THE WORKPLACE (*Baywood*)

PEOPLE SKILLS, third edition (*Palgrave Macmillan*)

Promoting Workplace Well-Being

Edited by
Neil Thompson and John Bates

Selection and editorial content © Neil Thompson and John Bates 2009
Individual content © contributors 2009

All rights reserved. No reproduction, copy or transmission of this publication may be made without written permission.

No portion of this publication may be reproduced, copied or transmitted save with written permission or in accordance with the provisions of the Copyright, Designs and Patents Act 1988, or under the terms of any licence permitting limited copying issued by the Copyright Licensing Agency, Saffron House, 6–10 Kirby Street, London EC1N 8TS.

Any person who does any unauthorized act in relation to this publication may be liable to criminal prosecution and civil claims for damages.

The authors have asserted their rights to be identified
as the authors of this work in accordance with the Copyright, Designs and Patents Act 1988.

First published 2009 by
PALGRAVE MACMILLAN

Palgrave Macmillan in the UK is an imprint of Macmillan Publishers Limited, registered in England, company number 785998, of Houndmills, Basingstoke, Hampshire RG21 6XS.

Palgrave Macmillan in the US is a division of St Martin's Press LLC,
175 Fifth Avenue, New York, NY 10010.

Palgrave Macmillan is the global academic imprint of the above companies and has companies and representatives throughout the world.

Palgrave® and Macmillan® are registered trademarks in the United States, the United Kingdom, Europe and other countries.

ISBN: 978–0–230–22192–5 hardback

This book is printed on paper suitable for recycling and made from fully managed and sustained forest sources. Logging, pulping and manufacturing processes are expected to conform to the environmental regulations of the country of origin.

A catalogue record for this book is available from the British Library.

A catalog record for this book is available from the Library of Congress.

10 9 8 7 6 5 4 3 2 1
18 17 16 15 14 13 12 11 10 09

Printed and bound in Great Britain by
CPI Antony Rowe, Chippenham and Eastbourne

for Beth and Harry

Contents

List of Tables and Figures	ix
Preface	x
The Editors	xii
The Contributors	xiii
Introduction: Work and Well-Being	xvi
Neil Thompson and John Bates	

Part 1   Workplace Problems   1

1 Stress   3
   Neil Thompson

2 Conflict, Aggression and Bullying   16
   Neil Thompson

3 Addressing Drug and Alcohol Use in the Workplace   27
   Iolo Madoc-Jones and Brian Heath

4 Mental Health Problems in the Workplace   42
   Suki Desai

5 Racism   54
   Gurnam Singh

6 Loss, Grief and Trauma   71
   Neil Thompson and Sue Thompson

Part 2   Promoting Well-Being   83

7 Promoting Workplace Learning: Challenges and Pitfalls   85
   John Bates

8 Leading to Well-Being   103
   Peter Gilbert

9	Managing Sickness Absence *Neil Thompson*	117
10	Women-Friendly Workplaces *Mary Tehan*	128
11	Spirituality in the Workplace *Bernard Moss*	141

Part 3   International Perspectives — 155

12	The Darker Side of the American Workplace *Seth Allcorn*	157
13	A Hong Kong Perspective *Siu-man Ng, Ted C. T. Fong and Xiao-lu Wang*	174
14	Death, Illness and Grief: Foundational Mysteries for Transforming and Humanizing Work *John Bottomley*	189
15	Promoting 'Labour Well-Being in a Classless Society': An Initial Examination of the Unfulfilled Prophecy. *Vassilis Ioakimidis and Georgios Bithymitris*	203

Index — 222

List of Tables and Figures

Tables

5.1	BME practice teachers' experiences of racism	64
10.1	Human rights standards related to palliative care	134
15.1	Classification by occupation	208
15.2	Proportion of employees against total employed within the Tertiary Sector by one-digit groups of individual occupations	209
15.3	Working hours per employment category	217

Figures

10.1	Three domains of an integrated approach to evaluation for grief support in the workplace	138
15.1	Employees need strong trade unions	210
15.2	Perceptions about unions	210
15.3	Belief that businesses are only interested in profits	211
15.4	Family and individual incomes	212
15.5	Perceptions of household current income	213
15.6	To what extent they control their own work	215
15.7	Work organization	215
15.8	Lack of time to cope with workload	216
15.9	Job requires very intensive work	216

Preface

The idea that an organization's most important resource is its human resource – its people – is a long-standing one, although it often remains at a rhetorical level without being translated into practice. The development of the notion of 'workplace well-being' is part of an attempt to take seriously the idea that people are indeed important. This monograph explores the significance of addressing people's occupational welfare needs as part of developing a more sophisticated, critical approach to human resource management. Drawing on contemporary research and theorizing, it adopts a problem-solving, empowering approach to workplace well-being issues.

Workplace problems, such as: stress; bullying and harassment; conflict; loss, grief and trauma; mental health problems; drug and alcohol problems and so on are generally dealt with in one of three ways (or a combination of them):

- *The ostrich approach.* This involves trying to pretend that the problems do not exist or that they are not important. This is a very dangerous strategy that can seriously backfire.
- *The occupational health approach.* This involves seeing the problems in predominantly if not exclusively medical terms. While there may indeed be a medical dimension (ill health as a result of stress, for example), a primary focus on occupational health presents a narrow and distorted view of the situation (for example, by neglecting key issues, such as power).
- *The psychological approach (workplace counselling and employee assistance programmes).* Again there is clearly a psychological dimension to workplace problems, but there are dangers involved in privileging the psychological dimension (for example, by assuming that counselling is the appropriate response in the vast majority of cases), as this too presents a narrow and distorted view of a much more complex field of study by failing to recognize the significance of the wider social and political context.

The book provides a platform for developing a critical understanding of a range of workplace problems without making the mistakes of these three approaches. It seeks to develop a holistic approach based on a multidisciplinary understanding of the complex issues involved. In particular, the book aims to:

- Establish the importance of dealing effectively with human relations problems in the workplace in order to:
  - Maximize organizational effectiveness;
  - Promote the health, safety and welfare of employees;
  - Contribute to broader family and community welfare issues (workplace problems carry over into broader family and community arenas);
  - Reduce the risk of industrial relations problems; and
  - Reduce the need for litigation, tribunals and other such costly and potentially stressful processes.
- Provide a multidisciplinary critical analysis of the problems commonly encountered in the workplace.
- Explore strategies for dealing with such problems as part of the development of a critical approach to 'workplace well-being'.

The book does not, of course, provide 'all the answers', but it should at least provide a platform for further discussion, debate and development.

The Editors

Neil Thompson is a director of Avenue Consulting, a company based in Wales offering training and consultancy in relation to various aspects of well-being (www.avenueconsulting.co.uk). He has held full or honorary professorships at four UK universities and has been a speaker at conferences and seminars in the United Kingdom, Ireland, Italy, Spain, Norway, Greece, the Czech Republic, the Netherlands, India, Hong Kong, Australia, the United States and Canada. He has over 100 publications to his name, including several best-selling books. Neil is a Fellow of the Chartered Institute of Personnel and Development, the Higher Education Academy, the Royal Society of Arts (elected on the basis of his contribution to workplace learning) and a Life Fellow of the Institute for Welsh Affairs. He currently edits the US-based international journal, *Illness, Crisis & Loss* and the quarterly e-zine, *Well-being* (www.well-being.org.uk). His website is at www.neilthompson.info.

John Bates EdD is an associate professor and the head of department of Social Work, Care and Justice at Liverpool Hope University. He has spent many years working in the human services and has a long-standing interest in adult learning. Recent research has focused on globalization and its impact on training and education in the human services. He has spoken at conferences in the United States, Canada, Hong Kong, Latvia and the United Kingdom. John is a fellow of the Higher Education Academy and is the author of a number of scholarly articles and book chapters, and is co-editor of a book on child protection. He is a member of the editorial board of *Illness, Crisis & Loss*.

The Contributors

Seth Allcorn PhD is the Vice-President for Business and Finance of the University of New England. Dr Allcorn has over 20 years of experience working with physicians, hospitals and academic medical centres. He has served as Associate and Assistant Dean for three schools of medicine and as a medicine department administrator at a fourth. He has worked for 25 years as a part-time and full-time organizational consulting specialist in the management of change, strategic planning and organizational restructuring. He is the author or co-author of 12 books and over 60 papers that have appeared in scholarly and practitioner journals. He is a founding member of the International Society for the Psychoanalytic Study of Organizations.

Giorgos Bithymitris is a PhD candidate in social policy at Panteion University of Social and Political Sciences. His main research interests concern the political sociology of trade union movements, labour history and organized interests in contemporary Greece.

John Bottomley is Director of Creative Ministries Network, an agency of the Uniting Church in Australia. After a congregational ministry in Melbourne's outer suburbs, his experience as a researcher for the union Shop Committee in a ship-building yard galvanized his interest in workplace issues. This interest has developed into a concern for addressing the trauma caused by the deep-seated violence in the way work is shaped by and shapes both our free-market economy and our political system of government. John seeks to integrate the arts and faith with a commitment to personal and social transformation for healing, justice and reconciliation.

Suki Desai currently works as a Senior Lecturer at the University of Hull. She has experience of working in multidisciplinary mental health settings including hospital, community-based teams and the voluntary sector. Suki has also previously worked as Regional Director for the Mental Health Act Commission and has sat on Mental Health Review Tribunals as a lay member.

Peter Gilbert is Professor of Social Work and Spirituality, Staffordshire University, NIMHE Project Lead on Spirituality, and Visiting Professor with both Birmingham and Solihull NHS Foundation Trust and the

University of Worcester. Peter is keen to ensure the integration of theory with practice. He has co-authored a training pack on *Supervision and Leadership* with Neil Thompson, and is the author of *Leadership: Being Effective and Remaining Human* (2005) and *The Value of Everything* (2003). Peter and his co-editors published *Spirituality, Values and Mental Health* in 2007. He is currently working on a position paper for the Social Care Institute for Excellence on leadership.

Brian Heath is Principal Lecturer in occupational and public health at Glyndwr University and is a Fellow of the Royal Society of Public Health, for whom he is also a registered tutor and examiner. In addition to lecturing, Brian has consulted extensively in a range of industries including aerospace, construction, petrochemical, pharmaceutical, process manufacturing, health care and engineering. The focus of this work has been on health and welfare in the workplace and on health protection systems.

Vassilis Ioakimidis PhD is a Lecturer in social work at Liverpool Hope University. His main research interests include international social work, history of Greek social welfare and radical approaches in social work theory and practice. Vasillis actively participates in the Social Work Action Network, a radical social work movement that opposes managerialism and promotes social work theory and practice based on social justice.

Iolo Madoc-Jones began his working life as a probation officer in the North West of England, working with a diverse client group, many of whom had problems in relation to alcohol and drug misuse. He then moved into academia and is currently Principal Lecturer in Criminal Justice at Glyndwr University in North Wales. He has published widely on issues related to justice and social inclusion and is currently completing his PhD looking at language issues in the criminal justice system. He has had articles published in the *British Journal of Social Work*, the *Howard Journal* and *Child and Family Social Work*.

Bernard Moss is currently Professor of Social Work and Spirituality at Staffordshire University, where he has been teaching social work students for 15 years. He has a multidisciplinary background, having previously been a probation officer, family mediator, university chaplain and faith community leader. He has published widely on the theme of contemporary spirituality. His teaching excellence has been recognized by the Higher Education Academy with the award of a prestigious Senior Fellowship and a National Teaching Fellowship. His latest multidisciplinary book is *Communication Skills in Health and Social Care* (2008) published by Sage. His website is at: www.bernardmoss.org.uk.

Gurnam Singh PhD is Co-Director of the Applied Research Group in Social Inclusion and Principal Lecturer in Social Work at Coventry University where he has been working since 1993. Prior to this he worked as a professional social worker in Bradford. He has been, and continues to be, actively involved in community-based activism and is a passionate advocate for social justice and human rights. He has published widely on the subject of racism, anti-racism and anti-oppressive practice. Linked to this is a deep commitment to critical pedagogy and popular education and emancipatory research.

Siu-man Ng is Assistant Professor in the Department of Social Work and Social Administration, and Associate Director of the Centre on Behavioral Health, The University of Hong Kong. **Ted C.T. Fong** and **Xiaolu Wang** are Research Co-ordinator and postdoctoral Fellow respectively at the Centre on Behavioral Health, the University of Hong Kong. Their common research interest is on management of nonprofit organizations, especially in relation to combating burnout, enhancing work engagement, meaning making and spirituality in the workplace. They have conducted extensive studies on the well-being of care staff working in rehabilitation services in Hong Kong.

Mary Tehan has held different positions in hospice/palliative/end-of-life care and social/restorative justice areas over many years. Her Master's in Public Health study has centred on compassionate leadership in the workplace in relation to employees diagnosed with a life-threatening illness or employed carers of a person with a life-threatening illness, including bereaved carers. Mary is also an educator in a public health/health promoting palliative care approach to spiritual care/grief, loss and bereavement. Mary is a member of a wide range of professional associations and vice-chair of the board of Creative Ministries Network. She has established her own consultancy service: Ultimacy.

Sue Thompson is a director of Avenue Consulting, a company offering training and consultancy around workplace well-being issues. She has experience as a nurse, social worker, mentor and educator and has written, or co-written, several books, book chapters and articles, including; *The Social Work Companion* (Palgrave Macmillan, 2008) and *The Critically Reflective Practitioner* (Palgrave Macmillan, 2008). She also has publications relating to ageing, spirituality and loss and grief and is currently involved in cross-cultural research into the significance of reciprocity in the care of dependent older people.

Introduction: Work and Well-Being
Neil Thompson and John Bates

'Workplace well-being' can be seen as a site of the confluence of various interests. By this we mean that promoting workplace well-being is something that offers benefits to all the stakeholders involved:

- Employees clearly have a lot to gain from being employed in an organization that values them, supports them and helps them to fulfil their potential.
- Employers also have much to gain from this, as well-supported employees are likely to be more committed and thus more productive. As Adams puts it: 'organizations that focus on the well-being of their human resources perform substantially better than their rivals' (2007, p. 39). There will also be additional benefits in terms of reduced levels of sickness absence, lower turnover of staff, fewer workplace conflicts and so on.
- Clients/customers/patients as well as suppliers and trading partners also stand to gain by having dealings with well-supported staff who are likely to be more responsive and helpful if they are not distracted by their own problems, unfulfilled needs, frustrations and grievances.
- Arguably, society as a whole can be seen to benefit from having a stronger focus on well-being, partly as a result of the boost to the economy that can come from more productive workplaces, but mainly from making a positive contribution to ensuring that the social world (of which the workplace is a key component) is premised, as far as possible, on dignity, respect, support, compassion and humanity.

To emphasize the common interests involved is not to deny that there will also be conflicts of interest. A focus on well-being should not be equated with a naïve, individualized humanist approach that neglects the wider socio-political operations of power and vested interests (Thompson, 2007). The value of focusing on areas of shared interest and benefit should therefore not be lost by dismissing it as apolitical. Gambles and colleagues capture the point well when they argue that: 'Workplaces as well as families and communities require people to have a sense of well-being if they are to be effective and sustainable' (2006, p. 38).

Our aim in producing this book is to make a contribution to the growing literature base in order to help develop fuller and deeper understandings of the complex issues involved. In this way, we are hoping to play a part in laying the foundations for a more enlightened approach to human relations issues in the workplace than is often to be found at the moment.

Work is a primary feature of human experience. Indeed, Stein makes the point that:

> For most people in Western industrialized (and post-industrial) society, work is part of who they are as well as what they do. It is far more than a job and a paycheck. Work is a central part of the meaning of one's life.
>
> (2007, p. 56)

This is an important observation in at least two major ways. First, it alerts us to the fact that, at a macro level, a civilized society – including its government, judiciary and civil society – needs to take a keen interest in the world of work to ensure that it is not a place where human dignity is compromised and human welfare disregarded. Second, at a micro level, an important implication is that employing organizations need to be characterized by a commitment to the well-being of their staff if they are to get the best out of them and prevent unnecessary problems – and that commitment needs to be a meaningful one, and not one that exists simply at a rhetorical level.

In exploring the sociology of work, Grint argues that:

> work is itself socially constructed and reconstructed. This implies that much of what we take for granted as inevitable or technically required or economically determined should be subjected to the most vigorous of critiques; if work is socially constructed then it is contingent and requires perpetual action by agents for its reproduction – it does not just happen but has to be brought off.
>
> (2005, p. 2)

What this means, in effect, is that the workplaces we characteristically have today do not have to be that way – they can be constructed differently by different actions and assumptions. The chapters in this book amount to an effort to develop our understanding of how the world of paid work can be different, how it can be both more humanitarian and more productive. Echoing the approach of Bolton and Houlihan

(2007a), we are interested in making sure that organizations recognize that their human resources are precisely that: *human*. They are not simply a resource and they will be a far from optimal resource if their humanity is not recognized, respected and supported.

In this regard, Casey's comments about changes in the twenty-first-century workplace are instructive:

> The manifest efforts in seeking expressions of self-identity, of spirituality, emotionality and meaningfulness occurring in organizational workplaces are signs of a wider cultural reaction against the totalizing ideology of modern, and post-industrial, productivism. The reduction of humans and their potentialities to instrumental resources as organizational producers and consumers is, in these new ways, being challenged from within, and beyond, the organizational sphere.
> (2002, p. 173)

This book is intended to be part of that challenge.

The chapters

The book is divided into three parts. Part One offers an overview of a range of workplace problems. The first of its six chapters is concerned with stress. Here Neil Thompson provides an overview of a range of key issues connected with this fundamental problem of workplace stress. Chapter 2 is also by Neil Thompson and is concerned with the damage that can be done by conflict, aggression and bullying. Where there are people together, there will inevitably be some degree of conflict. However, there can be serious dangers when such conflicts are allowed to overspill into aggression or even violence or manifest themselves as bullying and harassment.

In Chapter 3, Iolo Madoc-Jones and Brian Heath of Glyndwr University in Wales provide a highly informative and thought-provoking account of the challenges presented by drug and alcohol problems in the workplace. Large organizations can have a greater 'population' than small towns, and so it is not surprising that drug and alcohol issues will arise across such a range of people. But, of course, smaller organizations are not immune to such issues either. Chapter 4, by Suki Desai of the University of Hull, covers the equally challenging set of issues presented by mental health problems. Such problems can range from minor to quite severe, and can be quite varied in both their causes and effects. Good employers need to have an understanding of the issues involved if they are to be well equipped to respond to the challenges involved and remain supportive of their staff in difficult times.

Chapter 5 has as its topic racism in the workplace. The author, Gurnam Singh of Coventry University, examines how racism can be a major problem in the workplace. Next comes a chapter on loss, grief and trauma and their significance for the world of work. Written by Neil Thompson and Sue Thompson, it highlights how neglected an aspect of organizational life this is. It shows the significance of these challenging life experiences and the dangers of neglecting them.

While Part One focuses on workplace problems, Part Two of the book turns to potential solutions. The first chapter in this part is entitled 'Learning and Development' and is written by John Bates of Liverpool Hope University. This chapter argues that organizational learning can provide workplaces which can contribute significantly to well-being. However, traditional approaches to training and learning may need to be reviewed if organizations want to reap the rewards of a well-educated and motivated work force. This is followed by Chapter 8 on leadership by Peter Gilbert of Staffordshire University. He provides an overview of the vitally important role of leadership. His approach is captured in the comment from Collins (2004) to the effect that: 'If you find your boss inspirational, the chances are you will be far happier and more productive at work' (cited in Cranwell-Ward and Abbey, 2005, p. 20).

Chapter 9 addresses the topic of managing sickness absence. Written by Neil Thompson, it examines how the careful and well-informed management of sickness absence can make a positive contribution to workplace well-being. This is followed by 'Women-Friendly Workplaces' by Mary Tehan, a public health consultant from Melbourne, Australia. She uses the example of support for women experiencing life-threatening or terminal illness as a means of highlighting the importance of gender considerations as part of a commitment to promoting workplace well-being.

Chapter 11 addresses a key feature of well-being, namely the role of spirituality in the workplace. Here Bernard Moss of Staffordshire University shows just how important it is for employees to be able to find meaning in their work. Grint's point that 'Sievers (1984) argues that motivation becomes an issue only when meaning is eliminated from jobs' (2005, p. 120) shows well this link between meaning and spirituality on the one hand, and work and well-being on the other.

Part Three comprises a set of essays which demonstrate the breadth of international concern with workplace well-being. In the first of four chapters in this part, Seth Allcorn of the University of New England writes of 'The Darker Side of the American Workplace'. He provides a fascinating account of how organizational narcissism can act as a significant barrier to well-being. In Chapter 13, Siu-man Ng, Ted C.T. Fong and Xiao-lu Wang of the Center on Behavioral Health at the University of Hong Kong offer a perspective on the current state of play there in relation to the challenges of promoting workplace well-being. They raise some difficult issues of how Hong Kong workplaces, so long dominated by a Confucian culture which can encourage authoritarian management, may need to revisit some fundamental issues if the high cost of overwork and work/life imbalance is to be addressed.

This is followed by an Australian contribution: 'Death, Illness and Grief: Foundational Mysteries for Transforming and Humanizing Work' by John Bottomley of the Creative Ministries Network in Victoria, Australia. This well-crafted contribution gets to the heart of some key issues and offers a profound understanding of our workplace ills. In the final chapter, Vassilis Ioakimidis of Liverpool Hope University and Giorgos Bithymitris of Panteion University of Social and Political Sciences provide a Greek perspective and remind us that it is important to recognize the socio-political dimensions of work. Drawing on Greek studies, the authors argue that the discussion concerning workplace well-being should be reconnected to the examination of the class nature of employment. For the working poor, recent developments across the European Union have created workplaces that, far from contributing to well-being, have impoverished the lives of many low-paid workers.

Overall, the three parts provide a broad-ranging analysis which draws on a variety of theoretical approaches and disciplines and international perspectives. We hope that this breadth will stimulate further work on a variety of fronts in order to enable whatever progress can be made in (i) minimizing the dehumanizing effects of unenlightened approaches to work; and (ii)promoting a stronger commitment to placing human dignity and welfare at the heart of organizational life

References

Adams, J. (2007) *Managing People in Organizations: Contemporary Theory and Practice*, Basingstoke, Palgrave Macmillan.
Bolton, S. C. and Houlihan, M. (2007a) 'Beginning the search for the H in HRM', in Bolton and Houlihan (2007b).
Bolton, S. C. and Houlihan, M. (eds) (2007b) *Searching for the Human in Human Resource Management: Theory, Practice and Workplace Contexts*, Basingstoke, Palgrave Macmillan.
Casey, C. (2002) *Critical Analysis of Organizations: Theory, Practice, Revitalization*, London, Sage.

Collins, A. (2004) 'Where They Lead We Will Follow, The Sunday Times 100 Best Companies to Work For 2004', *Sunday Times*, 7 March.
Cranwell-Ward, J. and Abbey, A. (2005) *Organizational Stress*, Basingstoke, Palgrave Macmillan.
Gambles, R., Lewis, S. and Rapoport, R. (2006) *The Myth of Work-Life Balance: The Challenge of Our Times for Men, Women and Societies*, Chichester, Wiley.
Grint, K. (2005) *The Sociology of Work*, 3rd edn, Cambridge, Polity.
Sievers, B. (1984) 'Motivation as a Surrogate for Meaning', Arbeitspapiere des Fachdereichs Wirtschaftswissenschaft, no 81. Wuppertal Bergische Universitat. Quoted in Alvesson, M. (1987) *Organization Theory and Technocratic Consciousness*, Berlin, De Gruyter.
Stein, H. F. (2007) *Insight and Imagination: A Study in Knowing and Not-knowing in Organizational Life*, Lanham, MD, University Press of America.
Thompson, N. (2007) *Power and Empowerment*, Lyme Regis, Russell House Publishing.

Part 1
Workplace Problems

1
Stress

Neil Thompson

Introduction

It is no coincidence that this very first chapter addresses the question of stress in the workplace. This topic was deliberately chosen as our starting point, as it is a major – probably *the* major – way that other workplace problems manifest themselves. That is, other workplace problems can be difficult enough in their own right, but are also likely to add to people's pressures and therefore cause or exacerbate stress.

Stress is defined by the Health and Safety Executive as 'the adverse reaction people have to excessive pressure or other types of demand placed upon them' (2007a, p. 4). The same document highlights the extent of the problem by providing the following statistical picture:

- About 1 in 7 people say they find their work either very or extremely stressful (*Psychosocial working conditions in Britain in 2007*).
- In 2005/06 just under half a million people in Great Britain reported experiencing work-related stress at a level they believed was making them ill.
- Depression and anxiety are the most common stress-related complaints seen by GPs, affecting 20% of the working population of the UK.
- When stress leads to absence, the average length of sick leave is 30.1 days (Labour Force Survey 2005/06). This average is much higher than the average for work-related illness in general (21.2 days).
- A total of nearly 11 million working days were lost to stress, depression and anxiety in 2006/06.
- HSE research in 2003 into offshore work found approximately 70% of common work-related stressors are also potential root causes of accidents when they were caused by human error.

(2007a, p. 4)

This gives a helpful overview at a macro level of the problematic nature of workplace stress. However, this needs to be complemented by a more micro-level, qualitative understanding of how stress can wreck people's lives. People experiencing stress are not just part of a broad statistical picture; they are real live people whose health, relationships, confidence and career can all be significantly damaged by exposure to stress. It is therefore wise to ensure that we do not lose sight of this.

Stress can thus be understood as a significant problem in its own right, but also a reflection of other problems in the workplace, as stress will often be caused by such problems as bullying and harassment (Stephens and Hallas, 2006), conflict and/or aggression (Booker, 2004), discrimination (Baker et al., 2004), grief and trauma (Thompson, 2009) and poor leadership (Hooper and Potter, 2000). Organizations committed to promoting workplace well-being therefore need to take a close look at the question of stress to see what can be done to prevent it in the first place, to deal with it effectively when it does arise and to help people cope with the aftermath (for example, returning to work after a period of stress-related sickness absence).

This chapter begins by identifying and rejecting some common myths about stress in order to establish a clearer baseline of understanding undistorted by such misconceptions or misunderstandings. This paves the way for a discussion of my views about the steps organizations need to take to deal with the challenge of stress in the modern workplace.

Myths about stress

Here I am using the word 'myth' in its anthropological sense of meaning a belief which may be untrue or only partially true, but none the less influences behaviour, assumptions and interactions – that is, an idea which regardless of its dubious truth value, still holds considerable sway. Myths are not therefore simply 'errors' or 'misunderstandings' – they are much more significant than that because, despite their lack of foundation in truth, they have a powerful effect on shaping organizational experience, sometimes with quite detrimental consequences. My aim here, then, is to identify a number of common myths about stress and indicate why it is important not to let these influence our thinking or our actions in relation to tackling the problem of stress. I have chosen to focus on six myths in particular, but it should be noted that this is not intended to be a comprehensive or exhaustive list.

Stress is good for you

The Health and Safety Executive definition of stress quoted above is now generally accepted as the working definition of the concept in organizational attempts to promote well-being by keeping work pressures within manageable limits. This approach makes it clear that, by definition, stress is problematic by its very nature (consider, for example, the significance of the term *excessive* pressure'). However, before this definition became accepted, there was an earlier approach based on the work of, among others, Hans Selye (Selye, 1956; 1974; 1976) which adopted a different approach. This distinguished between 'eustress' and 'distress', the former being positive and life enhancing, while the latter was seen as harmful and problematic. The notion of 'eustress' is today captured by the idea of positive pressure. 'Pressure' in itself is a neutral term, in so far as it can be either positive (stimulating, motivating, rewarding) when kept within manageable limits or negative when allowed to become excessive – that is, when it overspills into stress.

The commonly stated belief that 'stress is good for you' can therefore be seen to be entirely inappropriate in the context of the current understanding of stress. Stress, by definition a harmful thing, cannot be 'good for you', as this is a contradiction in terms. Pressure, when kept within manageable limits, can indeed be 'good for you', but the key phrase here is 'when kept within manageable limits'. Those who respond to concerns about stress with a dismissive 'stress is good for you' are therefore likely to be contributing to the continuance of stress-related problems by refusing to take seriously the harm that excessive work pressures can do. Clearly such an approach is inimical to the notion of 'workplace well-being' as it fails to recognize the dangers stress presents. Organizations committed to promoting well-being therefore need to make sure that they are not muddying the waters by relying on outdated terminology that gives the impression that they are not concerned about the harm that stress can do.

Stress is inevitable

Stress, as we have noted, is a reaction to excessive work pressures and other such demands. No one can guarantee that circumstances will not conspire to create stress for particular individuals or groups at any one time. A stress-free working environment cannot therefore be guaranteed. However, this is a far cry from saying that stress is in any sense inevitable. In the vast majority of cases – that is, outside of highly exceptional circumstances – there is no reason why good management and leadership cannot ensure that employees' workloads and other pressures are kept at a manageable level.

Excessive workloads are counterproductive, in so far as giving people more work than they can reasonably cope with is not only to risk doing harm to their health and well-being, it is also likely to have the effect of demotivating them. Lowering morale is, of course, likely to make people less productive and effective, and so the net result of raising workload levels above a realistic threshold can reasonably be expected to be a reduction in both quality and quantity of work – with the added complication of risking further quality and productivity losses through sickness absence and recruitment and retention problems.

Stress is a sign of a weak individual

A very firmly established view of stress, despite its lack of grounding in reality, is that stress is experienced only by weak or inadequate individuals. This assumption is not only inaccurate, but also, for reasons I shall explain below, quite dangerous. Cranwell-Ward and Abbey capture well this unfortunate mentality when they comment that: 'Some managers have a macho approach to stress, taking the view that "stress is for wimps" and they fail to give the necessary support when a member of the team experiences stress' (2005, p. 56).

The reality is that anyone potentially can find him- or herself in a situation where, generally for a combination of reasons, their work pressures are exceeding their ability to cope at that particular time. While it is certainly true that some people are more highly skilled than others at managing pressures – for example, in relation to time management skills (Covey, Merrill and Merrill, 1999) – no one is entirely free of the dangers of stress. Even the most skilled, experienced and confident of employees may find themselves in a situation in which their pressures increase unexpectedly (as a result of a terrorist alert, for example – see Thompson and Thompson, Chapter 6 in this volume), while their coping abilities are diminished (as a result of illness, for example) and their usual level of support is decreased (perhaps due to their line manager being absent on sick leave): the net result of this can very easily be a significant experience of stress. In other words, in particular circumstances, *anyone* can be overwhelmed by their work pressures and experience stress. It is therefore inaccurate and misleading to state that stress is a sign of a weak or inadequate individual – the reality is far more complex and multidimensional than that.

To equate stress with weakness is highly dangerous because one major result of doing so can be that stress comes to be perceived as something to be ashamed of. This can then mean that people do not ask for support because they are frightened of being labelled as 'not up to the job'.

In turn, this can lead to a vicious circle in which not asking for support has the effect of increasing stress levels, which in turn can make the employee even more determined not to reveal their 'weakness'.

Stress is the organization's fault, not the individual's

In dealing with a topic as complex as stress it is not helpful to adopt a simplistic outlook that involves trying to attach blame. Stress is a multi-level, biological, psychological, sociological, political and organizational phenomenon, and so any attempts to develop single, linear causes are necessarily doomed to failure. What is needed is a much more sophisticated, holistic approach to the subject matter.

However, it is certainly true to say that organizational factors can be very significant in the development of stressful situations, and it would be a serious mistake not to include the role of the organization in our attempts to develop a fuller understanding of stress. This can arise in a number of ways, not least the following:

- Allowing excessive workloads to develop and be tolerated;
- Allowing bullying and harassment to feature as part of organizational life;
- Not addressing conflicts in the workplace, allowing them to fester and/or escalate;
- Being unresponsive in relation to personal problems (loss and grief, for example);
- Not valuing staff and thereby giving them a message that their work is not important;
- Allowing discrimination to undermine morale and make the workplace feel unsafe for members of minority groups;
- ... and so on.

I shall return to the question of organizational responses in the Conclusion below, but for present purposes it is important to note that it is necessary to move beyond an individualistic model of stress that fails to take account of its multidimensional nature. By the same token, we should not adopt a reductionist approach that conceives of stress as purely an organizational matter, replacing an individualistic pathology model with an organizational pathology model.

Stress is basically a matter of work overload

Having too much work to do in the time available can very clearly cause stress. However, it would be a gross oversimplification to reduce stress causality to a matter of work overload. As indicated above, in the discussion of organizational factors, there are various other ways in which stress can develop. Stress is a psychological response to excessive pressures, and those pressures can come from sources other than the amount of work. There can be problems with the nature of work (requiring a level of knowledge or skill the employee concerned feels he or she does not possess – for example, someone who lacks the confidence to do public speaking may become stressed if called upon to do so – especially if this is expected to happen extensively). Also, there can be problems arising from the level of responsibility associated with particular work processes or tasks (for example, someone working in the health or welfare fields where vulnerable people may depend on them). Furthermore, as the HSE management standards recognize, stress can be associated with unclear expectations – problems arising not from the workload being excessive (unrealistic expectations), but from poor communication about what is expected of the employee (unclear expectations). We should also not exclude the significance of workplace conflict, aggression and violence as potential sources of stress (see Chapter 2 of this volume). Nor, of course, should we neglect the significance of change – too many changes in too short a time or badly managed change can also prove to be significant sources of stress.

In addition, stress can arise from a combination of home pressures and work pressures. Given the organization's health and safety responsibility to safeguard employees from undue hazards, then it has to be recognized that, where employees are temporarily vulnerable as a result of pressures outside the workplace (going through a divorce, for example), what constitutes a realistic workload may have to be adjusted to take account of how the home pressures are affecting that employee's current work capacity. This does not mean that managers are expected to take responsibility for employees' personal problems, but failing to take account of their impact on the individual's capacity in terms of quality and quantity of work can be seen as a highly dangerous strategy. Distracted employees can be dangerous employees.

The answer to stress is learning how to relax / taking a holiday / taking more exercise / eating healthily
A whole industry of stress management products and services has grown up around the idea that the answer to stress is a combination of breathing exercises, relaxation, time out, exercise and diet. While all these can be seen as important parts of remaining healthy and therefore being in a stronger position to cope with life pressures, both within and outside the

workplace, there are dangers in seeing them as sufficient in themselves as a response to the challenges of stress.

These dangers include (i) reinforcing the reductionist individual pathology model of stress that fails to recognize the multidimensional nature of the phenomenon; and (ii) adopting a passive approach to stress (that is, one that takes the underlying causes of stress for granted and does little or nothing to address them) – the expectation is that the stressed individual 'adjusts' to the stressful situation rather than trying to resolve (or, if they cannot be resolved, come to terms with) whatever the difficulties are.

The 'lifestyle' approach to stress is not one that I would reject altogether, as it has its place in the overall scheme of things. The problem is that, for many people, their thinking about stress fails to go beyond this one aspect of the situation, again producing a reductionist oversimplified model. It is therefore important that organizations should not place all their workplace well-being eggs in the basket of providing training in relaxation, breathing and so on. The result can be considerable resentment. Imagine, for example, a situation in which someone who is highly stressed because they are being bullied raises this as an issue with their managers, only to be told that they are to be offered training in relaxation and breathing techniques. It does not take much imagination to work out how counterproductive such an approach is likely to be.

Dealing with stress

Having considered a range of myths that can distort our understanding of stress, we can now switch our attention to how organizations that are genuinely committed to promoting workplace well-being can deal with the problem of stress. We begin by exploring the 'official' approach to such issues as advocated by the Health and Safety Executive, before moving on to examine other related issues.

The management standards approach

In 2004 the Health and Safety Executive produced a set of 'management standards' as guidance in tackling stress (see HSE, 2007a). These incorporate the following six elements:

- *Demands.* This relates to issues of workload and working environment. The basic idea is that organizations should take seriously the challenge of making sure that employees have a reasonable and realistic workload. It may be a high workload (which can be stimulating and rewarding), but once it crosses the line and becomes *too* high, the results can be very detrimental for all concerned. Similarly, the working environment is a key factor as poor facilities can make working life even more pressurized, while good facilities can give a very positive message of support and appreciation (essential factors in preventing stress).

- *Control.* Having a degree of control and autonomy over one's workload and the demands involved in it has long been recognized as an important factor in fending off stress. Staff whose every movement is constrained and controlled by others are likely to be more prone to stress than employees who have a greater say in how their work is carried out. This is the basis of the principle of workplace empowerment (Thompson, 2007).
- *Support.* This includes both psychosocial support, such as showing encouragement and appreciation, and more concrete forms of support, such as the provision of the resources required to do the job. Both sets of issues can give either very positive messages (we value what you do – your work is worthwhile and a source of pride and dignity) where such support is forthcoming or a very negative one (we do not value what you do; we take you for granted and exploit you, so you can take no pride in your work or gain any dignity from it). Positive support is therefore crucial (Thompson, 1999).
- *Relationships.* This includes (i) avoiding conflict where possible and dealing with it effectively where it does arise; and (ii) responding appropriately to unacceptable behaviour if or when this arises. The absence of either of these can cause considerable ill feeling and can thus undermine morale, with adverse consequences in terms of both quality and quantity of work.
- *Role.* This relates back to my earlier comment about the importance of clarity of expectations. It also involves trying to ensure that there is no role conflict – seeing to it that there are no unnecessary tensions arising from conflicting aspects of an employee's duties, or at least keeping these to a minimum. Role conflict will undermine role clarity.
- *Change.* The point was made earlier that too much change or badly managed change can be potentially quite stressful. How change is managed and how information relating to change is communicated are therefore factors that are very relevant in determining whether or not stress will be experienced.

Beyond technical fixes

The management standards approach is premised on the idea that organizations should be aware of each of these six sets of factors and should do everything they reasonably can to ensure that there are positive outcomes in relation to each of them. This is an approach that I welcome partly because it helps to put the need to tackle stress firmly on the agenda and partly because it provides a well-informed practical framework that busy managers can use to make sense of some very complex and challenging issues. However, I believe that there is a danger in relying purely on such an approach, just as it is dangerous to rely on neat frameworks to address any complex set of problems. I see the management standards as a good starting point and a helpful one. However, it is not enough on its own. This is because organizations could work on each of the six management standards without getting any real grasp of the philosophy underpinning them – that is, a philosophy of workplace well-being, premised on taking seriously the notion that an organization's most important resource really is its human resource, its people.

I would therefore want to argue that the management standards need to be seen not in isolation as a technical fix for stress, but as a practical tool for implementing a much deeper commitment to promoting workplace well-being. Without the understanding of the complex psychological, sociological, political and organizational factors involved in workplace well-being, efforts to address stress could remain at a very superficial level and not really make a significant contribution to tackling the problems involved.

There are other technical fix-type approaches that fall into the same category that can be equally unhelpful if not part of a more adequate holistic understanding of stress in particular and workplace well-being in general. These include:

- *The ostrich approach.* This is sadly a common strategy – pretend the problem is not there and hope that it goes away. Sometimes it will simply go away, but there is a significant risk that the problems will get worse over time. Then the failure to deal with the issues is likely to be interpreted by the individual(s) involved as a lack of support or concern, thereby potentially making the situation much worse.
- *The medical approach.* There is a long tradition of treating stress issues as health concerns. In some respects this is quite legitimate, as stress can have a very adverse effect on health by exacerbating existing conditions (high blood pressure, for example) and/or introducing specific stress-related conditions, such as ulcerative colitis. However, there is a

danger in equating stress with health as the former is a much broader concept in terms of both causes and effects. See the discussion of the relationship between health and well-being in the Introduction to this volume.
- *The counselling approach.* People who are stressed will often find skilful counselling very helpful. However, it can be problematic when organizations come to regard the provision of counselling via employee assistance programmes (EAPs) as some form of panacea: 'Whatever the problem is, the solution is counselling.' EAPs clearly have a role to play, but again it is important not to fall into the trap of confusing one part of the situation with the overall situation.
- *The training approach.* This is sometimes used in place of the above or in addition to one or more of them. My argument is not that training is not helpful, but rather that it is not enough on its own. High-quality training can be an important part of an effective stress response (Thompson et al., 1996), but is no substitute for the other steps that need to be taken, the other issues that need to be addressed.

Responding to the stress challenge

What, then, should an organization committed to workplace well-being be doing in response to the challenges presented by stress? I would propose the following as the major elements of such a response:

- *Knowledge, skills and values.* The point has already been made that stress is a complex matter, and so it is important to develop a good understanding of it so that an adequate knowledge base can be built up over time. This knowledge base needs to incorporate at the very least an awareness of how to recognize the signs of stress and how best to respond. Similarly, stress is a sensitive matter and needs skilled handling. Someone rushing in without the required people skills and 'emotional intelligence' can make matters significantly worse. In addition to knowledge and skills, effective stress management requires commitment to particular values, especially that of recognizing workplace well-being as a sound foundation for human resource management and indeed for organizational leadership more broadly.
- *Strategy and policy.* Ideally organizations should have an overall well-being strategy with specific policies on particular aspects (such as stress prevention, stress remediation and dealing with the aftermath – see 'Training' below), or a generic well-being strategy with specific sections relating to the different aspects, including those relating to stress. Part of the overall strategy can potentially be a stress audit – that

is, an exercise for identifying levels of pressure and potential or actual stress 'hotspots'. This can be designed in house if the expertise exists or can be outsourced where no one with the appropriate level of knowledge and skills is available within the organization.
- *Supervision and appraisal.* For optimal effectiveness, appraisal should identify strengths to be built *on* and areas for development to be built *up*. This can help to ensure expectations are both clear and realistic and any obstacles (personal, organizational or other) to achieving these expectations should be discussed and, where possible, a plan for addressing them developed. Supervision can then be a key forum for taking those plans forward, monitoring workload levels to make sure they are reasonable, helping staff learn and discussing any other concerns that may get in the way of achieving optimal levels of work.
- *Employee assistance.* While occupational health and confidential counselling services have a part to play, there is also scope for a wider range of problem-solving and support services tailored to the specifics of the circumstances (Bates and Thompson, 2007). Thought therefore needs to be given to the range of help that can be offered rather than assuming that medical or counselling services are the only options to choose from.
- *Training.* All of the above needs to be supported by training. This should include basic training about self-care and stress-avoidance strategies (assertiveness and time and workload management skills, for example) for all staff and additional training for managers relating to:
  - *Prevention.* Keeping workloads at manageable levels; valuing and supporting staff; recognizing early signs of stress and trying to 'nip problems in the bud'; and so on.
  - *Remedy.* Responding positively and supportively when stress does occur; helping to find solutions to the problems encountered; signposting people in the direction of other forms of support; and so on.
  - *Dealing with the aftermath.* Dealing with sickness absence issues; managing a supportive return to work; preventing a recurrence of the problem; and related matters.
- *Leadership.* Much depends on having a workplace culture where people feel it is safe to ask for support, where they feel valued and appreciated and where they feel confident that problems facing them or the team will be dealt with constructively and in a spirit of teamwork. Creating and sustaining such a culture can be seen as a major challenge of leadership – see the Introduction and Gilbert, both in this volume.

These various elements do not comprise a comprehensive approach to responding to stress in the workplace – it would take more than one chapter for that, and probably more than one book – but it should none the less provide a sound foundation on which to build a fuller understanding of how an organization's response to stress can be a fundamental and meaningful part of their efforts to promote workplace well-being.

Conclusion

Stress can be seen as a warning sign – it is saying that all is not well. As such, it is rightly categorized as a health and safety issue, as the harm stress can cause to health, safety and well-being can be of major proportions. It can ruin lives, destroy teams and shake the foundations of whole organizations. In terms of trying to meet the challenges it raises, there have been many changes in recent years. On the plus side, there is now a much higher level of awareness of stress and the need to take it seriously as a matter of concern – as evidenced by the high level of attention given to the HSE management standards. There is also the increasing awareness of the significance of workplace well-being issues more broadly. However, on the debit side, there is still a preponderance of simplistic approaches that do not do justice to the complexities involved. For example, the dangerous mistake of assuming that stress is primarily a matter of individual failing or inadequacy still seems to characterize the approach and understanding of a significant proportion of people. There is also still apparent a strong tendency to brush stress issues under the carpet, especially when they are entangled in other complex and sensitive issues, such as bullying and harassment or mental health problems.

This chapter can therefore be understood as a plea for a fuller and more sophisticated understanding of stress as a fundamental underpinning of a concerted attempt to ensure that our workplaces are characterized more by well-being and support than by stress and suffering. To this end I have provided an overview of what I see as some key issues in relation to stress, its consequences and ways of responding to it. As such, this chapter should not only dovetail well with other contributions in this volume, but also provide a stimulus to wider reading, research and debate about these vitally important aspects of working life.

References

Baker, J., Lynch, K., Cantillon, S. and Walsh, J. (2004) *Equality: From Theory to Action*, Basingstoke, Palgrave Macmillan.

Bates, J. and Thompson, N. (2007) 'Workplace Well-Being: An Occupational Social Work Approach', *Illness, Crisis & Loss* 15(3), pp. 273–84.

Booker, O. (2004) *Averting Aggression: Safe Work in Services for Adolescents and Young Adults*, 2nd edn, Lyme Regis, Russell House Publishing.

Covey, S. R., Merrill, A. R. and Merrill, R. R. (1999) *First Things First*, 2nd edn, London, Simon & Schuster.

Cranwell-Ward, J. and Abbey, A. (2005) *Organizational Stress*, Basingstoke, Palgrave Macmillan.

Health and Safety Executive (2003) *Development of Internal Company Standards of Good Management Practice and a Task-Based Risk Assessment Tool for Offshore Work-Related Stressors*, RR107, London, Health and Safety Executive.

Health and Safety Executive (2007a) *Managing the Causes of Work-Related Stress: A Step-by-Step Approach Using the Management Standards*, 2nd edn, London, Health and Safety Executive.

Health and Safety Executive (2007b) *Psychosocial Working Conditions in Britain in 2007*, www.hse.gov.uk/statistics/pdf/pwc2007.pdf.

Health and Safety Executive (2007c) *Self-Reported Work-Related Illness and Workplace Injuries in 2005/06: Results from the Labour Force Survey*, www.hse.gov.uk/statistics/lfs/lfs0506.pdf.

Hopper, A. and Potter, J. (2000) *Intelligent Leadership: Creating a Passion for Change*, London, Random House.

Selye, H. (1956) *The Stress of Life*, New York, McGraw-Hill.

Selye, H. (1974) *Stress without Distress*, Philadelphia, PA, J. B. Lippincott.

Selye, H. (1976) *Stress in Health and Disease*, London, Butterworth.

Stephens, T. and Hallas, J. (2006) *Bullying and Sexual Harassment*, Oxford, Chandos.

Thompson, N. (1999) *Stress Matters*, Birmingham, Pepar Publishing.

Thompson, N. (2007) *Power and Empowerment*, Lyme Regis, Russell House Publishing.

Thompson, N. (2009) *Loss, Grief and Trauma in the Workplace*, Amityville, NY, Baywood.

Thompson, N., Stradling, S. and Murphy, M. (1996) *Meeting the Stress Challenge*, Lyme Regis, Russell House Publishing.

2
Conflict, Aggression and Bullying
Neil Thompson

Introduction

It is reasonable to assume that, where there are people, sooner or later there will be conflict. Indeed, it can be argued that conflict is part of the human condition and that it would be naïve not to account for it in trying to understand human experience. In the workplace, conflict can be seen to be particularly significant, partly because the workplace can be a major site of conflict (as we shall see below) and partly because conflict can be so problematic for the workplace in terms of inhibiting organizations in their attempts to achieve their goals and proving harmful for staff, managers and other stakeholders. Conflict can be a detrimental enough phenomenon in its own right. However, when we recognize that it can also lead to other, even more serious problems, such as aggression, violence, bullying and harassment, then it becomes even more apparent that conflict is a subject worthy of close attention. There is therefore much to be gained from giving conflict and related matters careful consideration in our efforts to make sense of workplace well-being and how best to promote it. These are very important issues, but unfortunately they are often oversimplified. A more sophisticated approach is called for, and this chapter serves to lay the foundations for developing such an approach by exploring some of the key issues involved.

The chapter begins with a discussion of the four levels of conflict. The aim of this discussion is to provide a conceptual framework to aid in the understanding of the complex issues involved. This is followed by an overview of current approaches to workplace conflict and the issues faced by organizations which draws on recent research and policy developments.

Next comes a consideration of aggression and violence in the workplace, aspects of working life that can be quite problematic in any organization, but which are not at all uncommon in some work settings. This leads into a discussion of the related topics of bullying and harassment, phenomena that are sadly much more common than most people realize.

The overall aim of the chapter is to show that conflict, aggression and bullying are potentially very harmful aspects of working life and to make the key point that organizations enlightened enough to be committed to promoting workplace well-being need to incorporate serious consideration of these factors into their analysis. Unless they do this, they run the risk of other aspects of well-being being undermined. For example, efforts to prevent stress may prove fruitless in an organization where conflict is at a high level and there is no concerted effort by managers or human resource professionals to deal with the challenges involved.

Conflict

Understanding conflict

A common conception of conflict is that it represents the breakdown of harmony, as if a lack of conflict is the norm and an outbreak of conflict is something that deviates from that norm by spoiling the underlying harmony or consensus. However, on closer inspection of this view, we can see that it does not match the reality of social life. A more accurate conception would be one that recognizes human existence as a mixture of harmony and conflict, with elements of both interacting on a daily basis. It is important to acknowledge this different conception for two reasons: (i) without it we have an oversimplified understanding of conflict, which, as we shall see, can be quite problematic in the workplace; and (ii) failing to recognize conflict as an everyday occurrence contributes to the tendency to regard conflict as something terrible to be avoided or even to be frightened of. This latter issue can, in turn, produce two unhelpful outcomes: (i) it can lead to people being reluctant to address conflict issues, thus allowing them to grow or fester; and (ii) it can mean that we miss out on realizing the positive potential of conflict. We shall return to these points below.

Conflict can be seen to apply at four levels as follows:

1. *Everyday interactions.* This is the level that many people miss by falling into the trap, mentioned earlier, of not recognizing the everyday nature of conflict. A queue, a traffic jam, two people trying to go through a doorway at the same time – these are all examples of conflict. This is because they involve the wishes, intentions, plans

or actions of particular individuals (or groups) conflicting with one another – getting in each other's way. This is a key point as, without this, there is a danger that people make the mistake of equating conflict with fighting. Fighting is what happens when conflict management fails. It is the result of earlier conflict that has not been managed successfully, rather than something that 'breaks out' from an otherwise harmonious situation. Managing conflict therefore begins with dealing with everyday interactions; it is dangerous, counterproductive and wasteful of effort to wait for the fighting to start before using conflict management methods and skills.

We tend to manage conflict successfully on an everyday basis. Traffic jams *can* result in 'road rage'; queues *can* result in people falling out with each other; two people approaching a doorway at the same time *can* end up pushing and shoving each other, but the crucial point is that, in the vast majority of situations, that is *not* what happens. Human beings by and large are very skilled and successful at managing conflict. We would be distorting the situation significantly if we were not to recognize this.

2. *Escalation of tensions.* To acknowledge how skilful we are at managing conflict, however, is not to say that there are no situations in which conflict becomes problematic. The second level of conflict therefore relates to situations in which tensions escalate, where the everyday conflict management processes are not fully successful. This can manifest itself verbally in terms of forms of language used that reflect tension and/or disagreement and nonverbally in terms of body language (tense posture, changes in eye contact, flushing of the face and so on). Very often this level is short-lived and quickly returns to the level of everyday interactions. However, there is also a danger that the tensions will escalate further, leading to the third level.

3. *Aggression.* This describes situations in which tensions have reached a point where people are being verbally and/or nonverbally aggressive, but without actually resorting to violence. This level is characterized by a clear element of hostility. As with Level 2, this can quickly 'peak' and return to the previous level, but also has the potential to escalate further into actual violence. Level 3 situations therefore have to be handled very carefully and sensitively to try and defuse the situation before it deteriorates further.

4. *Violence.* This is the level at which blows are struck or, at the very least, pushing and shoving occur. It can range from very minor to fatal. It is clearly important that staff and managers in the workplace should do everything they reasonably can to prevent tensions from

reaching this level. Some people would include threats of violence under this heading too, on the understanding that, even without actual physical contact, an explicit threat to do harm can, in effect, 'do violence' to the individual on the receiving end.

The majority of cases of violence reflect a movement through the four levels. Everyday interactions lead to an escalation of tensions, which leads to aggression which, in turn, produces a violent outcome. However, this is not always the case. For example, someone suffering from a psychotic disorder may resort to violence without any apparent movement through the levels. We have to be careful here, though, not to rely on stereotypical thinking and equate psychosis with sudden violence, as that would be a highly discriminatory assumption to make. The point I am making is that, except in highly exceptional circumstances, there is an element of predictability in the passage from everyday interactions to escalated tensions, to aggression and on to violence. Organizations therefore have much to gain from developing a fuller understanding of conflict and the methods and skills that can be used to manage it and prevent its escalation. Unfortunately, however, managing conflict is often not on the management or human resources agenda except in those situations where escalation has already taken place – for example, in relation to grievances, bullying and harassment and actual incidences of violence. Clearly, if we are to take seriously the challenge of promoting workplace well-being, this needs to change. Conflict and related issues need to feature much higher up the priority list for managers, leaders and human resources professionals.

Responding to conflict

Given the four levels of conflict highlighted above, approaches to managing conflict need to be quite broad based, including policies, problem-solving interventions, support services and training. Policy responses may be specific to particular aspects (for example, separate policies on dispute resolution), generic across the field (that is, one policy relating to the different aspects of conflict) or even as part of a wider staff care or well-being policy. Decisions about how best to address the issues will need to be made at a local level to try to respond to the specific circumstances, priorities and needs of that particular organization.

Problem-solving interventions can apply at different levels:

- *Mediation.* Independent, one-to-one dispute resolution services can be very effective in getting to the bottom of conflicts and creating

more constructive working relations. In this way, mediation can be a major contribution to both the well-being of the staff concerned and to wider organizational effectiveness.
- *Team development.* Often the conflict is not just between specific individuals, but is more deeply ingrained within the group dynamics across a whole team of staff – for example, as a result of poor communication within the group. The use of a skilled and experienced external facilitator (external to the team and possibly external to the whole organization) can be very helpful in identifying sources of problems and helping the group develop strategies for addressing them.
- *Organizational development.* This is partly team development writ large across the whole organization, in which case the role of an external facilitator can again be a very positive and helpful one, and partly a much wider issue about the place of the organization in the wider scheme of things, in which case interventions around reviewing, clarifying and reaffirming (or redirecting) strategy are likely to be potentially fruitful.

Support services are also important, as conflict is potentially a major source of stress. Those services used to prevent stress and/or deal with it when it does arise are therefore very important: supervision, counselling and, in some cases, occupational health services, for example.

Training can be seen to apply to three main levels: (i) conflict prevention (communication and interaction skills and so on); (ii) conflict responses (defusing tensions, preventing escalation and so on); and (iii) responding to aggression and violence (self-protection skills, for example). In addition, there is much benefit to be gained from considering whether there are further training needs for managers around the overall management of conflict issues in the organization and, furthermore, whether there is a need to have some staff trained as mediators.

Aggression and violence

Some organizations are much more likely to feature aggression and violence than others due to the nature of the work involved – for example, the police service. However, no organization is entirely free of the risk of aggressive or violent incidents occurring. Managers, policy makers and human resources professionals in all organizations across the full spectrum of work sectors therefore need to recognize the significant challenges involved and to be as prepared as possible for such eventualities.

In many respects, aggression and violence are at the extreme end of a continuum of conflict, Levels 3 and 4 of the four-level model discussed earlier in this chapter. In order to prevent reaching these levels, therefore, there is much to be gained by investing in appropriate conflict prevention and management policies, procedures and practices in order to be able to keep potentially very harmful incidents of aggression and violence to a minimum. However, this will not be enough on its own for two reasons:

1. Even the best efforts to prevent aggression and violence cannot be guaranteed to work in all cases – they cannot be entirely foolproof; and
2. Some incidents will arise without any apparent prior conflict. This would include some situations involving people who are in a psychotic state of mind as a result of a mental disorder or are under the influence of drink or drugs to such an extent that their behaviour is irrational and unpredictable. Also, Booker makes the point that: 'Ordinary people can act in extraordinary ways when they lose their temper' (1999, p. 10).

In situations like this members of staff cannot be held responsible for such incidents. They cannot be expected to have the expertise to deal with such complex and demanding behaviours. Indeed, it is potentially very unwise to seek to blame staff for incidences of aggression or violence in other circumstances. Ideally, staff should be sufficiently well trained (and therefore sufficiently knowledgeable and skilled) not to exacerbate tense situations and thus risk an escalation of conflict. However, even where they are, it is important not to lose sight that it is only the perpetrators of aggression or violence who can and should be held responsible for the harm done, unless staff have deliberately acted in a reckless or provocative way. It is therefore important to ensure that the pressures and tensions of such situations do not lead to 'blaming the victim' (Ryan, 1988).

The costs of aggression and violence are quite considerable for all concerned. Employees can suffer not only physical injury (or even death in some extreme circumstances), but also psychological trauma (see Thompson and Thompson, Chapter 6 in this volume). In fact, the psychological harm can be much greater and much longer lasting than any physical injuries suffered. Other staff can also suffer, even when not directly involved in the incident, as a result of the fear and insecurity such occurrences can generate. In some cases, there may be 'secondary' trauma – that is, a traumatic reaction on the part of people who were not directly involved (perhaps people who witnessed the incident or people who have previously been traumatized by an experience of violence, whose old wounds are opened by being exposed to the intense emotions generated by this latest event). However, in addition to the personal costs for staff, there are significant organizational costs, both financial and reputational. The financial costs include insurance premium increases as a result of damage to equipment and buildings; replacement costs to cover staff absences; and related administrative costs. Reputational costs can be quite significant in terms of recruitment and retention of staff on the one hand ('I'm not going to work there, it's too dangerous) and, on the other, services to clients/customers/patients who may be reluctant to engage with the organization as a result of what they perceive as a lack of safety or security. The cost implications all round are therefore potentially quite considerable.

The steps that can be taken to avoid such problems are many and varied. They include having appropriate policies and procedures in place; providing suitable and sufficient training to ensure that the policies are meaningful (and not simply pieces of paper gathering dust); the promulgation of safe working practices (International Labour Organization, 2007); and ensuring that appropriate support services are made available in the event of staff being exposed to aggression or violence. Given the risk of trauma, as mentioned above, the provision of appropriate psychological supports can be crucial in such circumstances for avoiding any enduring adverse reaction.

Practical guidance on preventing, and responding to, workplace and aggression can be found in the 'toolkit' provided by the Health and Safety Executive (http://www.hse.gov.uk/violence/toolkit/index.htm). It is intended for the licence and retail sectors, but much of its guidance is more broadly applicable. The International Labour Organization website also has guidance on workplace violence in their *SafeWork* programme (http://www.ilo.org/public/english/protection/safework/violence/index.htm). The Violence at Work (UK) website (www.violenceatwork.co.uk) also has helpful guidance and insights.

Bullying and harassment

Brimfield-Edwards helps us to understand the significance of bullying and harassment in the workplace when she points out that:

> A recent large-scale study carried out by the Department of Trade and Industry found that over two million British employees had encountered unfair treatment at work in the last two-year period, with almost one million of those reporting personal experiences of bullying and

harassment on the job (Grainger and Fitzner, 2007). The anti-bullying charity, The Andrea Adams Trust (2007), has estimated that over 18.9 million working days are being lost every year in the UK through incidences of workplace bullying and the Health and Safety Executive (HSE, 2007) have estimated a figure of over £2 billion a year as being the overall cost to British industry.

(2007, p. 4)

These figures clearly paint a worrying picture for modern workplaces in terms of threats to the potential for achieving high levels of well-being. The challenge of dealing effectively with bullying and harassment is one that all organizations need to be aware of and make a commitment to addressing (Thompson, 2000) if they are to be able to ensure humane workplaces in which employees are supported in fulfilling their potential and achieving the best they can in the circumstances.

What is of particular significance is the link between conflict and the problems of bullying and harassment. Bullying and harassment involve the abuse or misuse of power (Thompson, 2003). In cases of the *abuse* of power, the perpetrator deliberately uses his or her power to make life difficult for the person(s) targeted – for example, a racist worker deliberately making a black colleague feel unwelcome and of no value to the organization. In the case of the unwitting *misuse* of power, the perpetrator causes difficulties for others through insensitivity and a failure to think through the implications of his or her actions and attitudes – for example, a man who makes sexual remarks to a woman, not intending to cause her distress, but none the less doing so. (But note that this is not to say that racial harassment is always deliberate and sexual harassment never is.)

Whether the problems arise as a result of deliberate or unwitting actions, the consequences remain highly problematic. What is more, in both sets of circumstances, conflict can be seen as a key factor, in so far as the unacceptable behaviour is likely either to reflect conflict (in the sense that bullying and harassment will often arise where the perpetrator enters into conflict with a colleague – often, but not always, a subordinate – and then uses illegitimate means to establish dominance and thus render the conflict harmless to him or her); or to cause conflict; or, indeed, both.

Bullying and harassment are strongly detrimental factors when it comes to promoting workplace well-being due to the harm they are highly likely to do to morale, motivation, teamwork and learning. Where such behaviours become commonplace, there can also be significant problems connected with recruitment and retention – retention because both those people who are being bullied or harassed and others who witness and disapprove of such behaviour are more likely to leave; and recruitment because, if an organization develops a reputation for being 'macho' in its approach to employees, this can discourage many potential applicants for posts.

However, the issue of developing a bad reputation does not always apply. One of the difficulties associated with bullying and harassment is that the problems they generate can often remain invisible, especially if employing organizations are not attuned to the issues involved. As MacDonald comments:

> It is important for employers to be vigilant to the possibility of bullying and harassment in the workplace. Given that research shows clearly that the problem of bullying at work is widespread, it should never be assumed that, just because no one has complained, the problem does not exist within the organisation. Many employees are afraid to complain, especially if the person bullying them is their line manager or immediate supervisor. Alternatively, they may fear retaliation if they complain, or feel too embarrassed or distressed to speak out. Some forms of bullying are so underhand and subtle that they may leave the victim feeling that perhaps they are to blame.
>
> (2005, pp. 71–2)

Consequently, it is relatively easy for bullying and harassment to continue unabated if positive steps are not taken to address the problems and the underlying conflicts on which they are based – and, indeed, the additional conflicts they tend to cause.

One of the most positive steps that can be taken is to develop a policy of 'Dignity at Work'. This involves the organization making a formal strategic commitment to ensuring that employees (including managers) are free from threats, intimidation, victimization and related difficulties. It can form a separate policy in its own right or can be part of a broader staff care or workplace well-being policy (Thompson, 2000). Barber (2007) makes the point that dignity at work is a long-standing fundamental principle of the trade union movement. It is also something that human resource professionals would be wise to embrace as a professional value. Without a commitment to dignity the notion of workplace well-being would be a hollow sham, offering no real value to people involved in making the workplace both a more humane and more effective place.

The notion of 'dignity at work' has come to be closely associated with campaigns to challenge bullying and harassment in the workplace, but as Bolton (2007a) points out, dignity in the workplace is a broader concept than this. She helpfully distinguishes between 'dignity at work' and 'dignity in work':

> Dignity in labour via interesting and meaningful work with a degree of responsibility, autonomy and recognized social esteem and respect may be understood as *dignity in work*; structures and practices that offer equality of opportunity, collective and individual voice, safe and healthy working conditions, secure terms of employment and just rewards would lead to workers attaining *dignity at work*.
> (Bolton, 2007a, p. 8)

Tackling bullying and harassment can therefore be seen as part of a broader commitment to 'worker-friendly workplaces' (Andrea Adams Trust, 2007), rather than isolated concerns unconnected with a wider investment in workplace well-being as an enlightened approach to human resource management in particular and management and leadership in general.

Conclusion

Bringing people together in shared endeavour for the purposes of work can bring excellent outcomes as a result of effective collaboration, supportive teamwork, concern for one another and a commitment to shared goals. However, that is only part of the story. What can also arise is a wide range of conflicts, some minor and relatively easy to live with, but others quite significant and dangerous to ignore. As we have seen, some conflicts can even go so far as to produce instances of aggression and violence, while there is also the harm that can be caused by bullying and harassment – two very destructive phenomena that have their roots in conflict (and the abuse or misuse of power that so often accompanies conflict).

There can be no doubt, then, that conflict and its associated problems pose quite a challenge to any workplace, but a significantly bigger challenge to organizations that take seriously the need to promote workplace well-being. The negative effects of (unmanaged) conflict stand in stark opposition to the benefits to be gained from addressing the workforce's well-being needs. There is therefore a clear need for significant attention to be paid to the complexities of conflict, aggression, violence, bullying and harassment. No workplace can realistically expect to be entirely free of these dangerous aspects of human interaction, but there are steps that can be taken to minimize both their occurrence and their detrimental impact.

This chapter has made no claim to providing solutions, largely because the subject matter is too vast for that to be realistically covered in one chapter and partly because it is too complex to be amenable to such an approach. However, what I hope it has provided is a platform for developing a fuller and more sophisticated approach to the major challenges involved.

References

The Andrea Adams Trust (2007) *Factsheet on Workplace Bullying* London, The Andrea Adams Trust www.andreaadamstrust.org.
Barber, B. (2007) 'Foreword', in Bolton (2007b).
Bolton, S. C. (2007a) 'Dignity *in* and *at* Work: Why it Matters', in Bolton (2007b).
Bolton, S. C. (ed.) (2007b) *Dimensions of Dignity at Work*, London, Butterworth-Heinemann.
Booker, O. (1999) *Averting Aggression: Safe Work in Services for Adolescents and Young People*, 2nd edn, Lyme Regis, Russell House Publishing.
Brimfield-Edwards, S. (2007) 'The Continuing Problem of Workplace Bullying', *Well-being* 2(1), www.well-being.org.uk.
Grainger, H. and Fitzner, G. (2007) *Employment Relations Research Series No 63. The First Fair Treatment at Work Survey: Executive Summary – Updated*, London, The Department of Trade and Industry www.dti.gov.uk/publications.
The Health and Safety Executive (2007) www.hse.gov.uk/statistics/causdis/stress.htm2.
The International Labour Organization (2007) *SafeWork*, http://www.ilo.org/public/english/protection/safework/violence/index.htm
MacDonald, L. A. C. (2005) *Wellness at Work: Protecting and Promoting Employee Wellbeing*, London, Chartered Institute of Personnel and Development.
Ryan, W. (1988) *Blaming the Victim*, 3rd edn, New York, Random House.
Thompson, N. (2000) *Tackling Bullying and Harassment in The Workplace: A Personal Guide*, Birmingham, Pepar Publications.
Thompson, N. (2003) *Promoting Equality: Challenging Discrimination and Oppression*, 2nd edn, Basingstoke, Palgrave Macmillan.

3
Addressing Drug and Alcohol Use in the Workplace

Iolo Madoc-Jones and Brian Heath

Introduction

In exploring drug and alcohol use in the workplace, it is necessary to acknowledge that theoretical and terminological complexities abound. From a theoretical point of view, how a social issue is defined and, indeed, what counts or does not count as a social issue can change over time and across cultures. Accordingly, what constitutes a drug, a legal or illegal substance and what is problematic use of these has been subject to revisions over the centuries. This often reflects who has the power to make a particular issue seem important and particular definitions stick. Complexities arise with words like 'drugs' or 'substances', because they assume a homogeneity that does not exist. Drugs and alcohol vary so considerably in their nature and effects that to talk about 'drugs' or 'substances' in a generic way becomes itself problematic. While not minimizing the importance of theoretical and terminological clarity, this chapter proceeds on the assumption that enough common understanding exists about what does or does not count as a 'drug' and about what might count as a problem to make a generic exploration of alcohol and drugs in the workplace meaningful. This chapter therefore explores research in relation to the frequency and distribution of alcohol and drug use by employees, the issues that might arise in the workplace as a result of such use, and the policy and practical issues that arise for employers in relation to promoting well-being.

Frequency and distribution of alcohol and drug use in the workplace

Individuals have the right to enjoy a full social life away from their employing organizations and they are not required to organize their lives to maximize their work productivity. Increasingly, however, employers do take an interest in the extracurricular activities of their staff and, in particular, those that have the potential to affect organizational performance. This includes activities which might bring the organization into disrepute, as in the case of Arthur Redfearn who was sacked after West Yorkshire Transport Services discovered he was standing for election to Bradford Council as a British National Party candidate; high-risk sports that may lead to extended absence through injury or sickness, or use of drugs or alcohol which may directly affect short- or long-term role performance.

Alcohol and, in some cases, drug use is often accepted as a normal part of everyday living. Social drinking, as well as social drug taking, may be an antidote to the pressures of modern life and an effective way for individuals to relax. Individuals may subjectively experience alcohol and drug use, even use at levels that might be described by some as problematic, as helping them achieve a sense of well-being. Substances can give people confidence and make socializing less stressful, and they can pleasantly alter states of consciousness. While problems created by either alcohol or drugs may be overemphasized for political reasons, few would deny that alcohol and drug use can have negative effects on well-being and may become problematic for the person concerned, their family, friends and employer.

As Smith and colleagues (2004) indicate, there is little research that seeks to establish the prevalence and implications of drug and alcohol use amongst employees. Kemp and Neale (2005) indicate that there is a statistical correlation between hard substance misuse and unemployment, and so the dearth of research may reflect the belief that substance misuse is a problem for the unemployed, rather than the employed. However, according to Ghodse (2005) 70 per cent of people with alcohol-related problems hold some form of employment. The International Labour Organization (ILO) suggests that, globally 3–5 per cent of the workforce are alcohol dependent and up to 25 per cent are at risk of dependence because they drink heavily (ILO,1995). These global figures are likely to mask wide variations between countries and the problems that may be associated with non-dependent but binge drinking. The United Kingdom, for example, has one of the highest rates of alcohol use in Europe (EMCDDA, 2001). According to Parker and Williams (2003), weekend binge drinking is a leisure priority of the majority of young English adults; 65 per cent of 18- to 24-year-olds go pub drinking every weekend, 85 per cent every month and many of these drink to excess.

The authors link this to a work hard-play hard culture that predominates in the United Kingdom. Ghodse (2005) suggests 60 per cent of people who are drug dependent hold some form of employment. Ramsay and colleagues (2001) suggested that, in the United Kingdom, 1 in 4 workers under 30 reported having used drugs within a 12-month period. A year later the British crime survey put this at 28 per cent among 16- to 24-year-olds (Home Office, 2002). George (2005) also presented the results of his research into drug use in UK workplaces in 2002. From an analysis of 1617 urine specimens from 82 sources he found that 19 per cent were positive for illicit drug use. He suggests that the positive rate could be up to eight times higher because a one-off testing programme may only detect regular or daily users. The most common substance detected was cannabis (188 samples), followed by opiates (48) then cocaine (18), heroin as a sub-set of opiates (7) and amphetamines (6). Males were far more likely to test positive for any drug (284 versus 24). Smith and colleagues (2004) investigated drug use among employees by sending a questionnaire to 30,000 individuals living and working in South Wales. From 4620 returns they found 13 per cent had used drugs in the last year. This rose to 22 per cent of workers under 40 and 29 per cent of those under 30. Cannabis was the most reported drug, followed by ecstasy, amphetamines and cocaine (2.5 per cent, 2.3 per cent and 2.2 per cent).

Employees in some industries and occupations seem more prone to using alcohol and drugs. Accordingly, they are more prone, then, to experiencing problems relating to alcohol and drugs. For example, employees in bars and public houses are around twice as likely to die from alcohol-related illnesses as other employees (Romeri, Baker and Griffiths, 2007). Bar staff are closely followed by catering professionals and entertainers, seafarers, butchers and labourers (Berry et al., 2007) Some research identifies nurses at increased risk of drug dependency along with doctors (Lillibridge, Cox and Cross, 2002; Gossop et al., 2001). One common theme is accessibility to a substance. Bar staff have the same easy access to alcohol as medical staff have to drugs. Another theme identified is that staff whose lifestyles are disrupted by shift work or unsocial hours are also at increased risk of dependency (Collins, Gollnisch and Morsheimer, 1999). Other risk factors for men are being in men-only or male-dominated workplaces (Berry et al., 2007; Gamst, 1980; Moore et al., 2007), which tend primarily to be blue-collar occupational groups. Equally, however, studies such as those by Matano and colleagues (2002) have found that having a greater disposable income is a risk factor for men. Risk factors for women are being in occupations that are non-traditional in gender terms – for example, in managerial roles with all-male teams (Moore et al., 2007). Drug and alcohol misuse is also associated with stress at work (Stansfield, Head and Marmot, 2002). According to Danna and Griffin (1999) sources of stress include lack of participation and effective consultation with employees, poor communication between employees and employers, lack of clear expectations, bullying and unstimulating work environments. In a similar vein, Stansfield, Head and Marmot (2002) identified a number of factors giving rise to stress at work, such as having significant responsibilities, perceiving an effort/reward imbalance or having few decision-making responsibilities.

To explain different occupational rates of substance use with reference only to roles would be to provide a very partial account. Each occupational group recruits in general from particular socio-economic backgrounds, to be dominated by one or other gender and to have disproportionate numbers of younger or older workers. Alcohol- and drug-taking behaviour varies from country to country, according to gender, age and socio-economic status, and so complex 'other' social factors are likely to belie statistics about the variations in levels of usage reported between occupational groups. This does not mean that a workplace cannot promote healthy or unhealthy substance use behaviours, nor does it mean that it makes no difference that some workplaces are characterized by organizational structures and management approaches that leave employees feeling valued and empowered while others leave employees feeling undervalued, disempowered and stressed. As Miller and Rollnick (1990) argue, the environment can support or not a particular behaviour. Given that individuals normally spend half of their waking days in work, the workplace is an especially important environment in terms of the potential impact it could have on behaviour.

Consequences of alcohol and drug use and misuse in the workplace

While intuitively it might be thought that there are only a few occupations where it would be permissible for an individual to drink while 'officially' at work (for example, journalists who may hold meetings in bars), in many organizations the practice of going to the pub for lunch, especially on Fridays, and then returning to work is a cultural norm (*Sunday Times*, 8/7/2007). Lunchtime drinking sessions may promote team spirit in some settings, but clearly there are numerous roles that require those who perform them not to drink at work, or serious harm may arise. Considerable research (Curran 2000; Golding 1992; Smith et al., 2004) has suggested that even relatively small amounts of alcohol can have a significant impact on performance across a range of tasks that require concentration and precision.

The situation in respect of drugs, however, is more complicated. Many drugs impair performance, but it is well established that some can enhance performance as well. Amphetamines, when given in low doses, have been shown to improve performance and cognitive function (Ramaekers, 2006). It is for this reason that these and other so-called 'performance-enhancing drugs' are banned from sporting events. However, most drugs do not show such effects and even performance-enhancing drugs have been associated with a range of psychological and physical side-effects after repeated use (Ramaekers, 2006).

Research suggests that the effects of alcohol and drug taking can persist for some time (Block and Ghoneim 1993; Grant et al., 2003; Smith et al., 2004). Performance has been found to be undermined following single instances of alcohol or drug use for up to a week afterwards (Curran and Travill, 1997; Measham, Aldridge and Parker, 2001). As a result, air traffic controllers, school bus drivers, military leaders, mechanics and surgeons may be employees who need to be totally sober when at work and possibly for periods beforehand. The company rules of British Airways, for example, state that pilots cannot drink eight hours before a flight, and must drink in moderation 24 hours before departure. Mistakes by employees in critical positions arising from substance use may lead to serious or fatal injuries and particularly large private or public liability claims. The grounding of the Exxon Valdez off Canada in 1989, for example, and the shedding of 11 tons of oil into the sea, with long-term environmental consequences, were blamed partly on the ship's captain for being under the influence of alcohol. Equally, in 1987 in the United States a Conrail engineer admitted smoking marijuana just before a train crash which resulted in 16 deaths (*New York Times*, 24/7/2008).

Less obviously, accountants, bankers or teachers may cause economic or psychological harm if their performance is impaired. While the link between substance use and workplace accidents or losses are difficult to research, and for the most part the research that has been done is inconclusive (IIDTW, 2004; Veazie and Smith, 2000), there is some evidence of a broad link between substance use and workplace accidents (IILTDW, 2004; Pratt and Tucker, 1989; Single, 1998). For example, studies of lorry drivers in Australia suggest a link between drug use and road traffic accidents (Crouch et al., 1993). In addition, a study of almost 5000 Australian railway workers found that the workers believed in a link between alcohol and accidents (Zinkiewicz et al., 2000). A person prone to binge drinking is not necessarily dependent on alcohol. Binge drinking peaks at weekends, and so it might be considered that any problems associated with binge drinking (fights, injuries and hangovers) are confined to non-work days or in the home. However, a survey found a third of employees admitted to having attended work with a hangover and 15 per cent reported having been drunk at work (Norwich Union Healthcare, 2007). At the same time, any personal, relational or legal problems caused by binge drinking are likely to have physical or psychological influences that extend into the working week.

Across all industries there is evidence that absenteeism can be higher among those who are chronic and binge users of drugs or alcohol who then take a 'sickie' to recover (Normand, Salyards and Mahoney, 1990). Although stress is also associated with absenteeism (Cunardi et al., 2005) and excessive alcohol use, the precise direction of the relationships between substance use, stress and absenteeism is difficult to disentangle. Leontaridi (2003) suggests that between 6 per cent and 15 per cent of the 176 million days lost to sickness absence in 2001 was due to alcohol-related sickness. As well as absenteeism, 'presenteeism' – the phenomenon of a worker being present but not active – is also likely to be common among drinkers who are nursing hangovers in the workplace or drug users experiencing short-term or long-term symptoms of withdrawal. Both absenteeism and presenteeism are likely to have significant economic consequences for organizations and their staff, not least the additional pressure placed on others to carry the increased workload. According to the Institute of Alcohol Studies (2006), increased sickness absences and the inability to work through drinking account for an annual loss of £6.4 billion to the economy. According to Parker and Williams (2005) the costs are likely to escalate in the future because of the earlier onset of alcohol use amongst the young and the tendency for young people to delay entering transitional phases (home making, marriage and parenting) which traditionally play a preventative role.

Occasional and chronic use of alcohol and drugs are implicated in criminal activity, including acquisitive crime, violence, domestic violence, crimes associated with the purchase and supply of prohibited substances, and child neglect (Blackburn, 1993). Such crimes have an effect on the well-being of large numbers of individuals and may have effects on employees who may be victims of crimes related to alcohol and drugs, or may have to engage with the consequences of having employees who have to take time off from work to attend court, who spend time in jail, or whose lives are otherwise stressful because of relationship problems and court proceedings.

Relatively infrequent and minimal use of drugs and alcohol can have a deleterious effect on health and may lead to premature death (Godfrey and Parrott, 2005). The chronic effects of prolonged alcohol and drug use are many and, being chronic, are disproportionately likely to affect middle-aged people. They are disproportionately likely, therefore, to rob children of healthy parents and an organization of more skilled staff higher up the hierarchy (Pratt and Tucker, 1989). As long as the effects on health and productivity are not pronounced, family, friends and employers may choose not to interfere with the individual's right to make a particular lifestyle choice. However, while each individual has the right to engage in activities that may cause ill-health, they also have responsibilities in relation to the choices they make because of the implications for their family, friends, employers and wider society.

Legal and organizational issues

According to Zinkiewicz and colleagues (2000), employers have been slow to respond to the issue of drugs and alcohol in the workplace, despite the fact that a range of legislation and regulations set out a duty of care to employees. This legislation, however, focuses overwhelmingly on accident prevention and illness avoidance, rather than health promotion. It reflects a concern with specific industrial conditions and diseases. The responsibilities of employers in relation to drug and alcohol use remains largely unaddressed. That said, Section 2 of the Health and Safety at Work Act 1974 places a duty on employers to provide a safe place of work and, in this context, a failure to deal with an employee whose work is impaired because they are, or have been, under the influence of drugs or alcohol may constitute action which creates or fails to address a risk to other employees. Such failure could make the employers liable to prosecution. At the same time, Section 8 of the Misuse of Drugs Act 1971 and its subsequent amendments set down the penalties for possession and supply of various illegal drugs. Not taking reasonable action to prevent the use of drugs on premises has been legally found to constitute 'permitting' drug use. This was the case in the so-called 'winter comfort' incident when managers of a hostel were jailed for allegedly ignoring drug use. The Corporate Manslaughter and Corporate Homicide Act 2007 may also have important implications for employers, not only in terms of duties to act in the case of staff who are known to be performing their duties when under the influence of alcohol or drugs, but also

Organizational strategy and policy responses

Well-being is associated with more productivity (Russell, 2008), and so employers may wish to address some of the issues that can arise from drug and alcohol use. Because drug and alcohol use is largely understood within a medicalized discourse that locates problems at the level of the individual rather than at societal or organizational levels, the focus of interventions is often at the level of the individual. As Danna and Griffin (1999) highlight, however, what is often ignored is that problems can arise or be made worse because of the prevailing structures, management styles and cultures of an organization as much as out of any individual pathology. The tension-reduction hypothesis (Moore et al., 2007) holds that some individuals take substances as a way of managing stress. Use of alcohol or drugs may arise because of, or be exacerbated by, stress in the workplace and a failure by an organization to address such issues as excessive workloads or bullying. Lillibrige, Cox and Cross (2002), for example, found that many nurses who used substances stated that they did so to deal with stress.

Faced with such issues, organizations have tended to adopt one of two strategies. The first involves adopting a monitoring and disciplinary strategy. It is correctional in that it involves monitoring staff closely and taking formal action to address productivity failings caused by use or abuse of alcohol or drugs. Lillibridge, Cox and Cross (2002) identify that many nurses would have gone for help sooner had they been more robustly monitored and confronted by their employers.

A survey by law firm Browne Jacobson in 2007 suggested that 57 per cent of businesses in the United Kingdom banned the consumption of alcohol altogether during work time. Current drug policy in the US military mandates that anyone found to have used drugs is dismissed (Mehay and Webb, 2007). According to Klee, McLean and Yavorsky (2002) over a third of problem drug users said they had lost a job because of their drug taking. A monitoring and disciplinary approach, however, does not necessarily entail an employer adopting a zero tolerance approach to drug or alcohol use and dismissing individuals because alcohol or drug use was affecting their role performance. In 2007 the Chartered Institute of Personnel and Development (CIPD) suggested that, where people with substance use problems were provided with help, around 60 per cent were able to remain working after overcoming problems. Providing help may involve costs, but these costs would have to be weighed against the costs incurred in recruiting and training a replacement. Not providing help is an economically risky strategy. It is possible that an employment tribunal could decide that an individual was wrongly dismissed if an employer made no attempt to help a worker overcome a problem that was affecting work performance. Being dismissed form work may occasion greater alcohol and drug use on the part of the employee and therefore further social consequences for the wider community. According to Cebulla, Smith and Sutton (2004), the loss of work for individuals who were drug or alcohol dependant was associated with a loss of routine and distractions and therefore precipitated a more significant decline into dependency. Re-entering the labour market, even years after the alcohol and drug misuse had ceased, then became a problem. Employers are understandably wary of employing individuals with a known history of substance use who are thought to be unreliable, untrustworthy and unsafe (Klee, McLean and Yavorsky, 2002)

Rather than dismissing an employee, an organization operating a monitoring and disciplinary strategy might refer an employee for compulsory treatment. Whilst complexities arise in working with people undertaking any rehabilitative programme involuntarily (Trotter, 2006), without some form of compulsion individuals might not seek help for their problems. Gossop and colleagues (2001) found, in a study of 64 health care professionals referred for treatment, that only 9 had self-referred. No difference was reported, however, in completion rates between those who self-referred and those referred compulsorily by their employers.

A monitoring and disciplinary strategy may deter people from using alcohol or drugs, but it associates the behaviour with negative, punitive procedures, which may stop employees from seeking early help with their problems. Zinkiewicz and colleagues (2000) found that 80 per cent of their sample stated they would not talk to anyone within the organization about a problem with drink or drugs because of fears about jobs and promotion prospects. The focus of such an approach is also more likely to be at the heavier end of drug- and alcohol-using behaviour, when the substance use becomes very obviously disruptive. This may have the consequence of giving insufficient attention to the well-being of those who are chronically abusing substances and for whom the side-effects are less obvious. The monitoring and disciplinary approach also requires that managers be in place within an organization who are knowledgeable about drugs and alcohol and their effects, confident in approaching staff about substance use problems, and perhaps skilled in motivational techniques. Berry (2000), however, found that in a hospital setting over

50 per cent of managers lacked confidence in dealing with alcohol and drug misuse among staff.

The monitoring and disciplinary strategy may be associated with random testing. Pre-employment health checks are now fairly routine employment practices. Individuals subject to such checks may be asked about alcohol or drug use, and the answers they give may have a significant bearing on whether they are offered employment. It seems likely, however, that few potential employees would disclose levels of use that might be perceived as problematic. This may be because of awareness of the likelihood of such disclosures being perceived negatively but, equally, because individuals achieve objectives in social interaction through the accounts that they give of themselves and their lives. Stories are told in order to project a preferred self-image (Mischler, 1986). Organizations may therefore increasingly undertake drug testing of new and existing employees. Such a phenomenon is by no means rare and is routine in relation to airline pilots and athletes. According to George (2005), there is a growing trend towards workplace testing, but there are ethical and legal issues that arise in respect of random drug testing in the workplace. These relate to problems with specimen collection and the serious consequences that can follow from a false positive indication. In 2001, however, the UK laboratories guidelines for legally defensible workplace drug testing were published. According to George (2005), the establishment of these guidelines has led to workplace testing becoming a more routine aspect of the work of testing laboratories in the United Kingdom. The behavioural or deterrent consequence of this are as yet unknown, but Conway and Briner (2005) suggest that staff in organizations that monitor employees excessively tend to experience more stress and to have more negative attitudes towards work and to be less productive and happy as a result.

The second strategy an organization may seek to adopt to address the issue of alcohol and drug use in the workplace is a more universalist and rehabilitative health and well-being strategy. Such a strategy seeks to educate the workforce about health issues and provide assistance to those that need it to manage their behaviours. Such, so called 'employee assistance' approaches can be traced to the United States and to the work of members of Alcoholics Anonymous (Berridge, Cooper and Highly-Marchington, 1997). According to Cunningham (1994), employee assistance programmes (EAPs) seek to improve performance through the provision of formal and universal employee support services. Such programmes tackle a wider variety of health issues than just alcohol and drug use. Other health issues addressed might be obesity, smoking, stress and mental health. What distinguishes the health and well-being strategy from the monitoring and disciplinary strategy is that, theoretically, it is associated with less stigma because it can be offered confidentially, often by an external provider, and is more rehabilitative than disciplinary in orientation (Berridge, Cooper and Highly-Marchington, 1997).

Outside of the family, the workplace is often the most significant social system in people's lives (Ghodse, 2005). It therefore presents as an ideal site for therapeutic or educative intervention about alcohol and drugs to take place. For individuals with issues related to alcohol and drugs, continued employment can underpin recovery, assist in promoting abstinence, or at least prevent a further decline into drug and alcohol misuse (Cebulla, Smith and Sutton, 2004). Because individuals spend a lot of time at work and often make strong friendships, it is a site where extended interventions may be introduced, with peer support to help individuals manage their use of alcohol or drugs. Because work is important, some leverage may also exist to motivate those who need to engage in therapeutic processes. The benefits of addressing alcohol- and drug-related issues may obviously also extend beyond the workplace to the home and community.

Conclusions

Health and safety legislation can serve to promote workplace well-being. In this context, the lack of appropriate legislation in relation to drug and alcohol use in the workplace can be a significant impediment to improving provision. The reason for this absence may be traced back to weaknesses within the Health and Safety at Work Act 1974. The Robens Report (1972), upon which this legislation was based, largely expressed a preference for employer-led self-regulatory health and safety systems, leaving employers to develop and police their own practices. Currently, various understandings exist among employers as to the exact meanings and limits of the duty of care towards staff. While some employers define their duties broadly, as we have already seen most seem to associate it only with legislation and regulations relating to industrial disease and accidents (Norwich Union Healthcare, 2008).

Policy responses have therefore tended to reflect practical or legal concerns, rather than what might be prudent. Given the absence in many organizations of policies in relation to drugs and alcohol (CIPD, 2007), it seems likely that most employers have come to believe that it is easier to deal with alcohol and drug misuse through disciplinary routes than to take a holistic approach to workplace well-being or through creating shifts in the culture of the organization (Head et al., 2002). This may be short-sighted because, as discussed above, considerable economic benefit might arise from addressing alcohol- and drug-related problems in the workforce. A positive application of a duty of care might, at the very least, reduce claims against employers for stress, which at 16 per cent of all claims, now form the second largest basis for a claim (Peebles, Heasmin and Robertson, 2003).

Drug and alcohol misuse is often discussed or addressed within a pathological discourse that locates the source of the problem only at the level of the individual. This creates a stigma for many in relation to discussing their problems. Alcohol- and drug-related behaviours are closely associated with social arrangements, roles and positions, but they are also connected with the role an individual performs in an organization and the prevailing culture. Organizations wishing to promote well-being would therefore do well to begin with a thorough audit of the organization to address issues related to structures, management approaches and culture that may promote problems or fail to address problems in relation to alcohol and drug misuse. Following on from such an audit, organizations wishing to promote well-being would do well to introduce policies that educate employees and also encourages those with problems to come forward for help. Such a health and well-being strategy has been used widely to address problems related to drug and alcohol use in the United States. According to Zhang and colleagues (1999), the majority of employers offered such EAPs by 1999. By contrast, in the United Kingdom CIPD (2007) found that a large number of organizations did not even have an alcohol/drug policy in place. Clearly a need exists for more activity in this area. Policies should clarify the reasons for the legitimate interest of employers in the issue, be agreed with unions, be seen to apply to everyone, be associated with an EAP, make clear statements about confidentiality and its limits, and include training for line managers. There is evidence of support among workers to address issues of problems arising from alcohol or drug misuse and that EAPs have tended to increase workplace well-being when they have employee support (Zinkiewicz et al., 2000).

References

Alcohol Concern and DrugScope (2001) *Impact of Alcohol and Drug Problems on the Workplace: Glancesheet No 2*, London, Alcohol Concern/DrugScope.
Berridge, J., Cooper, C. L. and Highly-Marchington, C. (1997) *EAP and Workplace Counseling*. New York, Wiley.

Berry, C. B. (2000) 'Substance Misuse amongst Anesthetists in the United Kingdom and Ireland: The Results of a Study Commissioned by the Association of Anesthetists of Great Britain and Ireland', *Anaesthesia* 55(10), pp. 946–52.

Berry, J., Pidd, K., Roche, A. M. and Harrison, J. E. (2007) 'Prevalence and Patterns of Alcohol Use in the Australian Workforce: Findings from the 2001 National Drug Strategy Household Survey', *Addiction* 102(9), pp. 1399–410.

Blackburn, R. (2003) *The Psychology of Criminal Conduct: Theory, Research, and Practice*, Wiley: Chichester.

Block, R. I. and Ghoneim, M. M (1993) 'Effects of Chronic Marijuana Use on Human Cognition', *Psychopharmacology* 100, pp. 219–28.

Cebulla, A., Smith, N. and Sutton, L. (2004) 'Returning to Normality: Substance Users' Work Histories and Perceptions of Work During and after Recovery', *British Journal of Social Work* 34, pp. 1045–54.

CIPD (2007) *Managing Drug and Alcohol Misuse at Work: A Guide for People Management Professionals*, London, CIPD.

Collins, R., Gollnisch, G. and Morsheimer, E (1999) 'Substance Use Among a Regional Sample of Female Nurses', *Drug and Alcohol Dependence* 55(1), pp. 145–55.

Conway, N. and Briner, R. (2005) *Understanding Psychological Contracts at Work: A Critical Evaluation of Theory and Research*, Oxford, Oxford University Press.

Crouch, D. J., Birky, M. M., Gust, S. W., Rollins, D. E., Walsh, J. M., Moulden, J. V., Quinlan, K. E. and Beckel, R. W. (1993) 'The Prevalence of Drugs and Alcohol in Fatally Injured Truck Drivers', *Journal of Forensic Sciences* 38, pp. 1342–53.

Cunardi, C., Greiner, B., Ragland, D. and Fisher, J. (2005) 'Alcohol, Stress-Related Factors, and Short-Term Absenteeism among Urban Transit Operators', *Journal of Urban Health* 82(1), pp. 43–57.

Cunningham, G. (1994) *Effective Employee Assistance Programmes: A Guide for EAP Counsellors and Managers*, London, Sage.

Curran, H. V. (2000) 'Is MDMA (Ecstasy) Neurotoxic in Humans? An Overview of Evidence and Methodological Problems in Research', *Neuropsychobiology* 42, pp. 34–41.

Curran, H. V. and Travill, R. (1997) 'Mood and Cognitive Effects of MDMA (Ectasy): Weekend High Followed by Mid-Week Low', *Addiction* 92(7), pp. 821–31.

Danna, K. and Griffin, R. (1999). 'Health and well-being in the workplace: A review and synthesis of the literature', *Journal of Management* 25(3), pp. 357–79.

European Monitoring Centre for Drug and Drug Addiction (EMCDDA) (2001) *Annual Report on the State of the Drugs Problem in the European Union*, Luxembourg, Office for Official Publications of the European Communities.

Gamst, F. C. (1980) *The Hoghead: An Industrial Ethnology of the Locomotive Engineer*, New York, Holt, Rinehart & Winston.

George, S. (2005) 'A Snapshot of Workplace Drug Testing in the UK', *Organisational Medicine* 55, pp. 69–71.

Ghodse, H. (ed.) (2005) *Tackling Drug Use and Misuse in the Workplace*, Aldershot, Gower.

Godfrey, C. and Parrott, S. (2005) 'Extent of the Problem and Cost to the Employer', in Ghodse (2005).

Golding, J. F. (1992) 'Cannabis', *Handbook of Human Performance* 2, London, Academic Press.

Gossop, M., Stephens, S., Stewart, D., Marshall, J., Bearn, J. and Strang, J. (2001) 'Health Care Professionals Referred for Treatment of Alcohol and Drug Problems', *Alcohol and Alcoholism* 36(2), pp. 160–4.
Grant, I., Gonzalez, R., Covey, C. L., Natarajan, L. and Wolfson, T. (2003) 'Non-acute (Residual) Neurocognitive Effects of Cannabis Use: A Meta-Analytic Study', *Journal of Neuropsychology* 9(5), pp. 679–89.
Head, J., Martikainen, P., Kumari, M., Kuper, H. and Marmot, M. (2002) *Work Environment, Aalcohol Consumption and Ill Health. The Whitehall II Study, Contract Research Report 422/2002*, Norwich, Health and Safety Executive.
Home Office (2002) *The British Crime Survey 2001/2002*, London, The Stationary Office.
ILO (1995) *Code of Practice on the Management of Alcohol and Drug Related Issues.* International Labour Organisation.
Independent Inquiry into Drug Testing at Work (IIDTW) (2004) *Drug Testing in the Workplace: The Report of the Independent Inquiry into Drug Testing at Work*, York, Joseph Rowntree Foundation.
Institute of Alcohol studies (2006) 'Alcohol and the workplace', IAS factsheet, Cambridgeshire, IAS.
Kemp, P. A. and Neale, J. (2005) *Employability and Problem Drug Users*, *Critical Social Policy* 25(1), pp. 28–46.
Klee, H., Mclean, J. and Yavorsky, C. (2002) *Employing Drug Users*, York, Joseph Rowntree Foundation.
Leontaridi, R. (2003) *Alcohol Misuse: How Much Does it Cost?*, London, Cabinet Office.
Lillibridge, J., Cox, M. and Cross, W. (2002) 'Uncovering the Secret: Giving voice to the experiences of nurses who misuse substances', *Journal of Advanced Nursing* 39(3), pp. 219–29.
Matano, R. A., Wanat, S. F., Westrup, D., Koopman, C. and Whitsell, S. D. (2002) 'Prevalence of Alcohol and Drug Use in a Highly Educated Workforce', *The Journal of Behavioural Health Services and Research* 29(1), pp. 30–44.
Measham, F., Aldridge, J. and Parker, H. (2001) *Dancing on Drugs: Risk, Health and Hedonism in the British Club Scene*, London: Free Association Books.
Mehay, S. and Webb, N. J. (2007). 'Workplace drug abuse programs: Does "Zero Tolerance" work?', *Applied Economics* 39, pp. 2743–51. London, Taylor & Francis.
Mishler, E. G. (1986) *Research Interviewing: Context and Narrative*, Cambridge, MA, Harvard University Press.
Moore, S., Sikora, P., Grunberg, L. and Greenberg, E. (2007) 'Expanding the Tension-Reduction Model of Work Stress and Alcohol Use: Comparison of Managerial and Non-Managerial Men and Women', *Journal of Management Studies* 44(2), pp. 260–83.
New York Times (1987) 'Drug Trace Found in 2 Conrail Workers after Fatal Crash', 15/1.
Normand, J., Salyards, S. D. and Mahoney, J. J. (1990) 'An Evaluation of Pre-Employment Drug Testing', *Journal of Applied Psychology* 75(6), pp. 629–39.
Norwich Union Healthcare (2007) *Health of the Workplace Report*, Norwich, Norwich Union Healthcare.
Norwich Union Healthcare (2008) *Health of the Workplace Report 2*, Norwich, Norwich Union Healthcare.

Parker, H. and Williams, L. (2003) 'Intoxicated Weekends: Young Adults' Work Hard-Play Hard Lifestyles, Public Health and Public Disorder', *Drugs Education and Policy* 10(4), pp. 345–67.

Parker, H. and Williams, L. (2005) 'Intoxicated Weekends: Young Adults' Work Hard-Play Hard Lifestyles, Public Health and Public Disorder', *Drugs: Education, Prevention and Policy* 40(4), pp. 345–68.

Peebles, L., Heasmin, T. and Robertson, V. (2003) *Analysis of Compensation Claims Related to Health and Safety Issues Research Report 070*, Norwich, Health and Safety Executive.

Pratt, O. E. and Tucker, M. M (1989) 'Approaches to the Alcohol Problem in the Workplace', *Alcohol and Alcoholism* 24(5), pp. 453–64.

Ramaekers, J. G. (2006) 'Editorial: Drugs Promoting Wakefulness and Performance', *Current Pharamaceutical Design* 12(20), pp. 2455–6.

Ramsay, M., Barker, P., Goulden, C., Sharp, C. and Sondhi, A. (2001) *Drug Misuse Declared in 2000: Results from the British Crime Survey*, London, Home Office RDS.

Richmond, R., Wodak, A. and Heather, N. (1992) *The Workscreen Project – A Brief Intervention to Reduce Excessive Alcohol Consumption in the Workplace: The Australia Post Experience*, Sydney: National Drug and Alcohol Research Centre.

Robens, the Hon. Lord (1972) *Safety and Health at Work*, Cmnd.5043, London, HMSO.

Romeri, E., Baker, A. and Griffiths, C (2007) 'Alcohol Related Deaths by Occupation 2001–2005', *Health Statistics Quarterly* 35.

Russell, J. E. (2008) 'Promoting Subjective Well-Being at Work' *Journal of Career Assessment*, 16(1), pp. 117–31.

Shaw, M. F., Angers, D. H. and Rawal, P. (2004) 'Physicians and Nurses with Substance Use Disorders', *Nursing and Health Care Management and Policy* 47(5), pp. 561–71.

Single, E. (1998) *Substance Abuse and the Workplace in Canada. Report Prepared for Health Canada on behalf of the Canadian Centre on Substance Misuse*, Toronto, Health Canada.

Smith, A., Wadsworth, E., Moss, S. and Simpson, S. (2004) *The Scale and Impact of Illegal Drug Use by Workers*, Norwich, HMSO.

Stansfield, S., Head, J. and Marmot, M. (2000) *Work Related Factors and Ill Health. The Whitehall II Study, Contract Research Report 266/2000*, Norwich, HSE.

Sunday Times, The (2007) 'Lunchtime Drinking Could be Stopped Under New Plans To Make Britain More Healthy', 8/7 http://www.timesonline.co.uk/tol/life_and_style/career_and_jobs/article2041488.ece.

Trotter, C. (2006) *Working with Involuntary Clients: A Guide to Practice*. London, Sage.

Veazie, M. A. and Smith, G. S. (2000) 'Heavy Drinking, Alcohol Dependence and Injuries at Work among Young Workers in the United States Labor Force', *Alcoholism: Clinical and Experimental Research* 24(12), pp. 1811–19.

Zhang, Z., Huang and Brittingham, A. M. (1999) *Worker Drug Use and Workplace Policies and Programs: Results from the 1994 and 1997 NHSDA*, Washington, DC, Substance Abuse and Mental Health Services Administration.

Zinkiewicz, L., Davey, J., Obst, P. and Sheehan, M. (2000) 'Employee Support for Alcohol Reduction Intervention Strategies in an Australian Railway', *Drugs: Education, Prevention and Policy* 7(1), pp. 61–73.

4
Mental Health Problems in the Workplace

Suki Desai

Introduction

Mental health problems will be a common feature within the workplace, as it is estimated that one person in six is likely to experience a mental health problem (Department of Health, 2006). Research has shown that it is not necessarily having a mental health problem which is problematic; it is how people respond to those who experience mental health problems which is dependent upon how successful they are at gaining and maintaining employment (Curran et al., 2007; Hayton, 2002; Secker, Grove and Seebohm, 2001). In the United States it is suggested that between 55 per cent and 75 per cent of people who experience serious mental health problems can find, and keep, employment (Secker and Membrey, 2003). Anyone can experience mental health problems at any age. Mental health problems range, for example, from 'mild' forms of depression or anxiety that may be linked to loss or bereavement to more severe forms of disorder that could have devastating consequences for an individual, leading to added problems, such as loss of employment, housing problems or relationship breakdown that in turn could lead to further worsening of mental health (Social Exclusion Unit, 2004). Within the British context, Beddington and colleagues (2008) suggest that about 16 per cent of adults experience a common mental health problem, such as depression, and that the average annual economic cost of mental health problems in England alone is about £36 billion.

In order to gain a better understanding of mental health problems, as well as the solutions that could be offered to people who experience them, it is necessary to understand how the medical perspective of psychiatry has claimed the expertise on mental health and how this has an impact upon how we as a society deal with mental health issues, and the attitudes we have developed towards it. By drawing on two contrasting perspectives, those offered by Karl Marx and Michel Foucault, the chapter considers how psychiatry as a science was established in asylums or the 'Great Houses of Confinement' (Foucault, 1971) in nineteenth-century Europe. While psychiatry claims to retain its scientific episteme, the chapter also highlights the influence of changes in societal values and how these have an impact on the diagnosis of mental health disorders.

Previous research on employment and mental health problems has tended to promote the medical perspective where the onus on recovery, and the need to be symptom free, has dominated discussion of when, and whether, people with mental health problems can return to work (Grove, Secker and Seebohm, 2005). This research has not always promoted the experiences of those people who use mental health services and the difficulties they have encountered in gaining and retaining employment. This chapter also explores the current ideas relating to recovery, and how the ideas on recovery from mental health problems challenge workplace settings and emphasize the need for the creation of healthier workplace environments for all.

The medicalization of mental disorders

Marx believed that working and being in employment was an important factor in determining a person's consciousness, as it is through employment that people develop a key element of their identity in relation to others (Cockerham, 2000). The work environment is an important place where social relationships between people are created and developed. Hence, alienation from this environment can create a feeling of negativity in oneself, as well as loss of identity. For example, although many of us who are in employment may look forward to our retirement, when such retirement is imminent, it is commonplace to experience a sense of loss and anxiety. This is because, for the majority of us, our identity is heavily reliant upon how others perceive us and what we do.

On the other hand, Marx also believed that the work environment itself has the potential to create a negative self-concept and low self-esteem. For example, he believed that the introduction of automated machinery and technology within the production process would reduce the need for a human workforce and create inflexible work practices that would result in additional stress for those people left operating it. Marx claimed that maintaining a 'healthy' workforce was necessary in order to maintain capitalism, and that the role of medicine and psychiatry is to 'restore' the individual enough, so that they can contribute to the production processes underpinning capitalism. For Marx, the growth of asylums during the Western European industrial revolution is linked to this production process – hence the asylum was also the place initially where anyone who did not contribute to capitalism was confined. For example, women who gave birth to children out of marriage were commonly confined to asylums, and this practice continued in Britain until the 1950s.

According to Foucault, the growth of asylums, and what he calls the 'Great Houses of Confinement' in nineteenth-century France, was born out of the realization by the governments of the time that the most effective way to control and govern people was through categorizing them as 'populations' and not as people or 'subjects'(Foucault, 1971). He believed that sovereign power, with its ability to kill and punish the populace, was no longer perceived as effective. What was necessary was the ability to convince populations to monitor, control and discipline their own behaviours to the perceived 'norms' of the time, which could then be dictated by governments. In order to create 'disciplinary power', Foucault (1976) argued, it is necessary to define 'normality', and scientists, anthropologists and others have concentrated on certain types of scientific evidence gathering in order to analyse aspects, such as birth rates, the age that men and women should marry, the effects of unmarried life on individuals and so on, to arrive at conclusions about what are 'normal' practices. For Foucault, the rise in psychiatry and the medicalization of madness are not just linked to making a 'dysfunctional' individual fit for capitalism; it was also a matter of creating disciplinary power through which individuals freely subject themselves to the scrutiny of experts, such as psychiatrists, and where they engage in monitoring and regulating their own behaviour.

This form of self-scrutiny or surveillance for Foucault is epitomized in Jeremy Bentham's design in the late eighteenth century of an asymmetrical prison known as the 'panopticon' (Foucault, 1979). The panopticon contained a central inspection tower that allowed for constant surveillance of prisoners while they were in their cells. The significance of this form of 'watching' was that prisoners were unsure when they were being watched. The ultimate aim was to get the prisoners to police their own behaviour at all times and not just when they knew they were under surveillance. This resulted in: 'an automatic functioning of discipline and control' (Heir, 2004, p. 543). While Bentham's panopticon only remained as a concept, its contribution to the understanding of populations is significant for psychiatry because it allowed experts to observe those people who were deemed to be 'mad' within the confines of the asylum and to collect and analyse information that would define 'madness'. Through this process the general population also came to understood how they could monitor and regulate their own behaviour. Asylums also allowed experts to observe 'madness' and identify ways to discipline it, thus making psychiatry the sole domain of medical expertise in relation to mental health problems.

The scientific explanations or classifications for mental health problems are outlined in two significant texts: the Diagnostic Statistical Manual (DSM) and International Classification of Diseases (ICD). These are the two manuals used by psychiatrists in order to arrive at a diagnosis of mental illness (for a critical review of these see Kutchins and Kirk, 1999). Mental health problems are generally placed within two broad categories: (i) severe and enduring mental health problems, such as psychotic disorders (commonly known as schizophrenia and manic depression or bipolar affective disorder); and (ii) common mental health problems, such as anxiety, depression, phobias, obsessive compulsive disorders, panic attacks and eating disorders. There are other mental health problems that are currently not designated as a disorder within the DSM or ICD in their own right, such as self-harming. However, these may be linked to other disorders, such as depression.

It is estimated that about 1 per cent of the population experiences severe and enduring mental health problems (Golightley, 2004). However, the negative public perception of this small minority of people falsely identifies them as highly dangerous and a threat to public order. There have been some cases of people with severe mental health problems murdering or brutally attacking other people. However, these incidents are very uncommon. When these occurrences arise the media seize upon these stories, inflating them and creating within the public perception a shift from an individual incident to a generalized suspicion about all mentally disordered people being more violent than they actually are.

Within the mental health services, incidents such as these have created a whole discourse around risk and risk management of all people with mental health problems. The discourse on risk has become a significant feature in modern mental health care, and although it is argued that risk analysis is a contested concept, it is still represented as being scientific, measurable and calculable (Heyman, 2004). While in theory risk assessment and management are promoted as empowering processes for mental health service users, the actual identification of risk has become the subject for experts, and McCahill (2004) has argued that it is this expert knowledge that has become the overriding factor upon which everyone is dependent for security. Hewitt supports this assertion, claiming that 'violence, dangerousness, and mental illness have become embedded in cultural consciousness' of the public (2008, p. 186). The assessment of risk and the management of it therefore become less about taking risks and more about avoiding them. This in turn creates an over-reliance upon mental health professionals and, for those people who experience mental health problems, this means constant surveillance from mental health professionals.

Recovery and 'cure'

Within psychiatry the long-standing aim, and therefore definition of success, is 'cure' from a mental disorder, with cure being defined as the elimination or control of the symptoms of the illness to such a degree that it allows the individual to pick up their former life. The most common intervention within psychiatry in the treatment of severe mental health problems is medication. People who refuse to take medication, and whose mental health is perceived to be deteriorating, can be detained in hospital and treated without their consent under the relevant mental health legislation (for example, in England and Wales, under the Mental Health Act 2007). Some people who experience this form of intervention develop very negative views about mental health services and, depending upon how they were detained, this form of intervention may also affect relationships with other people.

While mental health professionals involved in the detaining of a person take this role very seriously, the impact that it has upon the individual should not be underestimated. Those people who have to rely on medication on a long-term basis in order to maintain their mental health can feel demoralized, especially where medication does not control all their symptoms, or the side-effects of the medication affect their capacity to lead a 'normal' life. The medical response is to keep refining medication and trialling new drug therapies where the person at the centre of it – the service user – often feels alienated from this process.

Psychiatry has continued to dominate the mental health field, and generally our expectation is that, when a person becomes distressed, we rely on medical intervention to resolve the problem. However, contemporary debates around 'recovery' are challenging medical discourse and its over-reliance on 'cure'. Shepherd, Boardman and Slade (2008) suggest that recovery is less about cure and more about meeting a person's full potential. In this respect, employment can be a positive factor in the journey to establishing one's own identity and self-respect. It is estimated that 35 per cent of people with mental health problems are inactive and would like to have the opportunity to work (Social Exclusion Unit, 2004). Perkins (2007) has noted that even people with severe mental health problems say that they want to work and, in addition, see employment as an important part of their recovery. The success of recovery is not always determined by returning to one's former self. It is about hope and building a meaningful life, with or without medication. The impact of mental health problems on a person can affect their perception and outlook on life, and some people do not necessarily want to return to their former lifestyle or indeed adopt the personality and values that they held prior to becoming ill, even though family and friends may want this outcome. Recovery has been described as:

> a deeply personal, unique process of changing one's attitude, values, feelings, goals, skills and roles. It is a way of living a satisfying, hopeful and contributing life, even with the limitations caused by illness. Recovery involves the development of new meaning and purpose in one's life as one grows beyond the catastrophic effects of mental illness.
>
> (Anthony, 1993, cited in Shepherd, Boardman and Slade, 2008, p. 1)

Shepherd, Boardman and Slade (2008) suggest that employment has to be a key priority in the promotion of recovery becoming a reality. These ideas on recovery suggest that complete cure from a mental disorder may not be necessary for people with mental health problems to undertake employment successfully. The decision as to whether a person with a mental health problem is ready for employment should not be the sole decision of mental health practitioners but, rather, should be driven by the needs of the individual, with advice and support from relevant practitioners (such as general practitioners, psychiatrists or social workers).

Creating a positive workplace environment

Foucault (1972) suggests that knowledge and power are interlinked, as knowledge can be constructed to define power over others. For example, one of the aims of psychiatry is to gather evidence-based knowledge about mental health in order to support its scientific episteme. Despite the fact that this knowledge is contested among psychiatrists, it still plays a significant role in the adoption of a medical discourse (or model). The medical model maintains its influence in society through the creation and preservation of inequalities between those people who are seen as 'sane' and those who are deemed as 'insane'. However, Foucault also argues that knowledge which informs mental health concerns is not static, as what is regarded as the 'truth' today about what constitutes 'insanity' may not be considered so in a decade's time. For example, a separate diagnosis for homosexuality first appeared in the DSM in 1968 and stayed as a mental disorder until 1973 when it was removed (Kutchins and Kirk, 1999).

The removal of homosexuality as a mental disorder was fiercely argued for by gay activists in the United States, which suggests that power does not just have one function – that is, to repress others. Power also has the capacity to produce knowledge. It is when power produces knowledge that it is most effective. In this respect, the debates on recovery and any other alternative forms of intervention are a significant development.

Foucault enables us to understand that mental health problems need not be the sole domain of psychiatry and mental health professionals, as we are all important elements in what constitutes sanity and insanity. Our understanding of mental health problems is influenced by societal values and assumptions and, in this respect, they are social judgements, often negative, which become institutionalized within organizational policies and procedures within which they are then practised. It is often the case that, when someone's behaviour is perceived as erratic or abnormal, our initial response is to rely on others to intervene, such as mental health professionals, as we do not generally perceive ourselves as a potential resource in enabling a person to regain control over their life. This is often the case in workplace environments where an expedient response to such problems is to refer a person to occupational health services or to offer counselling support through an employee assistance programme.

This is not to argue that such support is not necessary. People who experience severe mental health problems may, for example, require a lot of support, and the solutions that are required to address this can be complex. In order to achieve this, employers and other work colleagues have to engage with the person experiencing distress through a range of strategies. These include regular supervision or supervisory support, time out, perhaps sanctioning contact with relatives and friends during work hours and any other such forms of support as ways of engaging with the person concerned. People who experience mental health problems will generally know what type of support suits them, and it is useful to plan out what level of support is required before a crisis occurs.

Take, for example, Renee who experiences schizophrenia and has delusions in the form of 'orders' that enter her head. The orders are given by something she called the 'system'. Renee works as a secretary:

> At the same time I received orders from the System. I did not hear the orders as voices; yet while they were as imperious as if uttered in a loud voice. While, for example, I was preparing to do some typing, suddenly, without any warning, a force, which was not an impulse, but rather resembled a command, ordered me to burn my right hand or the building in which I was. With all my strength I resisted the order. I telephoned Mama to tell her about it. Her voice urging me to listen to her and not to the System, reassured me. If the System was becoming too demanding, I was to run to her. This calmed me considerably, but unfortunately only for a moment.
>
> (Sechehaye, 1964, cited in Cockerham, 2000, p. 44)

Renee's experience shows that people who experience severe mental health problems can show considerable strength of character. It is necessary to recognize these strengths and work towards building up this capacity. In this situation, as well as medical and professional support, Renee could also be helped by her employers if they were able to assist in planning with her how she might manage her delusions while at work, so that she could be enabled to carry out her job. It is very easy for people who experience severe mental health problems to become isolated from their colleagues. During the time when their symptoms become florid they find it difficult to separate their delusions, paranoia and hallucinations from reality, and it is precisely at these times that they need additional support. Often, other people are frightened of becoming involved with someone whose behaviour and responses have become bizarre and unexplained.

Responses to such situations include ignoring the person, finding them funny, avoiding contact with them, requesting not to be near them, and other ways of evading them. These responses are quite understandable in situations that may make people feel frightened and unsure as to how they should respond. In Renee's case, the command to burn down the building that she was in created an added dimension of fear. It is when this fear is institutionalized and the person experiencing the mental health problem is responded to in a punitive way (by taking action, for example, to have her detained under mental health legislation before any other solution is considered) that it promotes inequality.

Research that is focused on empowerment can enable a better understanding of the changes that are needed in enabling people with mental health problems to work successfully. Current research and government guidance (see, for example, Boyce et al., 2008; Department of Health, 2006; Sainsbury et al., 2008) identify a number of factors that both employers and employees can utilize in usefully supporting people with mental health problems at work or to support them in getting into employment. These include:

- Challenging stigma and negative attitudes;
- Having clear workplace policies; and
- Having access to support networks within the workplace.

Sainsbury and colleagues (2008) reported that stigma and the impact of being at the receiving end of negative attitudes were a major concern for people seeking employment as well as retaining it, especially when it came to disclosure of a mental health condition to an employer. Those people who did disclose their mental health condition to employers generally reported positive outcomes, especially from managers and supervisors. Not only was disclosure of a mental health condition linked to fear of negative responses from others, it was also the case that not all people with a mental health condition regarded themselves as 'mentally ill' or someone with a 'disability'. Boyce and colleagues (2008) suggest that employers might take a more planned and direct approach in enabling those employees who are reluctant to raise issues themselves. However, such responses need to be tackled sensitively, and any manager or supervisor is likely to require appropriate training and support in handling such interventions.

Stigma can also be apparent in the way that people with mental health problems are supported at work. For example, Seebohm and Secker (2005) found that mental health services did not fit around the working lives of many users of mental health services, and even though many service users felt that the support of mental health services was vital to them, they were reluctant to take time off work for appointments with their clinical practitioner. Stigma is a very important issue, as it is not just about tackling individual attitudes and societal values. These negative attitudes also become institutionalized in the ways in which policies are delivered, as well as the way that services are organized. For example, the ways in which the majority of support networks, such as having access to your own general practitioner or psychiatrist is still predominantly only available during the daytime and less available after office hours when it might be difficult to seek their support.

Mental health service users interviewed in a study by Seebohm and Secker (2005) also felt that the government needed to strengthen legislation, such as the Disability Discrimination Act 1995, in order to tackle stigma and negative attitudes. This supports the claim made by Secker and Membrey (2003) who have also argued that, even though legislation now requires employers to observe the needs of disabled people in the workplace, there are currently very few studies that specifically focus on mental health. The Department of Health (2006) has identified six principles for promoting mental health and ending discrimination within the workplace and have placed a specific onus on employers to:

- Demonstrate that employees are helped to look after their mental health by making them aware of the steps that they can take to preserve their own and others well-being;
- Promote a culture of respect and dignity for everyone, ensuring that staff are trained to recognise and be sensitive to mental distress or disability in others, whether they are workplace colleagues or customers;
- Encourage awareness of mental health issues;
- Demonstrate that no one is refused employment on the grounds of mental health problems or disability;
- Make reasonable adjustments to the work environment so that people with mental health problems can continue working; and
- Demonstrate that people with mental health problems are not disadvantaged.

These principles rely heavily on changing and challenging the cultural practices within workplace environments and addressing workplace policies. Changing long-standing beliefs about mental health issues cannot be achieved by adopting a minimalist approach to the problem – for example, by providing one-off training for staff or through superficial changes in policy. There must be long-term planning, with clear objectives for change.

Conclusion

It is important to remember that the vast majority of people with mental health problems are likely to experience common mental health disorders, such as anxiety, depression and obsessive-compulsive disorders. While these disorders may be more prevalent in the workplace than severe and enduring mental health disorders, such as schizophrenia or bipolar disorders, they can none the less be equally debilitating for the individual who experiences them. Allowing people to express their emotions at work in a way that promotes healthy discourse can seem like an unusual response for an employer to take but, as already highlighted, Marx's analysis of the workplace warns us that the work environment has the potential to create a negative self-concept and low self-esteem. Those people who are in employment spend a large proportion of their time in the workplace. It is not always possible to hold on to emotional distress until those times when it is appropriate to deal with it. Similarly, it is also important to recognize that people with mental health problems, including severe and enduring mental health problems, demonstrate a great deal of resilience. Renee's case example shows us how, in the absence of formalized support systems, people find alternative ways of dealing with crisis situations. The changing responses to psychiatry, especially attitudes towards recovery, not only challenge preconceived ideas and stereotypes of people with mental health problems, but also highlight the gaps within the currently available research.

This chapter has suggested that supporting people with mental health problems does not have to be the exclusive realm of psychiatry, and that we can all influence this process. Societal values in relation to people with mental health problems are changing (Department of Health, 2008), and there is increasingly more tolerance of mental health concerns, which can be helpful in leading to positive outcomes. However, training that challenges negative attitudes and raises awareness, together with policies that promote healthy environments for all workers and give access to support networks, still need to be strengthened if we are to have inclusive and stress-free workplace environments.

References

Beddington, J., Cooper, C. L., Field, J., Goswami, U., Huppert, F. A., Jenkins, R., Jones, H. S., Kirkwood, T. B. L., Sahakian, B. J. and Thomas, S. M (2008) 'The Mental Wealth of Nations', *Nature* 455, pp. 1057–60.
Boyce, M., Secker, J., Johnson, R., Floyd, M., Grove, B., Schneider, J. and Slade, J. (2008) 'Mental Health Service Users' Experience of Returning to Paid Employment', *Disability and Society* 23(1), pp. 77–88.
Cockerham, W. C. (2000) *Sociology of Mental Disorder*, 5th edn, New Jersey, Prentice Hall.
Curran, C., Knapp, M., McDaid, D., Tomasson, K. and the MHEEN Group (2007) 'Mental Health and Employment: An Overview of Patterns and Policies Across Western Europe', *Journal of Mental Health* 16(2), pp. 195–209.
Department of Health (2006) *Action on Stigma: Promoting Mental Health, Ending Stigma*, London, The Stationery Office.

Department of Health (2008) *Attitudes to Mental Illness 2008 Research Report*, TNS UK for the Care Services Improvement Partnership, London, Department of Health.
Foucault, M. (1971) *Madness and Civilization: A History of Insanity in the Age of Reason*, London, Tavistock.
Foucault, M. (1972) *The Archaeology of Knowledge*, London, Tavistock.
Foucault, M. (1976) *The History of Sexuality: Volume One, An Introduction*, Harmondsworth, Penguin.
Foucault, M. (1979) *Discipline and Punish*, Harmondsworth, Penguin.
Golightley, M. (2004) *Social Work and Mental Health*, Exeter, Learning Matters.
Grove, B., Secker, P. and Seebohm, P. (eds) (2005) *New Thinking about Mental Health and Employment*, Oxford, Radcliffe Publishing.
Hayton, K. (2002) 'Helping those with Mental Health Problems Access Open Employment – A Glasgow Case Study', *Local Economy* 17(1), pp. 35–49.
Heir, S. P. (2004) 'Risky Spaces and Dangerous Faces: Urban Surveillance, Social Order and CCTV', *Social and Legal Studies* 13(4), pp. 541–54.
Hewitt, J. L. (2008) 'Dangerousness and Mental Health Policy', *Journal of Psychiatric Nursing and Mental Health Nursing* 15, pp. 186–94.
Heyman, (2004) 'Risk and Mental Health', *Health, Risk and Society* 6(4), pp. 297–301.
Kemshall, H. and Pritchard, J. (eds) (1998) *Good Practice in Risk Assessment and Risk Management*, London, Jessica Kingsley.
Kutchins, H. and Kirk, S. A. (1999) *Making Us Crazy: DSM – The Psychiatric Bible and the Creation of Mental Disorders*, London, Constable.
McCahill, M. (2002) *The Surveillance Web: The Rise of the Visual Surveillance in an English City*, Cullompton, Willan Publishing.
Perkins, D. (2007) 'Improving Employment Participation for Welfare Recipients Facing Personal Barriers', *Social Policy and Society* 17(1) pp. 13–26.
Ryan, T. (1998) 'Risk Management and People with Mental Health Problems', in Kemshall and Pritchard (1998).
Sainsbury, R., Irvine, A., Ashton, J., Wilson, S., Williams, C. and Sinclair, A. (2008) *Mental Health and Employment*, Department of Work and Pensions Research Report No. 513, July 2008.
Secker, J., Grove, B. and Seebohm, P. (2001) 'Challenging Barriers to Employment, Training and Education for Mental Health Service Users: The Service Users' Perspective', *Journal of Mental Health* 10(4) pp. 395–404.
Secker, J. and Membrey, H. (2003) 'Promoting Mental Health through Employment and Developing Healthy Workplaces: The Potential of Natural Supports at Work', *Health Education Research* 18(2), pp. 207–15.
Seebohm, P. and Secker, J. (2005) 'What Do Service Users Want?', in Grove, Secker and Seebohm (2005).
Shepherd, G., Boardman, J. and Slade, M. (2008) *Making Recovery a Reality*, London, Sainsbury Centre for Mental Health. Also available online at www.scmh.org.uk.
Social Exclusion Unit (SEU) (2004) *Mental Health and Social Exclusion*, London, The Office of the Deputy Prime Minister.

5
Racism
Gurnam Singh

Introduction

Despite race relations legislation, racism continues to be a problem in contemporary society and organization. This chapter uses current research and thinking as a basis for exploring the important challenges faced by organizations committed to eradicating institutional racism.

Ten years have passed since the publication of the McPherson enquiry into the racist murder of Stephen Lawrence and the subsequent failures of the police in the United Kingdom. Many people felt at the time that the open recognition of institutional racism heralded a 'new deal' in terms of race equality. In a matter of days after its publication, the heads of many public and private sector organizations went public and recognized the reality of institutional racism and the need to act (*BBC News*, 25/3/1999). The British Government responded by introducing new legislation in the form of the Race Relations Amendment Act 2000, which extended the provisions of the Race Relations Act 1976. In short, this broadened the legislation to cover public sector organizations, such as the police and government agencies, hitherto exempt, and, to place a positive duty on organizations to promote diversity and equality of opportunity. Amongst other things, this placed a legal duty on organizations to develop and publish 'race' equality strategies, carry out comprehensive ethnic monitoring and conduct equality and diversity impact assessments. The purpose of these changes was to offer a mechanism whereby there was no discrimination in the way that policies, procedures and services were designed, developed and delivered.

In a major speech to mark the tenth anniversary of the Stephen Lawrence Inquiry, Trevor Philips, the former head of the now defunct Commission for Racial Equality suggested that, while public intolerance towards racist attitudes has grown considerably, British institutions have failed to keep pace, and deep inequalities remain where:

> ethnic minorities are twice as likely to be poor as white people. And it's getting worse. Children from ethnic minority groups – all ethnic minority groups – are even poorer than their parents, as well as their white counterparts.
>
> (Philips, 2009)

The overall purpose of this chapter is to uncover the important challenges faced by individuals and organizations committed to promoting racial equality and valuing diversity and to offer some pointers for overcoming these. The chapter represents a desire to understand the complex and slippery nature of racism and the possibilities for undermining it. Given the contested and complex nature of the central themes, namely 'race', 'racism', anti-racism and diversity, the chapter begins by looking at ways that these concepts have, over time, been understood and formulated. It then goes on to uncover the precise nature of organizational racism, which is done by drawing on general research findings and more specifically research that I conducted with experienced black professionals. The final section offers some concrete strategies for personal and organizational change.

What is 'race'?

Historically there are two pivotal moments that one can identify in the systematic study of 'race'; the first being the emergence of scientific racism in the late eighteenth century, the second being after the Nazi holocaust in the mid-twentieth century. In the first period, we see the study of 'race' as essentially the science of physical differences, designed to explain and justify racist practices. Although, as a literary term, to denote 'a class of persons or things', 'race' can be traced back to the early sixteenth century (Husband, 1987, p. 13), the word's emergence as a scientific tool for sifting out, categorizing, organizing and brutalizing *homo sapiens* really began to gain prominence in the late seventeenth century and continued to gather momentum up to the mid-twentieth century.

The second pivotal moment is the period following the horrors of the mass slaughter of Jews and other minorities on the grounds of 'racial' impurity during the twentieth century. While scientific racism managed to retain a long, albeit thin tail stretching throughout the twentieth century (Husband, 1987), we now saw a shift away from studying 'race' as a standalone idea to analyses aimed at uncovering the social, ideological, psychological and historical mechanisms associated with the production of racism. In rejecting the idea of 'race' as the basis for thinking about human diversity, we saw a discursive shift towards culture and ethnicity. For some this step represented a serious and progressive attempt to move beyond 'race' thinking altogether. Definitions of human difference, based on 'culture' and 'ethnicity' were felt to represent a progressive attempt to undermine 'race' thinking and ultimately racism itself. For others, the eradication of 'race' from the lexicon was not quite as easy or desirable as it may appear. Goldberg (2002), for example, has argued that 'race' matters, not because it provided a helpful means of describing human types, but because it forms an important component of the modern state. The crux of his position is that, since 'race' retains a presence in the structures of power, attempts to erase 'race', although well intentioned, are both mistaken and likely to fail.

What is racism?

From the above discussion, the key observation one needs to make about racism is that it can never be understood in isolation from the history of ideas and practices that gave birth to it. Although overt expressions of racism, in the form of biased and prejudiced attitudes, still prevail in our society, it would be a mistake to think that nothing has changed over the years. As a result of a combination of social and political struggles, legislation, social and cultural change and demographic change, in some respects we now see something of a positive transformation of the position of black and minority ethnic (BME) communities. Previously held and expressed beliefs of the inferiority of and negative stereotypical associations with 'non-Western' and 'non-white' communities and cultures have diminished significantly, and BME communities are much more organized and willing to celebrate their various ethnic identities with pride.

Looking at the emergence of Barack Obama as the first African-American president of the United States, one might be led to believe that racism is diminishing. If a black man from a single parent, mixed-heritage, poor background can become the leader of arguably the most powerful and racist nation of modern times, then surely this is proof that racism is no longer a barrier to progress? While there is every reason to celebrate such achievements and take hope, one needs to be tuned to another reality which is perhaps less evident in the prevailing attitudes of individuals, but hidden beneath the surface in the patterns of social exclusion that are exposed in the statistics about employment, health, educational attainment, criminalization, poverty, housing and so on. In this sense, the bigger picture reminds us that, while things can and do change, we need to be alert to the deeply embedded nature of racism and how it is able to reproduce and morph itself.

So what has changed? While the underlying mechanisms of racism in the twenty-first century will be no different from those in previous times, in the period following the attacks in New York, Washington, Madrid and London (to this add Islamabad and Mumbai) within the past eight years, and the so-called 'war on terror', new forms of racism have emerged. Kundnani (2007) suggests that these new manifestations of racism are based on misunderstanding of the links between global terrorism, neoliberalism, forced migration and their local manifestation. The racism that we are now facing, he suggests, is constructed around previously well-established patterns of demonization of asylum seekers and migrants being overlaid onto Muslim populations, in particular after 9/11.

Underlying the wider socio-political mechanisms that feed popular racism, some of which have been highlighted above, there are some broad features that one can safely assert underpin racism whatever the context:

- *A belief system.* That there is this thing called 'race' which is a significant factor determining human traits and abilities. It includes the belief that genetic or inherited differences produce the inherent superiority or inferiority of one so-called 'racial group' over another.
- *A theory of human difference.* Based on the assertion that any one or several of the different 'races' of the human family are inherently superior or inferior to any one or several of the others.
- *A denial of rights.* Any practice, action or inaction, intentional or unintentional, that denies access, recognition, protection, power, opportunities and benefits to any person or community on the basis of their membership or perceived membership of a racial, ethnic, religious or cultural group.
- *Prejudice and stereotyping.* Judging an individual based solely on a perception of his or her perceived affiliation to a different 'racial' group. Such affiliation, although historically linked to physical features, may be identified in terms of ethnicity, religion, nationality and language. The characterization, usually detrimental, of members of one group (usually minority) by members of other groups (usually majority).

- *Institutionalized structures.* Policies, procedures and practices that directly or indirectly result in unfair and unjustifiable discrimination and disadvantage against individuals and communities on the basis of membership of a particular 'race', religion or ethnicity.

What is anti-racism?

At the simplest level one may define anti-racism as any actions that seek to oppose, reduce and ultimately eradicate racism. This might be easy enough when one thinks of overt acts, such as hate crimes, but, especially in the context of organizations, the difficulty arises in that many forms of racism simply are not that visible or apparent. Moreover, at the ideological level, there may be disagreement about what indeed passes as a racist sentiment, as opposed to an expression of loyalty or allegiance to a group identity and/or set of belief systems – hence the need to develop conceptions of anti-racism that do not simply focus on behaviour or beliefs, but are linked to conceptions of power and powerlessness, social and economic justice and human rights.

The other way to think about anti-racism is to think of the reasons why somebody may want to oppose racism. In doing so, as Bonnett suggests, one can begin to understand 'the genesis of forms of anti-racist activism and consciousness' (2000, p. 4). He identifies seven different possible reasons, which are summarized here:

1. Racism is socially disruptive – it can have a damaging effect on good community relations.
2. Racism is foreign – it represents the worst, not the best, of our culture and society which is marked by tolerance and equality.
3. Racism sustains the class system – it forms part of the capitalist system which is inherently oppressive.
4. Racism hinders the progress of 'our community' – it marginalizes people who could make a positive contribution to benefit the whole.
5. Racism is an intellectual error – it is based on a false premise that human beings can be separated into distinct groups called 'races'.
6. Racism distorts and erases people's identities – based on myths and a false reading of history, it enables people to fabricate categories and assimilate identities.
7. Racism is anti-egalitarian and socially unjust – based on libertarian values of social justice and equality of opportunity, it is simply wrong.

What is most useful about these conceptions is that they help one to realize that motives for, and formulations of, anti-racism can take various forms and these conceptions also clarify the basis upon which different anti-racist perspectives may emerge.

Anti-racism as a social movement

Understanding racism is one thing; doing something about it is another. Although relatively short lived, anti-racism as a social movement within the United Kingdom has very distinct antecedents that are important to understand.

Since social movements often rely on mobilizing some all-encompassing identity for members to 'sign up' to, during the 1970s, in response to the many manifestations of what was perceived to be white racism, visible minority groups sought to appropriate and redefine the racial categories in order to take on the white racist power structure. For example, they began to organize themselves under the political concept 'black'. Against the backdrop of the American Black Power movement, the term 'black', hitherto acting as a signifier of 'racial' inferiority, became transformed into a key category of an organized practice of struggles based on building black resistance and new kinds of black consciousness (Anthias and Yuval-Davies, 1992).

This realization of a commonality of oppression led to the development of new alliances, both strategic and cultural, and what Sivanandan (1990) terms 'communities of resistance'. Brah (1992) offers a slightly different perspective in suggesting that the term 'black' emerged as a political challenge by activists from Afro-Caribbean and Asian communities to the colonial description of them as 'coloured' people, which they found insulting. The colonial code was now being 're-worked and re-constituted in a variety of political, cultural and economic processes in post-war Britain' (Brah, 1992, p. 127).

However, in the context of a perceived indifference by the established anti-racist movement to the feelings of Muslim communities and the growing Islamophobia, there began a questioning of the existing black/white binarism (Modood, 1992; Modood, Beishon and Virdee, 1994). It was argued that, at best for dealing with inequalities, 'black' is a very blunt instrument; at worst, it was felt the concept may actually perpetuate racism by masking considerable differences that exist in the socio-economic status of ethnic minorities (see Modood, Beishon and Virdee, 1994). As a consequence of complex socio-political changes and events, while debates about 'race' and racism never went away, mirroring the decline of the political Left in the United Kingdom, we saw a gradual fragmentation of the old anti-racist movement predicated on an emphasis on 'race' and class, to one that was built around a New Labour agenda of social inclusion and valuing diversity.

From race to ethnicity

More recently, the head of the Equality and Human Rights Commission, which replaced the Commission for Race Equality in the UK, Trevor Philips (2009) has suggested that demographic changes are leading to what he terms 'super-diversity' where 'race' and ethnicity have a much weaker influence on who somebody may choose for a partner, where the fastest growing 'ethnic' category is among mixed-heritage Britons. Supporting this assertion that our diverse population is becoming more diversified is a recent analysis by Platt (2009). Based on the Labour Force Survey data, her analysis suggests nearly 20 per cent of children under the age of 16 in the United Kingdom are from an ethnic minority, and almost 10 per cent of children live in a family which has multiple white, black or Asian heritages. Of course these changes do not mean that 'race' is dead, but that perhaps the language of anti-racism, as it has been traditionally articulated, needs to change.

Dominelli, Lorenz and Soydan (2001), for example, suggest that anti-racists have tended to ignore the complex range of ethnicities and hybridities among them. In his work on 'new ethnicities', Hall, once a firm advocate of the political black identity, offers an explanation for his own about turn:

> If the black subject and black experience are not stabilized by nature or by some other essential guarantee, then it must be the case that they are constructed historically, culturally, politically – and the concept which refers to this is 'ethnicity'.
>
> (Hall, 1992, p. 257)

In other words, while 'black' was only really capable of articulating one dimension of the marginalized/subaltern existence, 'ethnicity' is capable of encapsulating a much broader spectrum – history, language and culture – of factors that go into constructing lived experience and subjectivity.

The attraction of 'ethnicity' over 'race' was clear; it offered an opportunity to talk about human differences in non-essentialist ways, without setting some kind of deterministic hierarchy of abilities and traits. For these reasons, as well as giving birth to a vast literature, we saw the adoption of 'promoting and valuing diversity' as a favoured policy objective of many public and increasingly private sector organizations. However, as Ratcliffe suggests, like 'race', the term 'ethnicity' tended to be deployed in a very haphazard way, 'implying commonalities of language, religion, identity, national origin and/or even skin colour' (2004, p. 28). This is reminiscent of the Balkan wars during the 1990s when the term was used to catastrophic ends under the euphemistic notion of 'ethnic cleansing'.

The key question is to what degree 'ethnicity' can reflect a real identity as opposed to an imagined one. This highlights a fundamental philosophical problem about who we are. How is the present related to the past? And how can one understand human difference in a way that avoids slippage into essentialist conceptions which form the basis for racist ideas? Space does not allow a detailed exposition of these questions, but within the context of an analysis of feminist and anti-racist struggles, Brah (1996) offers a very useful taxonomy of difference in terms of four key strands:

1. *Difference as experience* – this relates to the everyday experiences that differentiates people's lives.
2. *Difference as social relations* – this refers to the ways in which difference is constituted and organized into systematic relations through economic, cultural and political discourses and institutional practices.
3. *Difference as subjectivity* – here difference becomes something akin to a lump of jelly – slippery and hard to pin down, contingent, shifting in time and space, never complete and never unitary, but fragmented, moving from one crisis to another.
4. *Difference as identity* – this represents our attempt to achieve some kind of resolution in response to the previous three categories.

In terms of practice, what the above description of the dynamics of difference provides is a basis for the construction of anti-racist change which is informed by a clear understanding of the mechanism for the production and reproduction of human subjectivities. It also points to a need to develop policies that move beyond simplistic notions of 'celebrating diversity' to practices that understand and work with the contingent and socially constructed nature of identity and difference. Now ethnicity is understood as multi-layered and stratified with fluid borders which are being constantly negotiated and renegotiated (Ratcliffe, 2004).

Racism in the workplace

Racism in the workplace can take many forms and manifestations but, broadly speaking, it consists of behaviours and/or practices which disadvantage people because of their actual or perceived membership of a particular racial, ethnic or religious group. Those behaviours and practices that appear to be rooted in institutional culture, policy and procedures are normally understood to manifest institutional racism, which has been defined by the Stephen Lawrence inquiry as:

> the collective failure of an organization to provide an appropriate and professional service to people because of their colour, culture or ethnic origin. It can be seen or detected in processes, attitudes and behaviour which amount to discrimination through unwitting prejudice, ignorance, thoughtlessness and racial stereotyping which disadvantages minority ethnic people.
> (McPherson, 1999, Section 46.25)

While institutional racism may be manifest in all aspects of the organization, most instances will be related to the following instances:

- *Recruitment and selection.* Disproportionate representation of the ethnic breakdown of the area from which recruitment takes place.
- *Promotion and career development.* May be evidenced in the nature of career development practices and the lack of BME staff in managerial and supervisory roles.
- *Harassment and bullying.* A workplace culture makes certain groups of workers feel uncomfortable.
- *Redundancy.* Disproportionate impact of redundancy schemes on some groups.
- *Dismissal.* Differential treatment of some groups in relation to the giving of final warnings and dismissals.

Although many public service organizations have made noticeable progress in promoting and protecting the rights of BME employees, there is considerable evidence to suggest that direct and indirect discrimination and, in some situations, harassment are still in evidence (Brockmann, Buttand Fisher, 2001; Gabe et al., 2001; Singh, 2004). A systematic review of literature by Bhavnani, Mirza and Meetoo (2005) found that, although organizations by and large had many diversity and racial equality documents and action plans, few organizations could provide any real evidence of what interventions reduce racism. They suggest that legislative changes have not significantly improved workplace conditions for people from black and minority ethnic groups; racial harassment is frequently unreported. Deitch and colleagues (2003), in a study on workplace discrimination, highlight talk about the prevalence of subtle and pervasive discrimination, what they term 'everyday racism' against 'blacks'. A very recent example of this can be seen in the highlighting by the Metropolitan Black Police Association (Met BPA) in the UK of a culture of hostility towards those officers that sought to challenge racism. The worrying irony of this situation is that, while the Metropolitan Police have been running powerful recruitment campaigns aimed at encouraging more BME recruits, the Met BPA announced plans to 'actively discourage' young black and Asian people from joining the force! (*Personnel Today*, 6/20/08). In my own research on the experiences of BME social work practice assessors across the United Kingdom (Singh, 2004, 2006), I uncovered five distinct spheres or forms of racism, which are summarized in Table 5.1.

One of most concerning and revealing aspect of these findings is the way in which BME professionals' career prospects can be blighted by the cumulative effects of direct and indirect racism. For example, while being valued for their experience of being black or the insights they brought to understanding racism, the respondents reported that, often, this was used as a justification for exploitation and/or providing a reason for white workers to be absolved of responsibility towards race equality.

Race experts

The identification of black workers as 'a race expert', irrespective of whether they were employed in a specialist role, is a recurrent theme in many research studies. Being seen as an expert represents something of a dilemma for BME workers and can in fact manifest some of the more subtle aspects of institutional racism, particularly in organizations where there may be a significant proportion of BME staff. Hence, while recognition of specialist knowledge and skills associated with diversity and culture can allow BME staff to feel a sense of power and authority, legitimation and importance, the downside is that the 'expert' tag may result in some negative consequences. For example, as well as putting BME staff under greater pressure to act as 'internal ethnic consultants', the tag of 'ethnic expert' may result in reinforcing stereotypes held by white colleagues about the limited range of their capabilities. Moreover, since the 'expert' tag is often seen as a product of a unique lived experience and perspective, BME staff may be deemed less able to make

Table 5.1 BME practice teachers' experiences of racism (Singh, 2004)

Themes	How this is manifest	Dynamics and levels of racism	Impact
Hostility from white service users	Refusal to have a black worker/carer Violence and abuse Undermining black workers	Conscious and unconscious racism Process of 'othering'	Isolation and marginalization Low self-esteem Conflict
Hostility from white workers	Lack of commitment to 'racism' Viewing black workers as deficient and/or untrustworthy Abuse Black workers feeling undermined	Conscious and unconscious racism Individualism 'Othering'	Conflict, polarization and mistrust Divided loyalties for black workers Low self-esteem Passivity Anger
Pathologizing of black service users by white colleagues	Stereotypical views of black service users Eurocentric approach to practice Under- and over-compensation for black service users' failings Control taking precedence over care	Common-sense racism Cultural racism Ethnocentrism Process of 'othering'	Loss of control Powerlessness Loss of esteem Conflict
Pathologizing of black professionals	Stereotypical views of black workers Reluctance to allow black workers to take a lead role/autonomy Recognition of black workers' expertise limited to sphere of 'race' and cultural diversity, i.e., as black experts	Common-sense racism Cultural racism Ethnocentrism Process of 'othering'	Passivity Anger Internalized oppression Loss of control Powerlessness Marginalization Conflict
Institutional racism	Glass ceiling Lack of encouragement Lack of support Burnout Having to work twice as hard or be exceptional Token gestures	Individualism Rational action Exploitation Displacement of the problem of racism to one of 'managing' diversity Racism as epiphenomena Racialized organization	Low expectation from white colleagues Stagnation Defensiveness Poor career development Conflict

objective judgements than their white colleagues. Unless organizations and employers are prepared to value the transferable and broad range of capabilities associated with diversity and equality work, there is a risk that staff, black or white, working in this arena may suffer a negative impact on their career development.

Career progression

A recurring theme is that, despite the quality of their work, the level of their qualifications or the depth of their commitment to the organization, career progression for BME staff is still something that cannot be taken for granted.

Lack of encouragement

Although one could not be categorical about whether this was a consequence of 'race', participants highlighted how their own careers seemed to be dependent on the good will of individual white managers, whereas the overall level of encouragement for staff development from the organization was poor.

Exploitation

A number of participants expressed a concern at being exploited by senior management within their agencies and, increasingly, by the Diploma/Degree in Social Work and practice teaching programmes. Given the relative scarcity of BME practice teachers, particularly those that are qualified or have considerable experience, there was a feeling that they were over-exploited as 'fixers' and 'creators' – that is, they were presented as being superhuman, thus creating a kind of mythological status.

Sources of support

Not all black workers will respond in the same way to racism. Some may respond by not challenging, by identifying with white norms, and by internalizing the oppression; others may resist, build alliances and develop anti-racist strategies. Whatever option is taken, there are positive and negative consequences associated with each. Passivity is likely to gain favour from the organization; it may be taken as a sign of loyalty for which career prospects may be enhanced. However, the downside is that this could lead to isolation from black colleagues and low self-esteem. Taking on an activist position is likely to build self-esteem, confidence and respect among black colleagues, although here the downside can be greater levels of stress and surveillance.

Conclusion and ways forward

Thus far the discussion has focused on identifying the multifaceted nature of organizational racism and, in particular, the insights one can gain from the experiences of those on the receiving end. In concluding this chapter, as well as summarizing some key points, I would like to offer some pointers for moving towards an 'anti-racist' organizational culture.

Before any change process can occur, one needs to be clear about the nature of the problem that one is seeking to tackle. Despite the fact that the language of 'race', racism and anti-racism is well entrenched, much of my research suggests that there still exists much misunderstanding of the complexity of racism. For any successful and deep change to take place, be it personal or organizational, there is a need to establish a clear understanding of the dynamics of racism. This should include understanding the various levels at which it works. Broadly speaking, one can identify three levels, namely personal, cultural and structural levels (Mullaly, 2002; Thompson, 2003). At this stage the focus is on taking the somewhat abstract conceptions of racism discussed earlier in this chapter and situating these within the social and psychological mechanisms that together shape our world. Here, the point is to isolate the various levels at which racism can operate and, most importantly, to appreciate the interconnections between the levels. Most importantly, at this point one is seeking to move from 'rigid' to fluid conceptions of racist oppression. Put another way, from intentional acts of discrimination to complex structures of oppression.

The reason is simple: rigid behavioural conceptions work to enable most people to distance themselves from being responsible; racism becomes located somewhere else. It becomes difficult to believe that 'enlightened people' and 'enlightened societies' can be 'inherently racist'. So, as Young (1990) points out, we need to appreciate that some people suffer from oppression not because of 'tyrannical power', but 'because of the everyday practices of a well-intentioned liberal society' (Young, 1990, p. 41). Racism therefore is understood as structural, embedded in norms, habits, processes and symbols; in short, it is understood as oppression without an oppressor.

In developing such a comprehensive analysis/model there is the everpresent danger of making the task of tackling racism appear to be impossible. While not underestimating the size of the challenge, it is critical to realize that anti-racist change is possible, and one way to do this is to identify the gains over the past 20–30 years. In this sense, rather than placing all the emphasis on 'dramatic' symbolic gestures, one seeks to go for a balance between pronouncements and gradual change. Such a strategy that 'mainstreams' and links the change process to good staff and organizational development processes is more likely to succeed. The key point is that one needs to move from reactive, defensive, token responses to ones that are built on creativity, critical thinking, and personal and organizational growth.

I present here a three-stage anti-racist change model designed to map some of the transitions that one may go through. The model can be used by individuals and/or teams to reflect on their own position along the continuum.

Stage 1   Critical unconsciousness

The first thing to say is that not all individuals, teams or organizations will be at this beginning stage. Indeed, given the current statutory framework, a stage of 'critical unconsciousness' would be clearly in breach of equality legislation. This stage represents a profound sense of complacency. It represents a sense that people working in most organizations, especially those with most power, are essentially good and well meaning, therefore the problem of racism, if it exists at all, is peripheral.

This stage is analogous to somebody who has a very unhealthy lifestyle and runs the risk of serious illness, such as cancer or a heart attack, but denies the link between their behaviour and the health risk. Given the reality of racism, something may happen to jolt this complacency. This may be a grievance by a member of staff or service user, a scandal (for example, Stephen Lawrence) or some personal learning experience where the status quo seems untenable.

Stage 2   Critical complacency

This stage is characterized by a shallow appreciation that there is a problem that needs to be addressed. However, the general attitude is one of seeing the problem in relation to superficial adjustments, or the need to be seen to be doing something. It also represents a defensive posture and a sense that the problem is primarily related to how individuals and groups are represented and talked about. Hence, characteristically one often observes an obsession with introducing the 'correct' words. However, far from signifying a great change, this simply acts as a smokescreen for a reluctance to consider or appreciate the need for a paradigm shift.

Such a position is not sustainable, since the problem of black marginality, powerlessness and racism is still ever present. Indeed, a sense of critical complacency, of 'window-dressing' is likely to have the effect of creating more tension, frustration and conflict. Of course, it may also simply mean that black staff leave or do not apply, and black service users do not demand the quality of service which is their right. However, not all have this choice; some will choose to take on the system or the problem simply will not go away.

Stage 3   Critical consciousness

This stage in the development of an anti-racist mindset represents an unconditional acceptance and appreciation of the endemic nature of 'racism' and the need to develop short-, medium- and long-term strategies to combat it. It involves not only a transformation of the make-up of the organization, but of the worldview that pervades among staff. This stage involves individuals and teams exploring new ways of framing realities, of engaging in critical two-way dialogue and, most importantly, of realizing the way that institutions, through complex mechanisms of regulation, surveillance and routinization can dehumanize all.

There is also a gradual realization of how much more pleasing it is to work from this perspective, of the excitement of growth, of the importance of laying bare power relations and of working towards anti-oppressive change, of developing new identities as professionals and human beings.

Human history is littered with many examples of cruelty and oppression against targeted minority populations. While this may reveal a dark side of humanity, one must not forget the other side, of care and compassion. Human beings and human societies have the capability to change and reform. Power is never absolute, and no human being is absolutely powerless, and therefore, there is always hope that things can be different. If one believes that racism is 'natural', that it occupies a permanent place in the human make up, then perhaps anti-racism might seem pointless. However, if one believes that racism is built upon myths and cognitive distortions, that it has its birth in history and materialism, then there is every reason to struggle for, and anticipate, a 'post-racist' society. While the nature of history is to depict struggles for social change in heroic and dramatic terms, the job of eradicating racism from organizations is going to be more mundane; it is about developing praxis out of which organizations and those that work in them can realize the unity of social, moral, professional and economic imperatives.

References

Anthias, F. and Yuval-Davies, N. (1992) *Racialised Boundaries: Race, Nation, Gender, Colour and Class and the Anti-racist Struggle*, London, Routledge.
BBC News (1999) *Special Report: Stephen Lawrence Enquiry*, BBC Online 25th March 1999, http://news.bbc.co.uk/1/hi/special_report/1999/02/99/stephen_lawrence/285357.stm [accessed 19.01.09].
Bhavnani, R., Mirza, H. and Meetoo, V. (2005) *Tackling the Roots of Racism: Lessons for Success by Reena*, Oxon and Bristol, Policy Press/Joseph Rowntree Foundation.
Bonnett, A. (2000) *Anti-Racism*, London, Routledge.
Brah, A. (1992) 'Difference, Diversity and Differentiation', in Donald and Rattansi (1992).
Brah, A. (1996) *Cartographies of Diaspora: Contesting Identities*, London, Routledge.
Brockmann, M., Butt, J. and Fisher, M. (2001) 'Article 1: The Experience of Racism: Black Staff in Social Services', *Research Policy and Planning* 19(2), http://www.elsc.org.uk/socialcareresource/rpp/browse2001vol19no2.htm.
Deitch, E. A., Barsky. A., Butz, R. M., Chan. S., Brief, A. P. and Bradley, J. C. (2003) 'Subtle Yet Significant: The Existence and Impact of Everyday Racial Discrimination in the Workplace', *Human Relations* 56, pp. 1299–324.
Dominelli, L., Lorenz, W. and Soydan, H. (2001) *Beyond Racial Divides: Ethnicities in Social Work Practice*, Aldershot, Ashgate.
Donald, J. and Rattansi, A. (eds) (1992) *'Race', Culture and Difference*, London, Sage.
Gabe, J., Denney, D., Elston, M., Lee, M. and O'Beirne, M. (2001) *Violence against Professionals in the Community*, London, Royal Holloway, University of London, http://www1.rhbnc.ac.uk/sociopolitical-science/VRP/Realhome.htm [accessed 23.08.04].
Goldberg. D. T. (2002) *The Racial State*, Oxford, Blackwell.
Gordon, P. (1985) *Policing Immigration: Britain's Internal Controls*, London, Pluto.
Hall, S. (1992) 'The Question of Cultural Identity', in Hall, Held and McGrew (1992).
Hall, S., Held, D. and McGrew, T. (eds) (1992) *Modernity and its Futures*, Cambridge, Polity Press.
Husband, C. (ed.) (1987) *Race in Britain: Continuity and Change*, 2nd edn, London, Century Hutchinson.
Kundnani, A. (2007) *The End of Tolerance: Racism in 21st Century Britain*, London, Pluto Press.
MacPherson, W. (1999) *The Stephen Lawrence Inquiry: report of an inquiry, by, Sir William MacPherson of Cluny*, London, HMSO, http://www.archive.officialdocuments.co.uk/document/cm42/4262/4262.htm.
Modood, T. (1992) 'British Muslims and the Rushdie Affair', in Donald and Rattansi (1992).
Modood, T., Beishon, S. and Virdee, S. (1994) *Changing Ethnic Identities*, Cambridge, Polity Press.
Mullaly, B. (2002) *Challenging Oppression: A Critical Social Work Approach*, Ontario, Oxford University Press.
Personnel Today (2009) 'London Mayor Sets up Racism Inquiry at Met Police', reported by Greg Pitcher, 06 October 2008, http://www.personneltoday.com/articles/2008/10/06/47766/london-mayor-sets-up-racism-inquiry-at-met-police.html [accessed 20/01/09].

Philips, T. (2009) 'Institutions Must Catch up with Public on Race Issues', http://www.equalityhumanrights.com/en/newsandcomment/speeches/Pages/Macphersonspeech190109.aspx, 19 January 2009 [accessed 20/01/09].

Platt, L. (2009) *Ethnicity and Family Relationships within and between Ethnic Groups: An Analysis Using the Labour Force Survey*, Institute for Social and Economic Research, University of Essex, http://www.equalityhumanrights.com/en/publicationsandresources/Pages/Ethnicityandfamilyrelationships.aspx [accessed, 20/01/09].

Ratcliffe, P. (2004) *'Race', Ethnicity and Difference: Imagining the Inclusive Society*, Maidenhead, Open University Press/McGraw-Hill.

Singh, G. (2004) *Anti-racist Social Work, Context and Development: Refracted through the Experiences of Black Practice Teachers*, Unpublished PhD thesis, Coventry; University of Warwick.

Singh, G. (2006) Supporting Black and Minority Ethnic Practice Teachers/Assessors: Practice Learning Taskforce, London, Department of Health, http://www.practicelearning.org.uk/index.php?id=95.

Sivanandan, A. (1990) *Communities of Resistance*, London, Verso.

Thompson, N. (2003) *Promoting Equality: Challenging Discrimination and Oppression*, 2nd edn, Basingstoke, Palgrave Macmillan.

Young, I. J. (1990) *Justice and the Politics of Difference*, Princeton, NJ, Princeton University Press.

6
Loss, Grief and Trauma

Neil Thompson and Sue Thompson

Introduction

There is a growing literature on the subject of workplace well-being, covering a wide range of workplace problems. However, two sets of issues that have received relatively little attention are those of loss and grief and the related subject of trauma. For example, MacDonald (2005), a book published by the Chartered Institute of Personnel and Development, the leading human resource organization in the United Kingdom, makes no reference at all to such matters.

However, despite this relative lack of attention paid to the subject, it remains a very important one. This is because the impact of experiences of loss and trauma (and the grief that they can both lead to) can be both profound and wide-ranging. They can have such a strong disorienting effect on employees that they may become dangerous – for example, by being absent-minded when operating machinery or failing to concentrate fully when making important decisions. This can be significant enough when it applies to individual employees, but the effects can be multiplied when an incident occurs that affects a whole workforce or a significant section of it – for example, when a member of staff is killed at work in front of colleagues. Similarly, as we shall see below, incidents involving terrorism or the threat of terrorism can also have a significant effect on the workplace because of the feelings of anxiety, vulnerability and panic that they can so easily engender.

It is also important to recognize that the effects of loss, grief and trauma can be very long lasting – it is not simply a matter of a grieving employee having a few days of compassionate leave after the death of a loved one and then returning to 'business as usual' shortly afterwards. The situation is much more complex than this for two reasons. First, in the case of a death, the effects of the grieving can apply over a much longer term than a few days – especially if the deceased was very close to the employee (his or her life partner, for example). Where there are other complicating factors, such as cumulative losses (several one after the other) or multiple losses (several at the same time), the timescale can be quite lengthy. Second, loss and grief issues do not apply only to death-related incidents. There are a whole range of other losses that can produce a strong grief reaction or even prove traumatic that may have no connection whatsoever with death. Examples would be divorce or the breakdown of a long-standing relationship, being a victim of crime and/or violence, becoming disabled, and being laid off or made redundant.

What we have, then, is a highly complex set of issues that can have a major detrimental effect on the workplace, causing major problems for staff, managers and the organization as a whole and potentially for other stakeholders as well. This chapter therefore makes the case for organizations to take seriously the challenges of responding to loss, grief and trauma in the workplace. We begin by considering how issues of loss and grief can arise within the workplace, before considering how they can be brought into work from outside. Finally, we explore the significance of trauma in the workplace, with a particular emphasis on how terrorism can be especially problematic.

Grief in the workplace

Given that change is such a central part of life in general and the workplace in particular, a sense loss is never far away, as change inevitably brings a mixture of gains and losses. As many of us spend a very significant part of our lives in our workplaces, it should come as no surprise that they should provide as likely a context for experiencing loss and grief as any other. And yet, if the lack of guidance and paucity of literature on the subject are anything to go by, it would seem that those experiences are either not recognized as such or are not seen as significant where they are recognized. So, if we are suggesting that loss is a common experience, rather than an occasional one, what forms might loss and grief in the workplace take?

The most obvious has to be that where a death has occurred. This might be the death of a colleague or significant member of a team or organization, or someone with whom there has been an investment of time and emotion – as with the death of a child in a school or a student at a college or a university perhaps. While the death of family members is usually sanctioned as an experience where empathy and time for mourning are seen as appropriate, the same considerations are not always extended to those experiencing a workplace-related death. Yet the loss of a colleague, client or indeed anyone else with whom one spends a lot of time or invests in some form of working relationship can be equally distressing, not only because of any ties of loyalty and friendship that might have existed, but also because of the potential for such an experience to have an impact on the very meaning of the workplace itself to the individual concerned.

In this regard, work can be seen as not just something people *do*, but also part of what they *are* – part of their identity (Stein, 2007) and, as such, it is a significant aspect of meaning making (see Moss, Chapter 11 in this volume). And, where it is a central part of someone's life, and endowed with meaning to that individual, it is not hard to see that a death in the workplace can be at best unsettling, but has the potential to be devastating. The work of Neimeyer and colleagues (Neimeyer, 2001; Neimeyer and Anderson, 2002) has shown the importance of 'meaning reconstruction' after a loss – that is, how it is necessary to rebuild our frameworks of meaning after they have been shattered by a major experience of loss. To ignore or trivialize a loss can therefore have a profound effect on the individuals concerned – in effect giving a message that their concerns are of no consequence. Such a negative message can be problematic at any time, but can be especially harmful at a time when people are feeling vulnerable as a result of their grief.

Thompson (2009) points out that, in some workplace contexts, such as hospitals, nursing homes and police and emergency service departments, the likelihood of having to deal with death and its aftermath exists on an almost daily basis. This does not mean, though, that this necessarily makes the experience any easier to deal with. What the event *means* to those involved remains an important issue. Workplaces that are not sensitive to this can therefore add to the pressures, rather than help to deal with them.

We can see, then, that far from being trivial events, easily 'sorted' with a few words of sympathy, death in the workplace can be a multilayered experience which can take a long time to come to terms with. But while we would argue that an unsympathetic and misinformed response to workplace-related deaths is an inadequate and potentially demeaning one, at least there is some form of recognition that they *are* loss experiences and, to some extent, there is a sanctioning of the outpouring of grief which is likely to follow them. However, we would suggest that, while other experiences of loss not directly associated with death can be equally devastating, they are less likely to be regarded as being grounded in loss, and the opportunity for them to attract empathy and understanding is lost as a result. Consider the following scenarios:

- Uri had worked for a local bakery for 32 years – ever since leaving school, in fact. It was a small family firm and he had played his part in sourcing local and ethically sound ingredients and upholding traditional methods. He took pride in his work and pleasure from playing a role in maintaining the character of his community and region as well as his workplace. Uri was given notice that the firm had been sold to a very large multinational company who would be making 'significant changes to the production methods and range of products' and that his new contract would be the standard one issued to their 15,000 UK-based workforce.
- Beth had worked at the school for many years and was admired by all of her colleagues for her energy, commitment to the school's ethos and her vision. She had played a major part in building up the reputation of the science department to the extent that it had become widely recognized as a centre of excellence and innovation in teaching. When a more senior position in the department became vacant she applied for the post but was not among the shortlisted candidates. No explanation was offered.
- This was the fourth time in less than nine years that the department in which Megan worked had been 'reorganized'. Every time this happened there was an atmosphere of chaos and uncertainty which took a long, long time to settle. Teams that had worked hard to establish good working relationships, shared goals and effective working practices found themselves disbanded with relatively little notice, even less guidance on what would be expected of them under the new system and nothing at all by way of a rationale for having made such drastic changes in the first place. Megan was beginning to feel like a chess piece rather than an employee.
- It was important to Winston that he felt respected in his workplace. This wasn't about arrogance or power but about self-esteem and job satisfaction. He knew what he was good at and worked hard at developing his knowledge and skills so that he could both perform his particular role to the very best of his ability and also act as a mentor to others in similar roles within the organization. When the company 'downsized', Winston found that his expertise had become redundant. As there were fewer employees to do the work, he was told in no uncertain terms to 'mind his own business' and concentrate on his own work.

While none of the above scenarios refer to grief relating to deaths, they can be seen as loss experiences nevertheless. They speak of loss of status, of a hoped-for future, of respect and dignity, and of security and stability in a place where one spends a lot of time and which provides the means to have a life outside of it. Such experiences can be just as difficult to come to terms with as the deaths of individuals and, in some cases, more so in accordance with the meaning attached to them. Where they are not recognized as such, employees are not given the emotional space they need or 'permission' to work through those losses – to grieve for what they have lost.

Grief enters the workplace

It is not uncommon to hear managers saying that employees should leave their 'domestic' problems at home when they enter the workplace, and there is something to be said for trying one's best to 'compartmentalize' home and work in order to, as far as possible, focus on workplaces issues while at work and domestic issues while at home in an attempt to be as effective as we can in each context. However, it is very difficult to maintain such strict boundaries, as workers are human beings who operate at an emotional as well as a cognitive level. And when we are talking about loss and grief experiences, emotions are often highly charged and very difficult to put to one side for any length of time, if indeed individuals are even aware of, or understand what, they are experiencing themselves. As Fineman comments: 'Emotional worlds often blur the distinction between the "public" and the "private", "work" and "home"; the domains can interact' (2000, p. 13).

And so, as well as the grief that arises *within* the workplace, those committed to workplace well-being must also strive to understand the grief that employees *bring into* the workplace, simply because it is asking too much for them to leave it behind them – it is part of who they are and what they are experiencing at a given time. To expect them to do otherwise is to see them as less than human. This point is made by a participant in a study by Frost and colleagues, who quote her as saying: 'I see lots of pain which people bring to their workplaces simply because they are human beings ... most people actually walk in the doors as wounded people' (2000, p. 25).

What wounds might we be talking about here? Once again, bereavement would seem to be the most obvious loss experience, although, even where a death has occurred, levels of compassion and understanding vary. Some organizations claim to have an equitable and compassionate staff care policy which allows employees a degree of paid leave, but only in circumstances where they are expected to be grieving after the death of a family member – supposedly time to get over the worst of the experience, so that they can return to work somewhat restored to their former capacity. Such a policy lacks insight into the meanings which people attach to relationships and so, while they can help in some circumstances of bereavement, they can be harmful in others. For example, consider the death of an employee's father. To one employee this could be a massive loss which shakes their very foundation – a shock which throws them into an existential crisis to the extent that their sense of identity and well-being is threatened in a major way. To another employee, whose father has always been absent from their life, with whom there has never been a sound relationship or in which the relationship has been an abusive one, the policy is likely to be unhelpful and even unwelcome, especially if not taking that compassionate leave makes them susceptible to being thought of by colleagues as callous or unfeeling. And what of the employee who has a pet or close friend as the mainstay of their life outside work? Does such a policy address the devastation they feel when that person or animal is no longer in their lives as someone who understands and values them and gives them unconditional love? Policies about such matters therefore clearly need to be flexible to suit the circumstances. The important issue is to be supportive of an employee at a time when he or she is very vulnerable, rather than mechanistically implement a fixed policy or protocol.

But, as we have discussed, bereavement is not the only cause of grieving in the workplace. For example, while divorce can be a positive experience for some, the potential for it to constitute a significant loss experience is high. As it is a relatively common occurrence (according to the Office for National Statistics, more than 244,000 divorces were granted in the United Kingdom between 2006 and 2007 – www.statistics.gov.uk), it is reasonably likely that a significant number of employees will be affected by it in some way. For some, the effect will be limited to a minor upset while new living arrangements and financial matters are sorted but, for others, divorce can involve a myriad of losses which can seriously shake the foundations of their life. It is very difficult to leave one's problems at home when you no longer have one, or the custody of your children, or the means to support them in the way that you would like to, or the future you had hoped or planned for.

Losses associated with illness can also have a huge impact on employees' lives, but remain largely invisible or poorly understood. The nature of an employee's illness may be such that he or she can continue to work, but may experience losses such as those of function, energy, concentration and so on – and sufferers may also be living with the knowledge that their condition could pose a threat to future employment, thereby opening up the potential for experiences such as loss of financial security, status and self-esteem. Quite a significant percentage of employees are also carers of dependent relatives (the 2001 Census for England and Wales recorded the fact that over 2.5 million people combine caring with paid work – www.carersuk.org). The caring role can also be underpinned by actual and potential losses, such as those of a hoped-for life and those inherent in changes in role and relationships that often take place when someone becomes dependent.

We can see, then, that while it may not be apparent to all, many employees will be dealing with grief in some form and they will be bringing it into the workplace, but will remain unsupported if a deeper understanding of what constitutes loss and grief continues to be left off the workplace agenda for discussion and policy making. We have suggested that a significant amount of grieving goes unnoticed, but would also make the point here that to notice it, but then deal with it inappropriately, can be harmful too. For example, it can be damaging to a grieving person's sense of spiritual and emotional well-being in situations where there is:

- a lack of understanding that people grieve in different ways and for different reasons;
- resentment from colleagues that someone has to be 'carried' because they are not working to full capacity;
- an avoidance of the grieving person or of discussion about their situation in case it upsets them; and/or
- an expectation that they will grieve to a prescribed timetable and then 'get on with the job' without recognizing that grief is far more complex than this.

For a variety of reasons, it is likely that at any one time there will be quite a number of people in any workplace who are grieving, and yet some employing organizations continue to behave as if workplaces are grief-free zones. We would suggest that such a strategy is both unrealistic and unfair – a far cry from the philosophy of workplace well-being.

Trauma and terror

Trauma is a concept that is closely linked to loss and grief. This is because trauma tends to produce a very strong grief reaction as a result of the immense and overpowering sense of loss involved (loss of security and stability, loss of normality and so on). A trauma, in the sense we are using it here (as opposed to the medical sense of a physical wound) refers to the type of situation in which the person or persons concerned experience a strong and lasting psychological reaction to a profoundly disturbing experience, such as being a victim of crime or violence, being abused or being involved in a disaster situation.

Trauma has profound and far-reaching consequences for the people affected by it. It can have the effect of seriously destabilizing our sense of reality, leaving the frameworks of meaning that give us our sense of self in considerable disarray – contributing further to our feelings of loss. As Bracken comments:

> The experience of very frightening events can have the effect of shattering any sense of living in an orderly world that has inherent structures of meaning and order.
>
> People describe a feeling of being set adrift from the rest of the world, of being completely on their own in a way which is beyond ordinary loneliness. The feeling of trust in the world, both human and natural, which is essential to ordinary life, has been broken apart and people describe living in a meaningless void, desperately seeking their old sense of order and meaning.
>
> (2002, p. 142)

With specific reference to the self, he goes on to say that: 'Post-traumatic anxiety also involves a profound realization of the self's fragility' (p. 142). This means that trauma can turn our world upside down, leaving us unsure of who we are and how we fit into the wider world. In this respect, it can be seen to bring about an existential crisis – a crisis of meaning and therefore of spirituality. Understandably, this tends to be accompanied by a strong grief reaction.

As with any grief reaction, the implications can be significant for both the individual(s) directly involved and for people close to them who can also be traumatized by the event (what is often referred to as secondary or vicarious traumatization – see, for example, Pearlman and Saakvitne, 1995). This means that trauma can be quite significant for the workplace, as it can affect a significant proportion of a group of staff – in some cases, the whole workforce (Tehrani, 2004; Thompson, 2009). Consider the following potential scenarios:

- An employee is raped on her way home from a late shift. Her colleagues are devastated by the event. Normal work patterns are severely disrupted.

- An employee is electrocuted as a result of faulty equipment. His death is witnessed by a large number of people. Everyone in the organization is unsettled by this tragedy.
- A gunman holds several employees of a bank hostage as part of a bungled robbery attempt. No one is hurt, but the potential for people to have died is enough to create a considerable shockwave throughout the workforce, not only at that bank, but also at other banks in the area.
- Members of the emergency services are strongly affected by being called to an incident in which a lorry driver lost control of his vehicle and ploughed into a young mother pushing a buggy containing her eight-month-old daughter. Mother and baby are both killed.

These are just some of the potentially very wide range of examples of how trauma can affect the workplace. Some people may argue that these eventualities can safely be ignored as the likelihood of their occurring in a particular workplace is quite low. However, we would contend that this is a short-sighted and dangerous attitude, as it means that organizations will not be prepared for what can be quite challenging situations. This attitude is the equivalent of the assumption that first aid training is not necessary, as there is no need for first aid interventions most of the time.

Traditionally, trauma has been regarded as an extreme psychological reaction to extreme circumstances and has been conceptualized in predominantly medical terms as part of positivist science. The fact that 'post-traumatic stress disorder' is included in DSM IV, the official definer of psychiatric conditions, tells us that there is a strongly medicalized approach to trauma. However, such a narrow approach is increasingly being challenged and regarded as an inadequate basis for understanding a phenomenon that has broader cultural and structural dimensions and is not simply a matter of an individualized psychiatric disorder (Bracken, 2002; Brewin, 2003; Summerfield, 2004). Bracken makes apt comment when he argues that:

> Positivist psychology downplays the importance of history and culture and, in relation to trauma, asserts that PTSD captures the universal nature of human emotional reactions to violence and horror. The individualist focus of contemporary psychology has also led to a neglect of attempts to understand social and communal dynamics in the wake of trauma. Because it is assumed that meaning is generated within individual minds these dynamics have not been theorized as

having a central role. As well as these positivist and individualist assumptions, contemporary psychology also works with a notion of linear causality.

(2002, p. 65)

This growing critique of an individualized, medicalized conception of trauma has significant implications for the workplace. This is because, in taking a more sociologically informed approach to trauma, we can see that such factors as environmental influences, interpersonal relations and power dynamics, cultural assumptions and norms (including workplace cultures) and social structures (race, gender, class and so on) can all play a part in the development of traumatic experiences and reactions to them. There is, therefore, a danger in conceptualizing trauma too narrowly, as such an approach would fail to see just how significant workplace factors could be in many such circumstances. Such a narrow understanding will therefore leave us ill equipped to deal with the challenges of trauma in the workplace.

What adds weight to the need to take trauma in the workplace seriously is the threat of terrorism. In the post-9/11 era, terrorism is clearly a significant concern. This can apply at two levels: (i) actual terrorist activity; and (ii) the threat of such activity, even when such a threat does not become reality. The latter can be a significant source of trauma, as it is the intense fear such a threat can generate that can prove traumatic. As Scraton puts it: 'To strike terror into the heart of an identifiable community is to frighten people so deeply that they lose trust and confidence in all aspects of routine daily life' (2002a, pp. 2–3). The threat of a terrorist attack reminds us of the fact that we may face death at any moment. In this regard, Brewin writes of: 'a fundamental human difficulty in comprehending and acknowledging our own vulnerability' (2003, p. 21). By this he means that so often people adopt an 'it won't happen to me attitude'. And, while this failure to take trauma as a feature of human experience seriously is clearly unwise, the threat of terrorism can have the effect of bringing it home to us quite brutally that we are not immortal.

To neglect the significance of trauma in the workplace, we would argue, is not a wise approach to workplace well-being in particular or to human resource management in general. But, not only is it necessary to put trauma on the well-being agenda, it is also essential to make sure that the approach to trauma we adopt is one that does justice to the complexities involved – that is, one that does not rely on a narrow, individualistic model that neglects the wider sociological aspects that can be so significant.

Conclusion

In this chapter we have sketched out the importance of including issues of loss, grief and trauma in our consideration of workplace well-being and highlighted the danger of neglecting such matters. In doing so we have shown how complex the subject matter is and how potentially harmful to individuals, to organizations and to their stakeholders. We have also seen that if we are to be serious about putting well-being at the heart of effective human resource management, then we must ensure not only that the relevant issues are part of our thinking, but also that our thinking is based on a sufficiently sophisticated understanding of the complexities involved to do justice to the sensitive and demanding challenges involved.

In terms of making progress, important steps will need to include the development of relevant policies (or the amendment of existing ones) to include adequate reference to loss, grief and trauma, and the development and delivery of appropriate training programmes or at least briefing sessions for key personnel. However, these 'technical' steps are only part of what is needed. If organizations are to be equipped to deal appropriately with the extremes of human experience that characterize loss, grief and trauma, then a lot of work needs to be done to ensure that the underlying culture is sufficiently supportive to carry people through. In some settings, this can be an undertaking of major proportions, requiring a high level of leadership expertise (see Gilbert, Chapter 8 in this volume). Other settings will already be sufficiently people focused to find the incorporation of these additional factors into their thinking and their HR practices relatively straightforward. Whichever is the case, the inclusion of loss, grief and trauma considerations on the well-being agenda is clearly a step that needs to be taken.

References

Bracken, P. (2002) *Trauma: Culture, Meaning & Philosophy*, London, Whurr Publishers.
Brewin, C. R. (2003) *Post-Traumatic Stress Disorder: Malady or Myth*, London, Yale University Press.
Fineman, S. (2000) 'Emotional Arenas Revisited', in Fineman (2000).
Fineman, S. (ed.) (2000) *Emotion in Organisations*, 2nd edn, London, Sage.
Frost, P. J., Dutton, J. E., Worline, M. C. and Wilson, A. (2000) 'Narratives of Compassion in Organizations', in Fineman (2000).
MacDonald, L. A. C. (2005) *Wellness at Work: Protecting and Promoting Employee Well-Being*, London, Chartered Institute of Personnel and Development.

Neimeyer, R. A. (ed.) (2001) *Meaning Reconstruction and the Experience of Loss*, Washington DC, American Psychological Association.

Neimeyer, R. A. and Anderson, A. (2002) 'Meaning Reconstruction Theory', in Thompson (2002).

Pearlman, L. A. and Saakvitne, K. W. (1995) *Trauma and the Therapist – Counter-Transference and Vicarious Traumatization in Psychotherapy with Incest Survivors*, New York, W. W. Norton.

Rosen, G. (ed.) (2004) *Posttraumatic Stress Disorder: Issues and Controversies*, Chichester, Wiley.

Scraton, P. (2002a) 'Introduction: Witnessing "Terror", Anticipating "War"', in Scraton (2002b).

Scraton, P. (2002b) *Beyond September 11: An Anthology of Dissent*, London, Pluto.

Stein, H. F. (2007) *Insight and Imagination: A Study in Knowing and Not-Knowing in Organizational Life*, Lanham, MD, University Press of America.

Summerfield, D. (2004) 'Cross-Cultural Perspectives on the Medicalization of Human Suffering', in Rosen (2004).

Tehrani, N. (2004) *Workplace Trauma: Concepts, Assessment and Interventions*, Hove, Brunner-Routledge.

Thompson, N. (ed.) (2002) *Loss and Grief: A Guide for Human Services Practitioners*, Basingstoke, Palgrave Macmillan.

Thompson, N. (2009) *Loss, Grief and Trauma in the Workplace*, Amityville, NY, Baywood.

Part 2
Promoting Well-Being

7
Promoting Workplace Learning: Challenges and Pitfalls

John Bates

> By three methods we may learn wisdom: first, by reflection, which is noblest; second, by imitation, which is easiest; and third by experience, which is the bitterest.
>
> (Confucius)

The promotion of well-being in organizations is inextricably linked to creating a culture in which people feel valued and can see their worth acknowledged in workplaces which provide opportunities for people to grow and develop. Of course, learning is something undertaken by individuals, but how organizations manage, encourage and ultimately capture the fruits of that process can either hinder or encourage workplace learning. There is something vaguely odd about the concept that an organization can have the adjective 'learning' attached to it, as a complex arrangement of buildings, people, machinery or whatever is surely unable to 'learn'. But workplaces are, of course, essentially the sum of the people working there and this chapter will contend that organizations can be places of genuine learning, but need to revisit the thinking behind the concept if they are not only to maximize the enormous potential people have to offer, but also provide workplaces where people feel valued and where their sense of belonging is enhanced. The benefits of a happier workforce have been recognized by David Cameron (2006) who has advocated the drive to 'ethical work' in which it is possible to have workplaces which are highly productive, but which are also supportive of well-being. One of the reasons for his concern is that recent evidence suggests that, for many people, workplaces are not healthy places to be. Stress and other mental health conditions are now among the main causes of employee absence, according to the CIPD absence management survey (2006). The Health and Safety Executive (HSE) (2000) estimates that stress costs business £3.8 billion a year. This chapter examines to what extent the development of learning in organizations might have a contribution to make to the goal of making workplaces better places to be.

Organizational learning or the learning organization?

The concept of organizational learning is not a new one (Gould, 2000; Grey, 2005; Thompson, 2006) and it has long been acknowledged that it plays an important role in maintaining morale and ensuring organizations meet their objectives. The idea is that organizations enhance learning processes: 'in order to improve individual and collective organizational knowledge and understanding' (Holt, Love and Heng, 2000). From this well-established concept has arisen the notion of 'the learning organization', which is defined by Pedler et al. (1988) as 'an organization which facilitates the learning of all its members and continually transforms itself (cited in Dale, 1994, p. 22). In other words, the learning organization focuses on the deliberate tactic of facilitating the learning of its people to improve the overall functioning of the workplace. The formation of the European Consortium for the Learning Organization (ECLO) according to Campbell and Cairns (1994): 'signals that the term "learning organization" has more or less officially entered the vocabulary of many managers' (1994, p. 24). However, they go on to argue that:

> entering the vocabulary of managers is not the same as operationalizing and implementing organizational learning to gain competitive advantage ... what is lacking is a convergence on a definition capable of application to many organisations plus guidelines to help implement the ideas.
>
> (Campbell and Cairns, 1994,
> cited in Reynolds and Ablett, 1998, p. 35)

Traditional ideas of a learning organization see it as a place where individuals, appropriately encouraged, learn new skills and capabilities, almost as autonomous learners who then enrich the workplace. Popular initiatives like Investors in People and the widespread introduction of National Vocational Qualifications (NVQs) have proved attractive to workplaces and, in many instances, are seen as the way to become recognized as a learning organization or, indeed, seen as synonymous with what a learning organization ought to be (Reynolds and Ablett, 1998).

The last two decades in particular have seen a major advance in the development of competency-based learning, biting further into areas where there is a technical and vocational element. Bates has conducted an extensive review of the history of the competence movement and finds how little meaningful scrutiny there has been over the years and how its development and penetration have outstripped our understanding of both its effectiveness and its social significance to the extent, she argues, that: 'It has become a colossus, skating on thin ice' (2002, p. 1). She develops the argument further and suggests that, somehow, its implications for education and learning have been immune from critical academic scrutiny. In 1993 Jones and Moore speculated that the silence in the academic literature may be socially constructed, in the sense that, by creating strong classifications and boundaries around the knowledge production of vocational programmes, it has produced almost 'no go' areas for academics. Bates develops this point further when she comments:

> If we define the competence movement more broadly to include the increasing use of performance criteria to manage and measure organizational and individual performance, it is even more starkly evident that we are dealing with a highly pervasive and seemingly relentless social trend.
>
> (2002, p. 8)

There is, however, a significant difference between a learning organization and an organization that simply pays attention to training – although the latter is important, and is almost certainly part of every learning organization, as are supervision, mentoring and appraisal (Thompson, 2006). But, in most organizations that have good training programmes, it is worth noting that training is something that is often given to employees by the organization. It is the organization (in the shape of the management, usually via the human resources department) that determines and then fulfils training needs. While, of course, there is a role for disseminating essential knowledge and required training programmes within any organization, employees who have some significant degree of self-determination of their own development, rather than simply having the training imposed on them from above, are more likely to become lifelong learners. An over-reliance on narrow, outcome-based, workplace learning runs the serious risk of a narrowness of learning based simply on occupational outcomes which, by themselves, stress the functional value of learning, which ultimately runs the risk of fostering a watered-down version of a learning process.

88 *Promoting Well-Being*

In reality, for many workers there is actually very little that is routine. Much of what many workers do is unpredictable and demands a capacity to 'think on one's feet' and an ability to improvise and combine ideas and themes in new and creative combinations. A learning culture based on a 'pedagogy of labour' (Field, 1991), which stresses a heavy reliance on National Vocational Qualifications (NVQ) or other behaviourist approaches to adult learning, should have a limited place in a learning organization. This emphasis on 'training' at the expense of education can never deliver what modern organizations and society actually need. Jeffs and Smith (1990) offer a biting critique of this approach to learning in the workplace, suggesting that:

> The problem with skills led training is that it is incrementally bolted on to a partial analysis of practice and purpose. Faulty and restricted perceptions of essential role, purpose and practice ensure that the skills taught must be inadequate to the task.
>
> (1991, p. 130)

They are not alone. Mezirow, as long ago as 1978, challenged this approach to the training of adults as: 'indoctrination to engineer consent' and of addressing: 'the wrong reality to begin with' (Mezirow, 1991). In addition, much of the literature on learning organizations approaches the issue from the perspective that learning is essentially good for business. For example, Cassels states:

> One may conclude that training and human resource management generally – may be seen working ... at a deeper level and concerns developing corporate capability so as to enable the company both to perform well immediately and to develop in the future in such a way as to improve its market position.
>
> (1991, p. 44)

In a similar vein, Senge writes in his seminal book *The Fifth Discipline*:

> As the world becomes more accessible and even the smallest companies can obtain whatever skills and technology they need at reasonable cost, the only source of competitive advantage is an organization's ability to learn and react more quickly than its competitors.
>
> (1990, p. 43)

Of course, organizations of any sort need to be clearly focused on their ultimate objectives, but the above quotations should caution that simply seeing the development of a learning organization as a means of reconstituting the worker to make him or her more 'productive' runs a risk of failure, as it encourages a learning regime with little understanding of how real learning takes place. In other words, an approach which tries to intervene and produce workers whose ambitions and outlook resonate with the organization may only lead to problems, as people resist the attempt to shape them into something they may not want, or are unable, to become. As Potter argues, 'In a world where people are vital in raising the value of goods and services, organizations must switch from managing workers simply as costs to managing them as valuable capital assets' (2006, p. 4).

The question of whether the 'learning organization' is a realistic, achievable, practical goal is an interesting and challenging one, as it often wishes out of existence the political realities many workers experience in their daily lives. I share the view of Thompson (2006) that perhaps there is an incremental process required which involves primarily the development of a 'learning culture' within a workplace. Gould is helpful here when he argues that:

> Although the literature on the learning organisation is relatively recent, it builds on a longer sociological tradition of theorisation of the relationship between organisational structure and behaviour.
>
> (2000, p. 2)

This allows a broader debate to take place which might examine organizational culture as well as its structures and systems. Cultures in organizations can be extremely influential in either encouraging or destroying attempts to make workplaces centres of enthusiastic learning which enhance well-being or centres of crushing inertia which destroy creativity and make workplaces unhealthy places to be.

Developing a learning culture: the first steps

We need to be clear at this point that developing a learning culture is different from the development of an organizational culture. During the early 1980s there were attempts at developing 'culture management' (Grey, 2005). This was seen at the time as the way forward to transform organizations by creating the idea of shared values within organizations – for example, by using a form of learning described by Kunda: 'The idea is to educate people without them knowing it. Have the religion and not know how they got it' (1992, p. 5). Grey goes on to use the example of how the privatization of public services throughout the last 20 years brought with it not only a change in ownership, but also attempts by managers to shift the organizational culture from one committed to public service to one driven by outcomes and performance targets – in short, a new efficiency that would mirror the assumed strengths of the private sector. For many in the public sector, for example, the experience over the last few years has not always been comfortable, making some former public bodies stressful places to work.

Staff within an organization where learning is seen as central to their mission should feel empowered to take responsibility for their own work area and/or work tasks and for their own career and personal development. The learning they undertake develops not only their direct technical and work-related skills, but also their social, organizational and communication skills. They learn, both directly and indirectly, to take responsibility for their work and for themselves.

Claxton argues that:

> Lifelong learning demands ... the ability to think strategically about your own learning path, and this requires the self-awareness to know one's own goals, the resources that are needed to pursue them, and your current strengths and weaknesses in that regard ... You have to be able to monitor your progress; if necessary even to measure it; to mull over different options and courses of development; to be mindful of your own assumptions and habits, and able to stand back from them and appraise them when learning gets stuck; and in general to manage yourself as a learner – prioritising, planning, reviewing progress, revising strategy and if necessary changing tack.
>
> (1999, p. 14)

A learning culture can be encouraged by a recognition that the organization:

- openly values individual and organizational learning as a prime means of delivering the organizational mission;
- involves all its members through continuous reflection in a process of continual review and improvement;
- structures work in such a way that work tasks are used as opportunities for continuous learning;
- needs to avoid a rigid hierarchical structure; and
- understands the learning process.

For many organizations developing a learning culture may require a serious revision of its practices. It is unlikely to develop in a 'traditional', heavily hierarchical organization in which a top-down structure is seen as the way to communicate and control, and where a highly formalized and evident command and control structure is used as the dominant managerial device. Similarly, the organization will not have the traditional view of the people it employs and the way in which it works. The organization is less likely to view the workforce as a collection of passive, hired hands and less likely to believe that new technology will automatically solve future organizational problems.

An organization which is developing a learning culture acknowledges that it must be adaptive and responsive to change in a world that seems to demand change almost on a daily basis, but manages that by valuing the concept of 'key professionals' and rewards personal development. People who are valued for the role they perform feed into organizational wellbeing, for work is integral to our identities and self-worth; our 'freedom to exercise informed judgement in work is a vital part of being human', argues Ozga (1999, p. 69).

Any workplace committed to developing a learning culture goes beyond the notion of simply valuing the individuals who make up the workforce by attempting to set individual learning in a framework that values all learning and attempts to discover additional lessons and add additional value to ongoing individual learning. The value of individual learning is maximized by systems that allow the organization itself to learn from the process of learning and to collect that learning for the benefit of others. Simply relying on the doubtful idea that 'experience is the best teacher' will produce workers who are stale, uninterested and often deskilled, as learning through practice is not how it happens (Bates, 2004. Nor is it sufficient to simply present a list of outcomes or competencies with the expectation that a person will 'learn' something. Being there does not equal learning. The crucial element in the process is what we do with any experience in terms of analysing it, reflecting upon it and learning from it. That process of reflexivity is not automatic, simple or quick, but is a technique of such value that the business of getting it right for both the organization and the well-being of the individual is worth the effort.

Developing reflexivity

Moon describes the process of reflexivity as: 'a set of abilities and skills, to indicate the taking of a critical stance, an orientation to problem solving or state of mind' (1999, p. 63). This nicely encapsulates the wide range of activities associated with thinking about one's learning. Seminal work by Kolb (1984) and Schön (1983) has given reflective learning higher prominence in recent years, using and applying a basic principle of reflecting on experience to improve action and practice in the workplace. The process is challenging, as it forces us to question what it is that we know and how we come to know it. Reflective learning involves moving away from traditional approaches to learning with the emphasis on 'technical rationality' and forces the individual to examine the basis on which he or she thinks something to be the case. The adoption of a more thoughtful and reflective form of learning may avoid developing a workforce that is inflexible and narrow in its perceptions and who are poor at problem solving. Reflective learning, done well, draws us into revealing and critically examining the values, assumptions, ideas, theories and strategies supporting our professional decisions and skills (Thompson and Thompson, 2008). It is essentially a process of elucidation.

In place of the rigidity of technical rationality, reflective learning proposes a more fluid approach in which there is a greater emphasis on integrating knowledge, theory and practice. Gould (1996) argues that:

> There is considerable empirical evidence, based on research into a variety of occupations, suggesting that expertise does not derive from the application of rules or procedures applied deductively from positivist research. Instead, it is argued that practice wisdom depends upon highly developed intuition which may be difficult to articulate but can be demonstrated through practice. On the basis of this reconstructed epistemology of practice, reflective learning offers an approach to education which operates through an understanding of professional knowledge as primarily developed through practice and the systematic analysis of experience.
>
> (1996, p. 1)

Good reflective learning underpins good practice in the workplace, as it provides the opportunity to review progress to date and helps the learner to identify areas of work which are in need of further development and those areas that have been successfully developed which, in turn, gives a good opportunity for that work to be shared throughout the organization, perhaps as models of good practice.

To facilitate this process Peters (1991) describes a four-step process called DATA: Describe, Analyse, Theorize, Act:

1. Describe: the basic elements of the problem, task or situation.
2. Analyse: identify assumptions, beliefs, rules, motives and any other factors underlying the current approach.
3. Theorize: what alternatives are possible? Comparative merits and drawbacks?
4. Act: try out the new approach, evaluate the results and share.

Essentially, our experience or skill in any particular sphere of activity depends on not just how much time we have been doing the job but also, more importantly, how well we have learned, adapted, innovated and implemented effective patterns of behaviour.

Roth (1989) suggested that the basic elements of a reflective process are as follows:

- keeping an open mind about what, why and how we do things;
- awareness of what, why and how we do things;
- questioning what, why and how we do things;
- asking what, why and how other people do things;
- generating choices, options and possibilities;
- comparing and contrasting results;
- seeking to understand underlying mechanisms and rationales;
- viewing our activities and results from various perspectives;
- asking 'what if ...';
- seeking feedback;
- using prescriptive models only when carefully adapted to the individual situation;
- analysing, synthesizing and testing; and
- searching for, identifying and resolving problems.

In summary, our 'experience' is often judged and quantified by how much time we have spent doing a particular job or role. However, a general observation shows that some people acquire, develop and continuously improve performance more effectively than others. Experience is not determined by how much time we spend on an activity, but by what we derive from the time we spend. Reflective learning, therefore, is a tool for:

- extracting more 'on the job' learning from our experiences;
- creating new understandings, fresh approaches;

- generating new ideas, new behaviour patterns;
- testing these new insights and ideas in the hot house of practical situations; and
- challenging uncritical routinization.

How can reflective learning be promoted?

Schön (1983) argued that the model of professional training referred to earlier as 'technical rationality' – that is, giving people material so that they can then apply it in practice – is fundamentally flawed, and does not encapsulate how most workers 'think in action'. It is therefore quite inappropriate in an ever-changing world. Not only that, but he went on to argue that, if we want people in the workplace to rise above superficial problem solving that only happens under pressure, some form of reflective learning has to become embedded within organizations that encourages staff to engage with deeper-level, potentially more meaningful and difficult enquiry.

This idea fits in well with what we know about how adults learn (Knowles, 1978). Essentially, adults have their own motivations for learning which involves making sense of, and building on, their existing knowledge base and experiences. For many adults their motivation for learning is related to their real lives and the practices and roles they engage in. Also, adults have a drive towards self-direction and towards becoming autonomous learners which often involves the learner initiating the task, with the role of the trainer/mentor providing a safe environment in which learning can take place without stress or humiliation. Another key feature of the adult learner is their ability to learn about their own learning processes which can often provide rich material for discussion and debate. Learning, then, is a characteristic of real-life activities, in which people take on different roles and participate in different ways, allowing people to learn by engaging in practice. Where the learning is seen as relevant, adults will engage. As Knowles (1978) points out, adults reflect and build upon their experience, using problems and issues in their real lives, and then articulate ways of resolving them.

These ideas resonate with the Canadian Centre for Management Development (2002), who argue that employee well-being involves:

- developing an attitude of mind that enables the employee to have self-confidence and self-respect, and to be emotionally resilient;
- having a sense of purpose, feelings of fulfilment and meaning;

- possessing an active mind that is alert, open to new experiences, curious and creative; and
- having a network of relationships that are supportive and nurturing.

This again argues powerfully for the benefits of reflective learning, since so much of what we learn arises out of the complexities of our own experience. A great deal of learning is therefore idiosyncratic and uniquely related to the learner, making it difficult to be planned in advance. Reflective learning enables people to reorganize experience and 'see' situations in new ways. In this way, adult learning is potentially transformative, both personally and socially. The problem is making it happen.

If reflective learning is to rise above a naval-gazing exercise, one of the key components is to develop a structure of organized supervision or mentoring. Learning through experience is not an easy option, but is a tough process that demands structure, a systematic approach to mentoring and a committed mentor. Even seasoned workers are often unable to offer insight into their actions without being guided through the process. One model to consider offers three elements:

- Supervision (mentoring/coaching);
- Structured reflections; and
- Utilization of a 'diary'.

Supervision/mentoring

Supervision is about guiding people through the process by supporting, challenging and providing vision. The latter concept is a metaphor for encouraging greater understanding by offering a 'map' through the maze of complexities, perhaps by making use of a structured 'diary'. Essentially, the approach encourages people to develop an attitude of open-mindedness where nothing is taken for granted and self-questioning is encouraged and seen as a sign of strength. Providing vision entails encouraging people to take responsibility for their work by moving beyond immediate 'everyday' questions to explore more diverse ideas. And, finally, providing vision helps people to develop a sense of wholeheartedness in which self-esteem, openness and commitment are explicitly valued. As Daloz argues: 'only by bringing our changes into consciousness can we be certain that they will stay put' (1986, p. 39). Acting as 'coach' demands both challenging and supporting, but if challenging is too thoughtless and robust without adequate support, then people will become intimidated and cease to be effective. Too little support and challenge leaves people in the comfort zone, while too little challenge and an over-supporting environment ensures that growth will never happen and real reflection will be illusory.

As mentioned earlier, if reflective learning is not conducted as a deliberate process, it can become a simple act of navel gazing. There are a number of models available to help supervisors and staff create a framework for reflection from a simple checklist through to more sophisticated, in-depth analyses dependent on the role and function of the member of staff and their level of understanding of reflective practice (see, for example, Bulman and Schultz, 2004; Gibbs, 1998).

A simple model might ask people to bring to a training session a brief account of an event or project listed against the following headings:

- What are you doing?
- What do you plan to do?
- What have you done?
- Why did you do it?
- What have you learned?

Trainers or mentors might want to make use of scenarios or case studies and then ask questions:

- Did our department/team act appropriately?
- Was the response too heavy-handed/too weak?
- Did we do the right thing by the way we acted?
- How should we have acted in this case to provide a better service?
- How might we do things differently next time?

Alternatively, a more structured approach can be adopted which asks people to complete a reflective log that focuses on one particular event chosen by the 'trainee' or by the supervisor/mentor. Alternatively, this approach can be used as a group training exercise that encourages people to begin the process of becoming reflective learners.

The Reflective Log – Cue Questions (based on Johns, 2000, and Carper, 1978)
1. Description of experience
- Describe the here and now experience
- What essential factors contributed to this experience?

- Who are the significant actors in this experience?
- What are the key processes (for reflection) in this experience?

2. *Reflection*
- What was I trying to achieve?
- Why did I work the way I did?
- What were the consequences of my actions for:
  - myself?
  - the client/customer?
  - my colleagues?

3. *Influencing factors*
- What factors influenced my decision – Knowledge? Skills? Values?

4. *Could I have dealt better with the situation?*
- What other choices did I have?
- Did I have a 'plan B' ready?
- What might have been the consequences of a different choice?

5. *Learning*
- How do I now feel about this experience?
- How have I made sense of this experience in the light of past experiences?
- How has the experience changed my way of knowing?
- How has my skill base been enhanced?
- Were my values compromised in any way?

The processes above all stress the importance of structured reflection which is fundamentally about developing:

> the capacity to draw back in order to reflect on what is happening almost as it happens ... enables learning to take place in a way which allows thought-less action to become thought-ful.
> (Yelloly and Henkel, 1995, p. 8)

But it is not a straightforward or linear activity. The journey to developing an organizational culture which encourages reflective learning is fraught with wrong turns and frustrations, but the journey is worth it for both the individual and the organization. The process is also messy, in the sense that people are being encouraged to engage with, and unpick, real problems and real issues, rather than being presented with prepared training materials that follow a neat logical sequence. It is through this process of thinking, challenging, reflecting and making connections that clarity can emerge from the fog and learning happens. As Claxton has suggested: 'learning to learn, or the development of learning power, is getting better at knowing when, how and what to do when you don't know what to do' (1999, p. 45).

Removing obstacles

Developing a learning culture in an organization is certainly time consuming and demands a reframing of the way organizations educate and train their workforce. But it can also generate huge savings in time and effort as a result of more sophisticated problem-solving techniques, wider accessing of resources and more efficient deployment of those resources. Another obstacle that can arise is claims of work overload and having no time to rethink training strategies in the workplace. These are not unreasonable responses, but what often underlies these is a defensiveness which may shroud instead a simple resistance to change. Making the changes, I would argue, is not the problem but, for many organizations, their unthinking adherence to training programmes dedicated to the inculcation of a limited range of competencies which gives the illusion of preparing a better skilled workforce is the real problem. After all, this approach brings with it the illusion of scientific credibility, with its language of behaviourist psychology and a range of taken-for-granted assumptions about how people learn and make sense of the world around them.

In addition, the skills approach allows us to measure not only the workers' learning outcomes, but the 'trainer's competence' as well as the cost effectiveness, all within a framework of fixed behavioural objectives. My point here is that the main obstacle to progress is a cultural one – a culture in which we have allowed a simplistic, if seductive, model of training to dominate our thinking. By exercising a shift from purely functionalist training approaches to a model of learning based on reflective learning techniques we can move towards de Bono's idea of *operacy:*

> In the real world there are people to deal with, decisions to be made, strategies to be designed and monitored, plans to be made and implemented. There is conflict, bargaining, negotiating and deal making. All this requires a great deal of thinking and a great

deal of operacy. ... Operacy involves such aspects of thinking as: other people's views, priorities, objectives, alternatives, consequences, decisions, conflict resolutions, creativity and many other aspects not normally covered in the type of thinking used for information analysis.

(1999, p. 11)

Another potential obstacle is that the development of a learning culture based on a 'bottom-up' approach requires a high degree of management trust, as the reflections and deliberations of workers may not always conform to what managers want. It is true that a learning culture will need to be managed, but essentially it is driven by everyone, which makes it more spontaneous. Wenger and Snyder (2001) suggest that this approach can be extraordinarily powerful, and their research suggests that large corporations have been transformed and the workforce engaged and enriched. They approach the issue by suggesting that learning teams become the heart of the organization, ensuring that teams grow together so that, if one member leaves, the wisdom acquired remains, and the team continues to experiment and push boundaries in an ever-expanding developmental process. This idea of the 'quality circle' is developed further by Wenger and Snyder who talk of 'communities of practice' where groups of people come together motivated by a shared expertise and enthusiasm. These communities of practice may exist in workplaces or by email networks, but essentially share their knowledge and experiences 'in free flowing, creative ways that foster new approaches to problems' (2001, p. 3).

Conclusion

There is a task to do and that is to continue training and teaching people in the workplace so that they become sufficiently engaged in the project that they want to become 'good', rather than 'correct' and remain enthusiastic learners for life (Thompson, 2006). The project will demand reframing the way training is approached by rethinking, for example, traditional routes, comfortable though they may be, in favour of embracing a model that challenges taken-for-granted assumptions. A revitalized learning framework in the workplace ensures that dialogue about work and what underpins that work is encouraged and rewarded by allowing people to step outside of the safety of the mundane and to take some responsibility for their own learning, which will involve an element of risk taking and inevitable mistakes. Trainers should not be 'rescuers', but instead encouragers of uncertainty, in the sense that staff are allowed to reframe situations in the light of past experiences and future hypotheses by burrowing down into their experiences in order to inform the present and the future.

This is a big project. Encouraging reflective learning in organizations cannot be an 'add on', but must, incrementally, become part of how an organization functions. Certainly both staff and trainers may want to resist, as the 'old ways' are comfortable and recognizable, but the potential for human development and well-being is worth the effort. Workplaces have the potential to lift people above the mundane and become places where learning is valued and openly encouraged, giving employees opportunities to become genuine lifelong learners. Through encouraging real learning, organizations can provide the foundations for people being valued and who, in their turn, see the workplace as a place of stimulation, reward and well-being.

References

Barnett, R. (1994) *The Limits of Competence*, Buckingham, Open University Press.
Bates, I. (2002) 'The Competence and Outcomes Movement: The Landscape of Research 1986–1996', *Education-line database*; http://education.leeds.ac.uk/devt/research/post-14.htm.
Bates, J. (2004) 'Promoting Learning through Reflective Practice', *British Journal of Occupational Learning* 2(2), pp. 21–32.
Brockett, R. (ed.) (1991) *Professional Development for Educators of Adults: New Directions for Adult and Continuing Education*, San Francisco, Jossey-Bass.
Buckler, B. (1998) 'Practical Steps towards a Learning Organisation: Applying Academic Knowledge to Improvement and Innovation in Business Processes', *The Learning Organisation* 5(1), pp. 15–23.
Bulman, C. and Schultz, S (2004) *Reflective Practice in Nursing*, Oxford, Blackwell Publishing.
Cameron, D. (2006) Speech to Google Zeitgeist Europe, http://www.guardian.co.uk/politics/2006/may/22/conservatives.davidcameron
Canadian Centre for Management Development (2002) *A Fine Balance: A Manager's Guide to Workplace Well-Being*, cited in *What's Happening with Well-Being at Work?* (2007), Change Agenda, CIPD publication.
Carper, B. (1978) 'Fundamental Patterns of Knowing in Nursing', *Advances in Nursing Science* 1(1), pp. 13–23.
Cassels, J. (1991) *Training and Competitiveness*, London, Kogan Page.
Claxton, G. (1999) *Wise Up: The Challenge of Lifelong Learning*, London, Bloomsbury.
Dale, M. (1994) 'Learning Organisations', in Mabey and Iles (1994).
Daloz, L. (1986) *Effective Teaching and Mentoring: Realising the Transformational Power of Adult Learning Experiences*, London, Wiley.
Davies, H. T. O. (2000) 'Developing Learning Organisations in the New NHS', *British Medical Journal*, April, pp. 998–1001.

De Bono, E. (1999) *New Thinking for the New Millennium*, London, Penguin.
Field, J. (1991) 'Competency and Pedagogy of Labour', *Studies in the Education of Adults* 23(1), pp. 41–52.
Fook, J., Ryan, M. and Hawkins, L. (2000) *Professional Expertise: Practice, Theory and Education for Working in Uncertainty*, London, Whiting & Birch.
Gibbs, G. (1998) *Realising Clinical Effectiveness and Clinical Governance through Clinical Supervision Practitioner*, Book 1, Oxford, RCN Institute, Radcliffe Medical Press.
Gould, N. (1996) 'Social Work, information technology and the post-fordist welfare state', in N. Gould, & I. Taylor, (eds) *Reflective Learning for Social Work*, Aldershot: Arena.
Gould, N. (2000) 'Becoming a Learning Organisation: A Social Work Example', *Social Work Education* 19(6), pp. 586–96.
Grey, C. (2005) *A Very Short, Fairly Interesting and Reasonably Cheap Book About Studying Organisations*, London, Sage.
Health and Safety Commission (2000) *Securing Health Together: A Long-term Occupational Health Strategy for England, Scotland and Wales*, Sudbury, HSE Books.
Holt, G. D., Love, P. E. D. and Li, Heng (2000) 'The Learning Organisation: Toward a Paradigm for Mutually Beneficial Strategic Construction Alliances', *International Journal of Project Management*, 18, pp. 415–21.
Jeffs, T. and Smith, M. (1990) *Using Informal Education*, Buckingham: Open University Press.
Jones, L. and Moore, R (1993) 'Education, Competence and Control of Expertise', *British Journal of the Sociology of Education* 14(4), pp. 385–97.
Johns, C. (2000) *Becoming a Reflective Practitioner: A Reflective and Holistic Approach to Clinical Nursing, Practice Development and Clinical Supervision*, Oxford, Blackwell Science.
Knowles, M. S. (1978) *The Adult Learner: A Neglected Species*, London, Gulf Publishing.
Kolb, D. A. (1984) *Experiential Learning: Experience as the Source of Learning and Development*, New Jersey, Prentice Hall.
Kunda, G. (1992) *Engineering Culture*, Philadelphia, PA, Temple University Press.
Mabey, C. and Iles, P. (eds) (1994) *Managing Learning*, London, Routledge.
Martyn, H. (2000) *Developing Reflective Practice*, Bristol, Polity Press.
Mezirow, J. (1991). *Transformative Dimensions of Adult Learning*, San Francisco, Jossey-Bass.
Moon, J. (1999) *Reflections in Learning and Professional Development*, London, Kogan Page.
Ozga, J. (1999) *Policy Research in Educational Settings*. Buckingham: Open University Press.
Palmer, A. M., Burns, S. and Bulman, C. (eds) (1994) *Reflective Practice in Nursing: The Growth of the Professional Practitioner*, Oxford, Blackwell Scientific.
Pedler, M., Boydell, T. and Burgoyne, J. (1994) *A Manager's Guide to Self-Development*, Maidenhead, McGraw Hill.
Peters, J. (1991) 'Strategies for Reflective Practice', in Brockett (1991).
Potter, J. (2006) *Smart Work*, London, Chartered Institute of Personnel and Development.
Redmond, B. (2004) *Reflection in Action*, Aldershot, Ashgate.

Reynolds, R. and Ablett, A. (1998) 'Transforming the Rhetoric of Organizational Learning to the Reality of the Learning Organization', *Learning Organization* 5(1), pp. 24–35.
Roth, R. A. (1989) 'Preparing the Reflective Practitioner: Transforming the Apprentice through the Dialectic', *Journal of Teacher Education* 40(2), pp. 31–5.
Schön, D. A. (1983) *The Reflective Practitioner: How Professionals Think in Action*, New York, Basic Books.
Senge, P. M. (1990) *The Fifth Discipline: The Art and Practice of the Learning Organization*, New York, Century Business.
Shor, I. (1987) *Critical Teaching and Everyday Life*, Chicago, University of Chicago Press.
Thompson, N. (2006) *Promoting Workplace Learning*, Bristol, Policy Press.
Thompson, N. and Bates, J. (1997) *Learning from Other Disciplines*. Norwich, University of East Anglia Monographs.
Thompson, S. and Thompson, N. (2008) *The Critically Reflective Practitioner*, Basingstoke, Palgrave Macmillan.
Wenger, E. C. and Snyder, W. M. (2001) 'The Organizational Frontier', *Harvard Business Review on Organizational Learning*, Cambridge, MA, Harvard Business School Press.
Yelloly, M. and Henkel, M. (1995) *Learning and Teaching in Social Work: Towards Reflective Practice*, London, Jessica Kingsley.

8
Leading to Well-Being

Peter Gilbert

Introduction

What we want and what we need are quite complex, stemming in part from our origins in small cohesive, tribal groups and our expansion into increasingly individual states of being within a globalized marketplace for labour and goods. Humans have perhaps moved from being big fish in small pools to small fish in a massive pool. In each human life we also have a continuing struggle between the twin desires of intimacy and autonomy. Within all of these often conflicting states, we have an increasingly complex struggle for identity. At one time, identity was formed for good or ill, often through group and community states; now we are increasingly having to make and remake who we are (see Bauman, 2005, 2007).

As Maslow (1943) pointed out, people look to meet some basic survival needs and then move on to address higher areas of need and attainment. The problem with taking Maslow too literally is that human processes are never as linear as a model suggests. As studies of art, anthropology, philosophy and theology demonstrate, humans have, from earliest recorded times, reached out for a sense of meaning, hope, connection and transcendence beyond the individual (see Coyte, Gilbert and Nichols, 2007, ch. 1).

As psychotherapist and concentration camp survivor Viktor Frankl (1959) opined: 'Man's [sic] search for meaning is the primary motivation in his life and not a "secondary rationalization" of instinctual drives.' We are indeed meaning-seeking creatures, and, Schultz (1994) states that humans have three major drives: to be liked, to have a measure of control, and to gain significance. Gaining a sense of meaning is partly individual, it comes from within us, but also arises in relation to others and the Other (see Haidt, 2006). So work, which takes up such a great deal of our lives, has to have a sense of meaning and purpose for it not to become mere routine (see Moss, Chapter 11 in this volume). Bunting (2004, 2005) has written persuasively about the culture of overwork. Sometimes the imperatives seem to come from without: work harder or you won't have a job; through consumerist drives, the implanted need to gain the latest 'must have'; or from within our need to be of significance (see Practice Focus 8.1). The actor Ian Holm is recorded as saying:

> I live for and through my work. Other than that it's quite difficult to know who I am ... I do think that there is an enormous hole inside me and that's why when there was a hiatus in the workload after *The Lord of the Rings* it was a shock. I suddenly felt: what am I going to do?
>
> (cited in Billen, 2004)

Practice Focus 8.1

Laura recently joined a retail, direct sales company, selling goods on a 'club' basis to clients. She found the firm very welcoming and encouraging and the training helpful and supportive. She was surprised to find that when she made a mistake, instead of being criticized, managers told her that it was their mistake for not training her up to the right standard. Gradually she became fully competent, able to train others, and described her workplace as having a good atmosphere and 'fun' to be in.

Closer to modern organizational life, we have the corporate scandals, such as Enron and WorldCom (see Goffee and Jones, 2006, and Mangham, 2004). Mangham argues in his case study of Enron that, as the pressure for success increased: 'the notion of personality began to replace that of character' (2006, p. 50). Mangham quotes Richard Sennett as stating that 'impatient capitalism' has corroded 'character', related to the ancient philosophical notion of virtue, which is essential in terms of human beings working ethically and doing unto others what they would have done unto them. Sennett sees the most essential aspects of character as those that 'bind human beings together and furnish each with a sustainable self' (1998, p. 17) and in Practice Focus 8.2 we have an example of personal insecurity undermining leadership. The corporate scandals and the naked greed attached to the credit crisis of 2008 have demonstrated that seeming success can disguise an ethical vacuum, and persuasive leadership, without an ethical foundation, and with insufficient leadership at all levels, can be leading the lemmings over the cliff.

> **Practice Focus 8.2**
>
> Dick had climbed to a relatively senior level in his organization, but remained in himself anxious and insecure. He felt worried if he wasn't doing something, and therefore often came up with new ideas before he and his team had actually completed the tasks they were already undertaking. Always worried about what those in more powerful positions were thinking about him, he was excessively anxious to placate them, which meant that he put increasing pressure on those working for him. Team members gained the impression that Dick was not particularly interested in their development or well-being, and trust began to erode. In the end the team members spent more time watching their own backs than looking towards the future, and the team's performance suffered. As it did, Dick became increasingly insecure, and a vicious circle developed.

Leadership: moving forward

If we read any major report concerning activities in the private or public sector, we will almost certainly find a reference to leadership. This is especially so if things have gone wrong, and usually the missing ingredient identified by the report's authors is a failure, or lack, of leadership.

Lord Darzi's report on the future of the National Health Service in England states that: 'Leadership has been the neglected element of the reforms of recent years. That must now change' (DoH, 2008). This comment is interesting in itself, in that the 1980s Griffiths reforms in the UK identified a lack of leadership focus, with responsibility in hospitals often divided between administrators, doctors and other professional groups. These reforms brought in general management, and now a different aspect of leadership has been identified, namely that, although there may be a clear management structure, what appears to be missing is leadership at all levels, with clinicians especially feeling disempowered (Moore, 2008).

In the private sector, Goffee and Jones state that: 'when we ask CEOs what is the biggest problem they face, they unerringly reply: "our organizations need more leaders at every level"' (2006, p. 9). Goffee and Jones stress that 'leadership is *non-hierarchical*'. Being given a particular managerial job 'may confer some hierarchical authority, but it certainly doesn't make you a leader. Hierarchy alone is neither a necessary nor a sufficient condition for the exercise of leadership' (2006, p. 13).

There is a common misconception that uniformed organizations (the armed forces, police, fire service and so on) have a purely command and control approach. Increasingly this is not so. Small-scale counterterrorism operations; the patrol officer on the beat; fire personnel in crises, such as getting people out from the ruins of the twin towers on 9/11, draw on remarkable feats of initiative as well as courage. To be effective an organization needs leaders at all levels (see Practice Focus 8.3). If not, then the organization tends to malfunction (see Practice Focus 8.4).

Practice Focus 8.3

After a first career in the British Army, including small-scale operations, Peter joined a social services office, which was fortunate to have leaders at all levels. The area director had a remarkable grasp of the issues, and had a primary aim of developing her staff to meet both the immediate and the future needs of the service. Peter's team manager was a woman of high emotional intelligence and great energy, who, while keeping a primary focus on casework issues, also pushed her staff towards community development. This developmental 'pushing' gave Peter a direction in terms of his social work focus which has remained with him all his career. Most of the practitioners in the office were also leaders, taking responsibility; developing areas of expertise; being prepared to share that expertise and support others to grow and develop.

But if everybody calls for leadership, what is it? It is often helpful to go back to the roots of words. 'Leadership' is derived from the Old English 'laed' which means a path or a road, and is related to the verb *lithan*, to travel or to proceed. The *Oxford English Dictionary* defines 'lead' as: 'To show the way to (an individual or a group) by going with or ahead; to guide, control and direct; to direct the course of; to give an example for others to follow'. Adair (2002) points out that the metaphor of 'travelling with' as an image of leadership appears in a number of other languages; and the Roman word for leader, *dux*, gives rise to the English word 'education' – leaders being educators as well as 'direction finders'. So, leadership is about finding a direction of travel and walking with people on that journey: sustaining the vision, nurturing and developing the people; going step by step towards a goal.

'Management' comes from different root words; the Latin noun 'manus' – a hand and its derivative, the Italian word 'maneggiare' – to handle or train. It epitomizes control, but also a 'hands-on' coaching to increase skills, to produce from something or someone with raw talent a controlled source of power and skills. Although this has many positive connotations, it has a more static ethos than leadership (see Gilbert, 2005, ch. 1; and Adair, 2002).

There are many theories of leadership (see Alimo-Metcalfe, 2008; Gilbert, 2005, ch. 4; Storey, 2004, ch. 2) ranging from the leadership characteristics or trait theory, to behavioural, through situational, to the new leadership paradigms. One of the major theoretical culs-de-sac in recent years is that of overstressing 'leadership', sometimes called 'transformational leadership', and underemphasizing management, sometimes termed 'transactional leadership'. Viscount Slim, the leader of the British Army in Burma during Second World War put the difference thus:

> Leadership is of the spirit, compounded of personality and vision; its practice is an art. Management is more of the mind, more a matter of accurate calculation of statistics, of methods, timetables and routine; its practice is a science. Managers are necessary; leaders are essential.
>
> (cited in Adair, 2002, p. 243)

Kotter (1990) has delved into the differences and convergence of leadership and management in some detail. He talks about leaders: establishing a vision; aligning people and communicating that direction; and motivating and inspiring in keeping people moving in the right path. Managers need to plan and budget; organize structures and staffing; monitor, review and problem solve. Organizations, and the people who work in them, need both leadership and management. It is also my experience that not many people are good at both these aspects, because they are in some ways temperamentally different, and therefore the organization needs to ensure that both sets of attributes are there in an enduring sense (see Practice Focus 8.4).

Practice Focus 8.4

Anne was the head teacher of a failing comprehensive school in a deprived area. In three years she turned the school around, creating a strong desire to learn and achieve in her pupils; getting staff, parents

> and governors on board; forging strong links with the local education authority and with the local community including employers and putting the school on the map. Her deputy, Fred, was a quiet, dedicated man who had been in the school through all its tribulations for many years, and had plugged away at making sure that the staffing, IT and financial systems were sound and robust. When Anne left to work for the government, Alistair, the chair of governors was unsure whether to go for somebody with Anne's skills, or to promote Fred. In the end they promoted Fred to head teacher. He was very much aware of his natural talents and his temperamental inability to be another Anne. The governors made sure that Fred's skills were best used, and that the more charismatic elements of Anne's leadership were now carried forward by the chair of governors and the growing cadre of leaders at all levels within the school.

In a recent study of transformational and transactional leadership, Peck, Dickinson and Smith (2006) considered the current climate in both the public and private sectors, especially the accent on rapid change in a global environment, and the increased predilection for mergers and acquisitions and their subsequent consequences. Peck and colleagues conclude that transformational characteristics may be more appropriate in the early stages of the transition process.

What is abundantly clear from the research is that, for organizations to become effective and for staff to be engaged, developed and supported, both transformational and transactional approaches need to be adopted by the organization as a whole, even if these attributes cannot be contained in the chief executive. If we return to the original meaning of leadership, and its metaphor as a journey, clearly nobody in their right mind goes on a journey with somebody they do not trust. At the heart of leadership is the integrity of the leader at whatever level that person may be. As Goffee and Jones point out, we do not want to work for mere apparatchiks. They pose the vital question: 'Why should anyone be led by you?' Peters and Austin put the directional approach concisely when they wrote:

> You have got to know where you are going, to be able to state it clearly and concisely – and you have to care about it passionately. That all adds up to vision, the concise statement/picture of where the company and its people are heading, and why they should be proud of it.
> (1995, p. 284).

Goffee and Jones suggest that the leaders we need today display a consistency between words and deeds – they do not just talk about values, they live them; they have a capacity to display coherence in role performances, communicating a consistent underlying thread of vision and values; and they are personally secure in themselves.

Swings and roundabouts

Leadership is often complicated by the expectations of staff working in organizations or of people generally in society. In the United Kingdom, Margaret Thatcher was widely recognized as having stopped the economic decline with a particularly robust form of leadership which left her with as many detractors as admirers. In retrospect, many current Conservative thinkers believe that some of the harsh economic decisions may have accelerated some aspects of the social decline that is now causing so much concern. In 1992 when Thatcher was toppled by an internal coup within the Conservative Party, many people welcomed John Major as more of a 'One Nation' Conservative. But, within a fairly short space of time, many of the same people who had called for a change began to pine for the more explicit leadership of his predecessor. Senior managers need to make the vision *live* for people (see Practice Focus 8.5)

Practice Focus 8.5

Jeanette was a divisional head in a large organization and had got to her position by diligence, hard work and attention to fine detail. She found it difficult, however, to translate what everybody felt were solid values into anything which felt like a vision for the future and a team ethic that would get her division to that future. If leadership was about putting things right, keeping things going and doing new things, Jeanette was very good at the second but floundered with the other two elements. Increasingly, people asked 'Where is the division going?', and Jeanette seemed to have no answer to this. The fact that a number of other women managers within the organization seemed to exemplify the transformational behaviours that put Jeanette in the shade made her division feel that they were struggling to keep up with the other divisions in the organization.

Roffey Park Management Institute produces an annual management survey collating the feedback from managers of different levels in organizations as to their actual experiences. One of the major themes over the past few years has been the pace and extent of change and the need for leaders to provide meaning (see Holbeche with Springett, 2004) and tell a story which resonates with those being encouraged to go on that journey (see Bates and Gilbert, 2008).

What do staff want from their leaders?

In 2008 the UK Healthcare Commission surveyed each trust in England and asked specific questions about senior management (Santry, 2008). The result was not encouraging, as 47 per cent did not think that senior managers involve staff in big decisions and only a third say managers encourage them to suggest ways to improve services; 8 per cent of staff reported having been bullied or harassed by managers; 65 per cent of staff in the worst performing trusts did not think that care of patients was their organization's top priority; and 47 per cent of staff generally said that they did not have time to carry out their work. The Healthcare Commission Chief Executive, Anna Walker, stated sadly that 'Staff in the NHS provide vital, often life-saving, care. Yet they do not feel their work is valued by their trust; and communication with senior management is poor. These are the things that can and must change' (Santry, 2008, p. 4).

NHS manager, Ken Jarrold in a speech in 2005, evaluated the peaks and troughs of the health service changes under New Labour. Many of the peaks were around leadership issues, such as putting in place national service directors who would champion and push through reforms in a range of issues, such as cancer, primary care, mental health and so on; better partnership working; and a higher priority for patients and their safety. Some of the troughs were the plethora of changing organizational structures. Jarrold highlighted the positive side of leadership as the national service directors giving a clear vision of a better future and being on hand to support people. In mental health, for example, Sheehan set up the National Institute for Mental Health in England, which provided support for service development at a national, regional and local level, one of the first times when governance had actually sought to hit these three crucial levels of activity and governance at the same time. But Jarrold (2005) warned about the dark side of leadership where, as he put it:

> I am very concerned about some of the behaviours in today's NHS. There is bullying and harassment at all levels. The drive to deliver has become, in some places, an opportunity for inappropriate behaviour. Performance management is not a value-free zone. Everyone in the

NHS, from the most senior people to the most junior, are accountable for the way we behave towards other people.

But what is sometimes called 'the soft' side of management is not 'soft as we tend to understand it. Listening, for example, is not an end in itself, though it is always valuable. But, as leaders, we have to be able to listen, hear, respond and act. Sometimes the vision of a bright future is not an easy one for people to see and accept. When I became Director of Social Services in Worcestershire in 1997, I was very encouraged by the staff attitudes in our residential homes for older people. I was shocked, however, by the fact that the buildings and equipment had clearly not been invested in for many years. These homes for vulnerable elderly people were rapidly deteriorating. The question was: Could a historically cash-strapped council invest in extensive refurbishments? The clear answer was no! The second question was: Is the council the best organization to run a specialist service? and the answer was that there might well be viable alternatives. Understandably, residents, staff, relatives and politicians were unhappy and anxious about the idea of the council moving out of this area of activity. A small team worked extensively with people, sometimes facing angry meetings, considering whether the present was sustainable. People realized and accepted that it was not. Through intensive work and some specialist consultancy we worked with all parties, including the unions, and came up with a not-for-profit specialist housing and care provider who, a few years later, now provides considerably improved care, with a staff group who feel much more empowered within a specialist and less bureaucratic organization.

Compare this with another public sector organization, an acute general hospital striving for foundation status. When consultant Gerry Robinson had his work with the trust filmed by the BBC in 2007 (*Can Gerry Robinson save the NHS?*) one of the aspects he had to tackle was the chief executive's apparent inability to realize that getting out of his office and talking with staff was a positive thing to do. In the follow up series it was clear that the chief executive had learned a great deal from his staff, and the staff were encouraged to see their chief executive consulting with them around the changes.

Although the seminal work by Peters and Waterman (1982) has come in for some criticism, their initial observation that the behaviour of employees in the front line may well be a pointer to the culture of the organization, still holds true. One of the ironies of public sector organizations is that the stated values are often around a shared understanding of humanity, and yet the mirroring of the I-Thou relationship is often fractured, so that staff are not receiving from their managers a model in which to follow (see Gilbert, 2007). Bunting quotes Mike Harris of the Internet bank Egg, as saying:

> We ask employees to bring their humanness to work. Most people hang up their personalities at the door on the way into the office. [But], we want your humanness, and with that comes your creativity, commitment and personality.
>
> (2005, p. 81)

In her 'transformational leadership questionnaire' (TLQ), Alimo-Metcalfe considers three main leadership areas:

1. Leading and developing others: showing genuine concern; empowering staff; being accessible; encouraging change and welcoming questions.
2. Personal qualities: being transparent; acting with integrity; being decisive; inspiring others; resolving complex problems.
3. Leading the organization: networking and achieving; focusing team effort; building a shared vision; supporting a developmental culture; facilitating change sensitively.

(Alimo-Metcalfe and Alban-Metcalfe, 2004)

Such an approach is being taken at a number of hospitals where leadership at all levels is encouraged to demonstrate qualities such as engagement; being focused; questioning the what and the how; facilitating and motivating – considering the 'we' as stronger than 'I'; modelling and championing; and demonstrating empathy and a sense of humour. Allied to this was political adeptness in knowing who to influence and how, and an ability to take appropriate risks to move services on (see Buckley, 2008).

As leadership extends to all levels of an organization, there is a symbiotic relationship between leadership and followership. All leaders have at some stage and at some times also to be followers. Someone who simply sticks to their own agenda no matter what, and pushes their own team vision above that of the organization as a whole, is not likely to serve the organization to the full. Kelly (1988) once wrote 'In praise of followers', where he mapped four quadrants containing the effective follower, who manages him- or herself, and does what Goffee and Jones describe as 'being yourself with more skill'; the sheep who simply follow blindly; 'yes people' whose lack of questioning quite often embeds leaders in their worst characteristics; and alienated followers, who are critical and independent, but sometimes sink into disgruntled acquiescence, or subterranean mutiny.

To develop leaders at all levels, there needs to be a robust system of supervision (see Gilbert, 2005, p. 90) which brings together the goals of the organization, the development needs of the individual (both current and future) and their support needs. Also useful, especially at times of major change, is the promotion of learning sets for groups of people, as well as coaching and mentoring. When staff from social care agencies moved into NHS trusts in mental health services from 2001, the National Institute for Mental Health in England and the Social Care Institute for Excellence set up learning sets for directors of social care and senior managers in social care (see Sewell and Gilbert, 2006).

Conclusion

In their management agenda surveys coming up to the millennium and after, Roffey Park found an interesting surge in the issue of 'spirituality' or as they put it 'meaning' in the workplace (Holbeche and Springer, 2004). Holbeche felt it was to do with a need to reconnect with themselves and with something other than immediate concerns, otherwise in a world of constant and ever-increasing change, to quote Shakespeare's Othello, 'Nothing can or shall content my soul'.

Issues of work are not essentially divorced from issues of life in general (March and Weil, 2005). Work may be an increasingly pervasive part of our lives, but it should not be the whole of it, nor should it warp our personalities; dampen our inner spirit; undermine our sense of virtue and citizenship. Ethical leadership provides a vision towards a genuinely better future.

As human beings become increasingly individualistic, and the prevailing culture becomes more self-centred, leaders at whatever level will have increasing need to weave the thread of a compelling story (see Bates and Gilbert, 2008) through the tapestry of the working life. They will need to embrace and channel all the creativity that each individual worker brings to their employment role.

At Staffordshire University, Vice-Chancellor Christine King, at each graduation ceremony, tells the story to the gathering of why people seek higher education; how the support of families and groups is important to individual students; and how those individual students, give back to the community through the educative process. Many students come from deprived areas, and are the first person in their family ever to go to university. Many have to work long hours to support themselves through the three years of their degree. This is recognized by the Vice-Chancellor and celebrated. We link the graduation ceremony right back to the induction process for new entrants, so this sense of being professional and being human, and serving the needs of a community is instilled in the value base right at the beginning of that journey.

As we have seen, leadership is not just something carried out from the top, though it is essential there. It is carried out at all levels. Jacques Rogue, the chief executive of the Beijing Olympics 2008, stated intriguingly: 'A good organizer is a humble organizer.' One of the leadership examples in Goffee and Jones's book is Marcia, a Puerto Rican American woman who leads a team of office cleaners:

> She is intensely proud of her origins and yet a subtle reader of the many cultures represented by her team ... her passion is for the office workers to notice and comment favourably on the cleanliness of the offices. With all this, members of her team know that she cares about them and about getting the job done right. In unpromising circumstances she has forged a high performance team.
>
> (2006, pp. 18–19)

I recently had the task of picking up the poor performance of an individual. We sat down quietly and looked at the work that had been done and the performance standards required. If one is sensitive, then both giving and receiving criticism are uncomfortable. It was a difficult meeting. A day later the individual returned to me and said: 'I found yesterday very difficult. But I'd like to thank you for valuing me enough to take the time to tell me what I needed to do. Now I know where I'm going.'

As we have seen from the Healthcare Commission survey, staff often feel that they do not have time to do what they need to do. But, often what we are forgetting is the small moments, the moments when we know that we are human beings, not human doings; that we have duty to ourselves and to other people to ensure that we are all growing. Sometimes it is taking the trouble to seize an opportunity to say something important to another person which can have a lasting effect. We also know through our experience that people might well display leadership abilities if they were given different opportunities. General Marshall, the American chief of staff during the Second World War once remarked that there were no bad generals, just generals that he had not put in the right place at the right time. One of my school teachers, Father Michael Smith, a Benedictine monk, was a very unremarkable teacher, he was in the wrong place. He knew it, we knew it. But, when he went out to Peru to work with communities in the Andes, his quiet, unassuming faith and courage, and sheer persistence, earned him a heroic status. When he faced death, years later, his Abbot (community leader) said to him: 'Michael, you have climbed many mountains in your life and now you have to climb the highest one of all.' 'Yes, I've often thought of it like that', he replied, 'and the best part of climbing a mountain is the view from top' (obituary in *The Times*, 3 February, 2004).

The novelist George Eliot, in her novel, 'Middlemarch',writes of her heroine, Dorothea thus:

> Her finely touched spirit had still its fine issues, though they were not widely visible ... But the effect of her being on those around her was incalculably diffusive, for the growing good of the world is partly dependent on *unhistoric acts* and that things are not so ill with you and me as they might have been is half owing to the number who live faithfully a hidden life and rest in unvisited tombs.
>
> (1871, p. 838, emphasis added)

References

Adair, J. (2002) *Inspiring Leadership*, London, Thorogood.
Alimo-Metcalfe, B. (2008) *Leadership and Gender: A Masculine Past; a Feminine Future?*, Thematic paper for CERFE Project.
Alimo-Metcalfe, B. and Alban-Metcalfe, J. (2004) 'Leadership in Public Sector Organizations' in Storey (2004).
Bates, P. and Gilbert, P. (2008) 'I Wanna Tell You a Story: Leaders as Story Tellers', *The International Journal of Leadership in Public Services* 4(2), August, pp. 4–9.
Bauman, Z. (2005) *Liquid Life*, Cambridge, Polity Press.
Bauman, Z. (2007) *Consuming Life*, Cambridge, Polity Press.
Billen, A. (2004) 'Yes, I Do Fear Madness. Very Definitely I Do', *The Times*, 28 September, p. 12.
Bradley, M. and Alimo-Metcalf, A. (2008) 'Leadership: Best Actors in a Supporting Role', *Health Service Journal*, 8 May, pp. 28–9.
Buckley, T. (2008) 'How to Fire up Your People with Enthusiasm', *Health Service Journal*, 19 June, pp. 32–3.
Bunting, M. (2004) 'I Work Therefore I Am', *The Guardian*, 14 June, pp. 2–3.
Bunting, M. (2005) *Willing Slaves: How the Overwork Culture is Ruling Our Lives*, London, Harper Perennial Press.
Coyte, M. E., Gilbert, P. and Nicholls, V. (2007) *Spirituality, Values and Mental Health: Jewels for the Journey*, London, Jessica Kingsley Publishers.
Department of Health (2008) *High Quality for All* (Lord Darzi's Report), London, Department of Health
Eliot, G. (1871/1994) *Middlemarch*, London, Penguin Books.
Frankl, V. E. (1959/2004) *Man's Search for Meaning*, London, Ryder Press.

Gilbert, P. (2005) *Leadership: Being Effective and Remaining Human*, Lyme Regis, Russell House Publishing

Gilbert, P. (2007) '(Nobody noticed): Leadership and Issues of Workplace Loss and Grief', *Illness Crisis & Loss* 15(3), pp. 219–31.

Goffee, R. and Jones, J. (2006) *Why Should Anyone be Led by You?: What it Takes to be an Authentic Leader*, Boston, MA, Harvard Business School Press.

Haidt, J. (2006) *The Happiness Hypothesis*, London, William Heinemann.

Holbeche, L. with Spingett, N. (2004) *In Search of Meaning at Work*, Horsham, Roffey Park Management Institute.

Jarrold, K. (2005) 'The NHS – Past, Present and Future', *The Sally Irvine Lecture*, 23 November 2005.

Kelly, R. E. (1988) 'In Praise of Followers', *Harvard Business Review*, November–December, pp. 142–8.

Kotter, J. (1990) *A Force for Change: How Leadership Differs from Management*, New York, Free Press.

Mangham, I. (2004) 'Leadership and Integrity', in Storey (2004).

March, J. G. and Weil, T. (2005) *On Leadership*, Oxford, Blackwell.

Maslow. A. H. (1943) 'A Theory of Human Motivation', *Psychological Review* 50(4), July, pp. 370–96.

Moore, A. (2008) 'Darzi Drives Doctors to Scale the Dizzy Heights', *Health Service Journal*, 10 June, pp. 12–13.

National Institute for Mental Health in England (2002) *First Year Strategy for NIMHE: Meeting the Implementation Challenge in Mental Health*, Leeds, NIMHE.

Peck, E., Dickinson, H. and Smith, J. (2006) 'Transforming or Transacting? The Role of Leaders in Organisational Transition', *The British Journal of Leadership in Public Services* 2(3), September, pp. 4–14.

Peters, T. and Austin, N. (1985) *A Passion for Excellence*, New York, Random House.

Peters, T. and Waterman, R. (1982) *In Search of Excellence*, New York, Harper Collins.

Santry, S. (2008) 'Communication Breaks Down as Staff Feel Left in Dark by Leaders', *Health Service Journal*, 10 April, pp. 4–5.

Schultz, W. (1994) *The Human Element*, San Francisco, Jossey-Bass.

Sennett, R. (1998) *The Corrosion of Character: The Personal Consequences of Work in the New Capitalism*, New York: W. W. Norton.

Sewell, H. and Gilbert, P. (2006) 'Leading and Learning', *The British Journal of Leadership in Public Services* 2(1), March.

Storey, J. (ed.) (2004) *Leadership in Organizations: Current Issues and Key Trends*, London, Routledge.

Travis, A. (2008) 'The Making of a Violent Extremist: Anger, Rejection – and Vulnerability', *The Guardian*, 21 August, p. 11.

9
Managing Sickness Absence
Neil Thompson

Introduction

For many people the topic of sickness absence is quite straightforward: people on sick leave fall into one of two categories, those who are 'genuinely' ill and who deserve support and those who are 'malingering' who deserve contempt, if not actual punishment. The reality of the situation is far more complex than this. In this chapter, we shall see that what constitutes 'sickness' or 'illness' is subject to debate and competing theoretical understandings, especially when *mental* illness is the topic under consideration. We shall also see that the reasons for sickness absence are many and varied, and that there are various factors involved at various levels. I shall therefore be arguing that simple solutions are unlikely to work and may actually prove counterproductive. A much more sophisticated understanding is called for, one that connects with the wider field of workplace well-being and the emerging knowledge base about such matters.

I shall begin by examining the nature of 'sickness' before considering some key factors in relation to sickness absence. This will lead to a discussion of potential solutions, or at least a framework of understanding that can help us develop appropriate responses that are both consistent with a commitment to workplace well-being and effective in ensuring that as little time as reasonably possible is lost to sickness absence.

Understanding sickness

The dominant model of sickness (what Foucault would call an 'episteme' – see Faubion, 2000) is a biomedical one. That is, it is based on the analogy of the human body as a form of organic machine, and sickness or ill-health is equated with some form of bodily dysfunction – a part of the machine that needs to be repaired where possible. It is this model which gives us the simple, if misleading, dichotomy between genuine sickness (there really is something wrong with the bodily mechanisms) and malingering (or 'swinging the lead' – pretending that there is something wrong when, in reality, there is not). However, this narrow biomedical approach has been heavily criticized over the years for being too simplistic and for neglecting the significance of a range of psychological and sociological factors that shape the experience of (ill-)health. As Foucault's (1973) work has shown, this model rests on a discourse of health that constructs particular power relations with regard to health issues, both in the workplace and in wider society. But Foucault's voice of criticism is not the only one to make itself heard. Turner reflects a widely held view when he argues that:

> The basic position in the sociological approach to illness and disease is that being sick is fundamentally a social state of affairs rather than being a narrowly defined biochemical malfunction of the organism. Sociology is concerned to explain the social causes of sickness, the character of sickness as a social role and the human response to sickness in terms of feeling, language and social action.
>
> (1995, p. 37)

What determines whether or not someone attends work or takes sick leave will be a complex set of biopsychosocial factors which interact in complex ways. These will include:

- *Biological.* The presence or otherwise of injury, infection, physical pain and so on are clearly key factors in many, but not all, cases. These can be 'caused' or exacerbated by lifestyle choices, such as consumption of alcohol, smoking and lack of exercise.
- *Psychological.* Among the psychological factors will be level of motivation and commitment and self-esteem, as well as the presence or absence of such emotions as anger, resentment and disappointment or pride, loyalty and enthusiasm. An employee who feels valued and supported may well be prepared to work on despite being in pain, whereas someone who feels undervalued, unsupported and exploited may be ready to take sick leave at the first sign of any pain or other such symptoms.
- *Sociological.* This will encompass such factors as level of income and status; gender; culture and ethnicity; religion and so on. Particularly

important will be power relations – for example, who has the power to define someone as 'sick' or 'fit for work'? What channels exist (in terms of policy, law and industrial relations processes) for challenging such definitions in certain circumstances? And so on.

Distinguishing between health and sickness is therefore clearly not a simple or straightforward matter. When we turn to the question of *mental* health problems, the situation becomes even more complex. This is because the very notion of 'mental illness' is a contested one. This is not to say that those who challenge the label 'mental illness' deny or disregard the existence of mental conditions that cause great suffering to people. Rather, it is a question of disputing the validity of regarding such conditions as illnesses and thereby creating the assumption that the most appropriate response is a medical one – predominantly through medication and the adoption of the sick role (Thompson, 2003a). Space does not permit a fuller discussion of these issues (interested readers are advised to consult the following texts to develop their understanding further: Bentall, 2004; Crossley, 2006; Fawcett and Karban, 2005 – see also Desai, Chapter 4 in this volume, for a fuller discussion of mental health in the workplace), and so I shall limit myself to using these complexities as an example of the need to avoid relying on oversimplified notions of sickness as predominantly, if not exclusively, a biomedical matter.

Whether we are concerned with physical or mental health, we should not lose sight of the psychological and sociological dimensions. Fineman offers an important perspective on this when he discusses the significance of emotions in the workplace. He makes the point that:

> As emotional arenas, organizations bond and divide their members. Workaday frustrations and passions – boredom, envy, fear, love, anger, guilt, infatuation, embarrassment, nostalgia, anxiety – are deeply woven into the way roles are enacted and learned, power is exercised, trust is held, commitment formed and decisions made. Emotions are not simply excisable from these, and many other, organizational processes; they both characterize and inform them.
>
> (2000a, p. 1)

The workplace is not an emotion-free zone, and so efforts to understand workplace health will need to incorporate consideration of emotion. Without this element of understanding steps taken to address sickness absence will lack a crucial dimension.

120 Promoting Well-Being

The problem of sickness absence

Sickness absence can be seen as a significant workplace problem in a number of ways:

- It puts additional pressure on remaining staff and can therefore contribute to potential work overload problems;
- It can reduce quality of service for both internal and external stakeholders – partly for quantitative reasons (fewer staff available) and partly qualitative (for example, lack of service continuity where a member of staff becomes unavailable);
- It can contribute to recruitment and retention problems (for example, as a result of the detrimental effects on morale);
- It can also lead to tensions and conflicts;
- Deadlines can be missed;
- The organization's reputation can suffer; and
- There are financial costs – estimated to be £666 per employee per annum on average (CIPD, 2008).

There is therefore considerable incentive for organizations to address the challenges presented by sickness absence. To be able to do this there is a need for a fuller understanding of the problem. The distinction I mentioned above between 'genuine' illness and 'malingering' is not a false or unhelpful one, it is just too simple to reflect the complexities involved. For one thing, a simple black and white dichotomy between genuineness and malingering does not take account of the range of possibilities in between or the ways in which psychological and sociological issues can shape employees' responses to their circumstances. In reality, there are (at least) six main ways in which sickness absence can arise. These can be summarized as follows:

1. *Incapacity.* This refers to those situations where, due to injury, infection or other such reason, the employee is unable (or feels unable) to attend work. No doubt much of the sickness absence that occurs is for genuine reasons of this kind, although, as we shall note below, even here there are psychological and sociological factors to take into consideration. As noted in Chapter 1, stress can exacerbate existing health problems as well as create new ones – see 'Embodiment of distress' below.
2. *Excuse.* This covers those occasions that are commonly referred to as 'malingering'. The practice of 'taking a sickie' as an illegitimate means

of, in effect, increasing one's leave entitlement is not uncommon. This can happen when employees are disaffected by the particular working situation they are currently employed in (where their level of engagement is therefore low), or it can be a characteristic of some employees whose attitude towards work is a negative one in general. In the latter case, this is not simply a matter of having a 'bad egg', an untrustworthy individual, as this begs the question of leadership – the ability of the leader(s) concerned to create and sustain a working culture where people feel uncomfortable about 'letting the side down' by playing the system. Again the situation is a complex one, with causation being linked to a range of factors, rather than simply either a 'bad' employee or a 'bad' leader.

3. *Escape.* This refers to situations where staff feel the need to absent themselves from time to time, just to cope with the pressures. Where this occurs, it is likely to be a situation characterized by stress, bullying and harassment, conflict, aggression and the threat of violence and/or high levels of emotional pressure. In such cases, the absence does not have biological roots, but nor is it a cynical way of seeking additional time off. Indeed, in such circumstances the time taken off may feature so much tension and such a strong sense of guilt that the use of such a strategy to ease pressure may completely fail. It may, in fact, make the situation worse.

4. *The last straw.* This is similar to the 'escape' situation, but is less deliberate. It refers to high pressure situations in which somebody has a minor ailment: a cold, mild back pain and so on. If work circumstances were not so pressurized, the individuals concerned may be quite prepared to work on regardless of their minor health problems. However, in situations of high pressure (and particularly where morale is low), employees may find that a minor ailment is enough to render them unfit for work – to feel that, with the added burden of the health problem, they are not able to cope with the level of pressure associated with their job at that time. In effect, the ailment, however minor in the overall scheme of things, becomes the last straw.

5. *Embodiment of distress.* In some respects the idea of 'embodiment of distress' is a more extreme version of 'the last straw'. It refers to situations in which levels of stress reach such a point that they manifest as either: (i) physical symptoms; or (ii) mental health problems. In terms of (i), highly stressed employees may experience intense headaches, stomach aches and so on – physical manifestations of psychologically distressing circumstances. In terms of (ii), experiences of depression or

high levels of anxiety can arise from stressful situations being allowed to persist.
6. *Balance shifting.* Here what I have in mind is work–life balance, as it has come to be known (Johnson, 2004). Some people feel the need to take additional time off unofficially because they have caring responsibilities at home, whether care of children or care of dependent relatives (Clarke, Evandrou and Warr, 2005). This differs from 'excuse' above, as the cynical element of trying to exploit one's employer is absent. It is more a case of trying to be creative in managing the combined pressures of work and home life – perhaps bending the rules rather than breaking them.

These should not be seen as exclusive categories – that is, they do not necessarily exist in their pure form. Many circumstances may contain elements of more than one of these.

This typology helps us to appreciate the multidimensional nature of sickness absence by taking us away from a simplistic, individualistic conception of sickness. Writing about 'the dark side of behaviour at work' (that is, how employees can behave in disloyal ways), Furnham and Taylor make important comments when they argue that:

> Many organizations can appear faceless, soulless and uncaring. To those running the institution, it is often hard to accept that they have a responsibility for specific employee problems. To them, it is the individual through his or her act of leaving, whistle-blowing or sabotage who is to blame. Little attention is paid to how the institution as a whole, and senior managers in particular, might have contributed to that individual's breaking away and severing the bonds of trust and loyalty.
>
> (2004, p. 2)

To this list of 'leaving, whistle-blowing or sabotage' we can perhaps add some aspects of sickness absence – especially those under the heading of 'excuse'. The authors go on to offer a partial explanation for this when they argue that:

> Part of the problem is that it is difficult to talk about organizational factors and processes as causal agents in the story of any individual. We are all psychologists in the sense that we choose to explain events at the level of the individual; not the group, not society as a whole but the individual. People are the origins of causes. Thus, confronted

with different types or levels of explanation we often choose the most familiar. In this sense, betrayal is explained in terms of the betrayer; not that which is betrayed.

(Furnham and Taylor, 2004, p. 2)

In other words, much of the difficulty arises from an individualistic approach that fails to take account of wider social, political and organizational factors. Here we have a parallel problem with that discussed in Chapter 1 in relation to stress – the lack of a holistic understanding of some very complex multi-level issues.

One example of a wider set of issues that is generally given scant attention in relation to sickness absence is the role of organizational politics. Vigoda (2003) argues that this is a topic that has a massive impact on well-being within organizations. The fact that people have different agendas and different interests within any organization makes the workplace a *political* place. Sometimes, the organizational politics can be so intense or so destructive in how they are acted out that people feel the need to leave – either permanently by resigning or perhaps temporarily through sickness absence (see the discussion of 'escape' above). One important question organizations committed to promoting workplace well-being need to ask is: Are we confident that the way organizational politics are played out is not a factor contributing to sickness absence?

If we are to think in terms of potential solutions to the problems presented by sickness absence, we clearly have to go beyond the level of reductionist explanations that see only individual perspectives. The example of organizational politics is just one of the aspects of organizational life that offers a broader perspective – and one that we would be foolish to neglect.

Potential solutions

In terms of direct practical solutions there is now a growing stock of resources that can be drawn upon to guide human resource professionals (see, for example, the 'toolkits' available at http://www.cipd.co.uk/subjects/hrpract/absence/absmantool?vanity=http://www.cipd.co.uk/absencemanagementtool; the booklet available from ACAS at http://www.acas.org.uk/index.aspx?articleid=1361 or the practical guidance offered in Spurgeon et al., 2007). However, given the complexity of the issues involved as outlined in this chapter, there is clearly a need for a more strategic approach to the issues, one that goes beyond technical fixes and relies on a more sophisticated and holistic understanding of the issues involved (see the discussions of stress in Chapter 1 of this volume).

The development of a culture premised on a genuine commitment to workplace well-being, I would argue, should be seen as a key plank in the organizational response to sickness absence. It is far too easy (and far too dangerous) to adopt an individualistic approach to the subject that basically amounts to ascribing people to one category or the other: either genuinely ill and in need of support or 'swinging the lead' (parallel with the distinction between the 'deserving' and 'undeserving' poor in nineteenth-century social policy – Lister, 2004). As we have seen, the actual situation is not so clear cut, and a far less reductionist understanding is needed to act as a platform for developing strategies for addressing the problems.

An example of how a culture of well-being can be of benefit in this regard comes from the work of MacDonald (2005), who argues that employees who have been on long-term sick leave are more likely to return to work sooner if they feel that their employing organization is adopting a supportive attitude towards them.

An organizational culture cannot 'heal the sick' in miraculous fashion, but it can help to keep the problem to a minimum by:

- *Keeping workloads at realistic levels.* As noted in Chapter 1, excessive workloads give rise to stress; stress can give rise to illness. Keeping workloads at reasonable levels is therefore an important part of preventing sickness absence. Workplace cultures that condone or even encourage work overload can therefore be seen as inimical to keeping sickness absence to a minimum.
- *Addressing conflicts constructively and not allowing them to fester.* The discussions in Chapter 6 lead us to realize that brushing conflict under the carpet is a dangerous and unwise strategy. Conflicts are likely to cause tensions that can have significant consequences in terms of sickness. By contrast, a culture that is premised on the open and constructive management of conflict is likely to have a far less detrimental effect on people's health – as well as their well-being.
- *Promoting dignity at work.* As Bolton (2007) explains, not tolerating bullying and harassment is an important part of promoting dignity, but the concept is actually much broader than that, in so far as there are other aspects of working life that can undermine dignity (a punitive attitude towards sickness absence, for example). By creating and sustaining a culture in which dignity is not undermined, leaders can play an important role in reducing sickness absence.

- *Being responsive.* This means adopting a helpful response to personal problems or other such factors that stand in the way of achieving personal and professional goals. The difference between a responsive and a non-responsive culture can be immense in terms of the impact on morale, job satisfaction, productivity and so on. Such factors can, in many cases, make all the difference in terms of whether someone feels able to deal with the demands of work at that time.
- *Providing confidential support services.* The value of giving a clear message of support and concern, especially when staff are having difficulties of some description can be quite significant. This can be done through the provision of:
  - **Occupational health.** This is now a well-established form of support that can be very helpful.
  - **Counselling.** Although many employees can be suspicious about counselling, it can be very effective in the right circumstances.
  - **Occupational social work.** A relatively little-used facility in the United Kingdom, but more widely adopted elsewhere, occupational social work offers a range of problem-solving activities, advocacy and related supports (see Bates and Thompson, 2007).

  It is important that a culture that mocks or devalues support services is not allowed to develop.
- *Offering appropriate training.* It is essential that staff are sufficiently well equipped to do the jobs to at least a basic level of competence if they are not to be placed under unnecessarily high levels of pressure. Training therefore has an important part to play. Consequently, a culture that values and supports training in particular and ongoing learning in general is a valuable asset to have at one's disposal.
- *Keeping the channels of communication open.* As in so many matters to do with people, communication is a key factor. Poor communication can create or exacerbate tensions, while effective communication can be a great strength to draw on for any team of staff (Thompson, 2003b). A culture premised on high levels of communication can therefore be a great help when it comes to reducing the pressures that can lead to sickness absence.

The emphasis on culture here reflects the fact that high-quality leadership can be identified as a basic ingredient of an organization's efforts to develop a constructive and effective approach to the challenges presented by sickness absence.

Conclusion

The point was made in the Introduction that well-being should not be equated with health. The two are inter-related, but they are not the same thing. This chapter has explored some aspects of the significance of that inter-relationship, in so far as it has examined how a range of well-being issues can, and often do, have an impact in terms of health in general and sickness absence in particular. A key message of this chapter, therefore, is that managing sickness absence is an important part of promoting well-being and, equally, promoting well-being in general can be a major contribution to addressing sickness absence.

Managing sickness is basically about managing people. As Johnson so aptly puts it:

> Dig deeply into organizational problems and you will always get to people. Conflict, stress, misunderstanding, poor communication, demotivation, resistance, low morale, all have their origins in people and their lifestyle needs not being met. These are leadership issues. Organizations are only as effective as the people in them. People are only as effective as their leaders enable them to be.
>
> (2004, p. 104)

Health problems are about people too, and so leadership needs to be a key aspect of effective sickness management. As we have noted, a simplistic approach based on a reductionist and individualistic understanding of sickness and the ways in which it leads to absence is a far from adequate basis for developing such leadership. A more holistic, multi-dimensional approach drawing on a wide range of theoretical insights places us in a much stronger position for making sense of the complexities involved. This chapter can therefore be seen as a plea for developing more sophisticated levels of understanding so that we can move away from the problems caused by adopting too basic an approach premised on looking for simple technical fixes.

References

Bates, J. and Thompson, N. (2007) 'Workplace Well-Being: An Occupational Social Work Approach', *Illness, Crisis & Loss* 15(3), pp. 273–84.

Bentall, R. P. (2004) *Madness Explained: Psychosis and Human Nature*, London, Penguin.

Bolton, S. C. (2007) *Dimensions of Dignity at Work*, London, Butterworth-Heinemann.

Bracken, P. and Thomas, P. (2005) *Postpsychiatry: Mental Health in a Postmodern World*, Oxford, Oxford University Press.
Chartered Institute of Personnel and Development (CIPD) (2008) *Absence Management: Annual Survey Report 2008*, London, Chartered Institute of Personnel and Development.
Clarke, L., Evandrou, M. and Warr, P. (2005) 'Family and Economic Roles', in Walker (2005).
Crossley, N. (2006) *Contesting Psychiatry: Social Movements in Mental Health*, London, Routledge.
Faubion, J. D. (ed.) (2000) *Power: Essential Works of Foucault 1954–1984*, London, Penguin.
Fawcett, B. and Karban, K. (2005) *Contemporary Mental Health: Theory, Policy and Practice*, London, Routledge.
Fineman, S. (2000a) 'Emotional arenas Revisited', in Fineman (2000b).
Fineman, S. (ed.) (2000b) *Emotion in Organizations*, 2nd edn, London, Sage.
Foucault, M. (1973) *The Birth of the Clinic*, London, Tavistock.
Furnham, A. and Taylor, J. (2004) *The Dark Side of Behaviour at Work: Understanding and Avoiding Employees Leaving, Thieving and Deceiving*, Basingstoke, Palgrave Macmillan.
Johnson, M. (2004) *The New Rules of Engagement: Life-Work Balance and Employee Commitment*, London, Chartered Institute of Personnel and Development.
Lister, R. (2004) *Poverty*, Cambridge, Polity Press.
MacDonald, L. A. C. (2005) *Wellness at Work: Protecting and Promoting Employee Wellbeing*, London, Chartered Institute of Personnel and Development.
Spurgeon, P., Mazelan, P., Barwell, F. and Flanagan, H. (2007) *New Directions in Managing Employee Absence: An Evidence-Based Approach*, London, Chartered Institute of Personnel and Development.
Thompson, N. (2003a) *Promoting Equality: Challenging Discrimination and Oppression*, 2nd edn, Basingstoke. Palgrave Macmillan.
Thompson, N. (2003b) *Communication and Language: A Handbook of Theory and Practice*, Basingstoke, Palgrave Macmillan.
Turner, B. S. (1995) *Medical Power and Social Knowledge*, 2nd edn, London, Sage.
Vigoda, E. (2003) *Developments in Organizational Politics: How Political Dynamics Affect Employee Performance in Modern Work Sites*, Cheltenham, Edward Elgar.
Walker, A. (ed.) (2005) *Understanding Quality of Life in Old Age*, Maidenhead, Open University Press.

10
Women-Friendly Workplaces
Mary Tehan

Preamble

Creating and maintaining women-friendly workplaces can be a particular challenge for employers, at local, national and international levels. As a means of demonstrating some of these challenges, this chapter will focus on Australian workplaces, within a broader global social policy context. With over 50 per cent of carers being women, emphasis will be placed on the needs of employers, employed carers of people with a life-threatening/terminal illness, carers ceasing work (temporary or permanent) and carers returning to work, including bereaved carers. The concept of a 'compassionate workplace' is explored in response to the accompanying grief and loss associated with illness, loss and carer responsibilities having an impact on workplace productivity, profits and retention of valued staff.

What is the challenge and how does it affect women?

The ill person

Globally, it is predicted that by 2030, non-communicable conditions will cause over three-quarters of all deaths; deaths due to cancer, cardiovascular diseases and traffic accidents will collectively account for 56 per cent of the projected 67 million deaths due to all causes (WHO, 2001, p. 29). World Health Organization (2008) global health indicators highlight similar patterns of mortality and burden of disease across Europe, the United States, the United Kingdom and Australia. Projected life expectancy and ageing population trends are on the increase; which consequently has workplace health and well-being implications for employers across the life course, including end of life (WHO, 2008, pp. 35–45).

Regardless of the illness or site of care (home or institutional), the above statistics suggest that government, business and health care sectors all need to be framing policy, programmes and practices that support employers, carers, ill people and their work colleagues through life course transitions. This support needs to include the end-of-life, death and bereavement trajectory (cessation from, and return to, work period). Since the majority of carers are women, addressing the needs of women in relation to work will benefit the businesses within which they work, and ultimately, the economy (Carers Australia, 2008). According to Carers Australia, employers who support carers, predominantly women, benefit from greater stability, skill retention and improved workplace morale, which in turn leads to increased productivity. These gains have flow-on effects to the whole economy (Carers Australia, 2008, p. 15).

The carer

For working carers in Australia, the Taskforce on Care Costs has reported that nearly half (44 per cent) of working carers have selected a role at work below their skill level because it provides greater flexibility and that costs of care can also impact on relationships at work. (cited in Carers Australia, 2008, p. 13). The National Survey of Carer Health and Wellbeing found that: 'the physical, mental and emotional health and wellbeing of most carers was poorer because of their caring responsibilities' (National Centre for Social and Economic Monitoring (NATSEM), 2006, p. 17). Loss of sleep, stress and the constant pressure of caring may result in loss of concentration, mistakes, and misunderstandings at work. Consequently, for women in, or seeking, employment, stigma and discrimination may occur at any point along the illness/carer continuum. In the longer term, the economic and social costs to businesses, government, communities and individuals could be very high if policies, practices and interventions do not address this aspect of support need in the workplace.

The largest Australian survey of carers' health and well-being, undertaken jointly by Deakin University, Australian Unity and Carers Australia, found that carers (mostly women) have the lowest well-being of any population group surveyed so far (Department of Health and Ageing, 2007, p. 19). The Australian Unity Wellbeing Index (AUWI) measures personal well-being in relation to health, personal relationships, safety, standard of living, achieving in life, community connectedness, and future security. It also includes outcome measures taken from the Depression, Anxiety and Stress Scale. One key finding was that carers have an average rating on the depression scale that is classified as moderate depression, and over one-third have severe or extremely severe depression (AUWI, 2007, cited in Carers Australia, 2008, p. 19).

Women who are ill or in a carer role who are trying to negotiate transitions and are experiencing stress may require a particular workplace culture or ethos to help them make the transition safely and compassionately. In Victoria, Australia, lost productivity through absenteeism and 'presenteeism' is a significant burden on the Victorian economy, to the same extent as the risk of chronic disease is for the broader community (WorkSafe, 2008). 'Presenteeism' refers to the phenomenon of employees being at work, but not functioning because of illness or injury to themselves or others (Econotech, 2007, p. 3). According to Econotech, in a report commissioned by Medibank Private, 'presenteeism' was estimated to cost the Australian economy $25.7 billion in 2005–06, four times as much as absenteeism (2007, p. 4). Medibank Private, in conjunction with this study, also surveyed its staff in three call centres across Australia, in order to better understand their health needs. The survey showed that normal workplace tasks were affected when employees were suffering from a health-related condition at work, with the top two factors being: difficulty in thinking clearly when working (78 per cent); and difficulty in doing their work without making mistakes (66 per cent). Grieving also commonly gives rise to 'lack of concentration' and 'making mistakes' (James and Friedman, 2003); this is an area not addressed in the Econotech or Medibank Private 2007 studies.

Europe has framed its policy responses in language that emphasizes rights and responsibilities (Howe, 2007, p. 122). As Howe appropriately highlights, if there is no entitlement to vary hours because of family responsibility, each crisis at home becomes a crisis at work (p. 122). Similarly, a crisis at work is likely to have negative consequences at home. If, in addition to addressing the education-work-retirement trajectory, the system could also address the emerging reality of carer-illness-death-work life transitions, it will benefit businesses, individuals (especially women) and communities.

In Australia, the WorkHealth initiative is the response of the Victorian Government to the rising trend of an unhealthy workforce. This initiative is an excellent example of public health promotion and health-promoting palliative care in the workplace, and is likely to be of particular benefit to women. For a five-year period beginning in July 2008, approximately $40 million will be spent on addressing the health of Victorian workers (WorkSafe, 2008). By 2009, education; support services for 'at risk' workers; screening for chronic disease risks; well-being programmes; and support for Victoria's employers are to be introduced free of charge to small and medium-sized businesses. Large-sized businesses with a well-being programme in place will benefit through subsidized programmes. According to WorkSafe, the Victorian economy expects to save in excess of $100 million per annum through improved productivity and reduced health expenditure associated with chronic disease (Victorian WorkCover Authority, 2008).

What have been the responses to the challenges in various parts of the world?

The global context

The United Nations Millennium Development Goal Number Three is to promote gender equality and empower women (UN, 2008). In September 2008, the United Nations agreed to ratify and implement the Convention on the Elimination of All Forms of Discrimination against Women, and International Labour Organization (ILO) Conventions on Equal Remuneration, Discrimination, Workers with Family Responsibilities, and Maternity Protection. It resolved to increase efforts to implement work principles, such as social protection and freedom from harassment (UN, 2008).

In addition, in *Closing the Gap in a Generation*, the World Health Organization Commission on Social Determinants of Health, in August 2008, recommended the following goals: fair employment, decent work, social protection across the life course, gender equity, market responsibility and tackling the inequitable distribution of power, money and resources (WHO, 2008). For example, under the Declaration on the Promotion of Patients' Rights in Europe, promoted by a WHO European Consultation: 'patients have the right to enjoy support from family, relatives and friends during the course of care and treatment and to receive spiritual support and guidance at all times' (Item 3; art. 5.9; cited in the OSI Resource Guide, 2007, p. 35). In relation to the workplace, this statement highlights the right of ill people and their carers, including ill employees and employed carers, to remain available to each other at the time of a life-threatening/terminal illness, and throughout the bereavement period. Item 5 also highlights the need for employers to provide a non-discriminatory environment based on equality when an employee has either a life-threatening illness or is an employed carer of a person with a life-threatening illness.

With the majority of carers being women, these human rights standards are particularly pertinent to female carers, either employed, seeking paid work or returning to it. According to the National Centre for

Social and Economic Modelling, internationally, a 'sandwich generation' is emerging – that is, people, mostly women, supporting and caring, at the same time, for their semi-independent adult children and their ageing parents (NATSEM, 2006, pp. 2, 21). With the additional financial costs of medical treatment, pharmaceuticals, home modification and transport costs involved in the provision of home-based care, the 'right to work' of many carers can become a necessity.

Howe states that women tend to take part-time or casual work in order to manage work–life balance, and in doing so, often find themselves in a marginal labour force position (2007, p. 68). In addition, he argues, that insufficient attention has been given to helping people, individuals and communities to: 'anticipate and prepare for the uncertainties and risks inherent in a modern society' (p. 19). The time has come, he states, for government, businesses and communities to think in terms of: 'integrated policy responses linked to key transitions – [to] make it easier for everyone to combine paid employment with care activities' (p. 29). For example, he suggests that it may be helpful to explore these needs through a life course approach within a social policy framework.

An example of good social policy to support employed carers through an end-of-life transition can be found in Canada. Compassionate Care Benefits permits carers of a person who is gravely ill to take six weeks funded leave under Canada's Employment insurance programme. These benefits, in the short term, are a good example of 'shared responsibility', between government, business and individuals-in-community, as per Kellehear's (2005, p. 50) compassionate cities model. However, from a life course perspective, Canada's policy on its own is insufficient. Grief, loss and bereavement support needs for female carers are not adequately addressed through the Canadian policy. The process of grieving involves emotional repair work that takes time. It may take years to recover from a bereavement and adjust to a new reality (James and Friedman, 2003; Renzenbrink 2002).

What have been the responses in Australia?

The Australian context

There are two million carers in Australia, many of whom want to work. In their survey, the Taskforce on Care Costs (Australia, 2007, cited in Carers Australia report (NATSEM, 2006), p. 21) estimates that one in three Australians expects to care for an aged person and/or a person with a disability in the next five years. Women in the 35–54 age group typically provide this community care; workforce participation is therefore a critical issue for women in this age group (Taskforce on Care Costs, cited in Carers Australia report (NATSEM, 2006), p. 21). There is a need to maximize workforce participation, particularly of women. In Victoria, Australia, a new Equality Act for a Fairer Victoria, is currently being proposed (Dept. of Justice, 2008). In addition, the Victorian Equal Opportunity and Human Rights Commission has developed guidelines for employers and employees: *Building eQuality in the Workplace – Family Responsibilities* (July, 2008). The Commonwealth Equal Opportunity for Women in the Workplace Act (1999) is another piece of legislation designed to prevent discrimination against women at work. Interestingly, grief, loss and bereavement are not mentioned in any of the documents. Still to be specifically addressed are the central issues related to 'presenteeism', trust, confidence, resilience and capacity *within* the workplace, for vulnerable individuals, such as ill employees, employed carers, their work colleagues and employers.

For Australian employers, addressing death, grief, loss, bereavement and trauma needs in the workplace is becoming an unavoidable reality. In *Compassionate Cities: Public Health and End-of-Life Care*, Kellehear argues for a new public health approach that supports and strengthens a more compassionate society (2005, pp. 94–5). Kellehear suggests that it is communities of all types – including workplaces, and how they care for and support people in end-of-life circumstances that constitute this approach (p. 95). He also suggests that a concern for equality needs to begin with a commitment to inclusion (p. 90). In addition, death, loss and health need to be located in the context of continual changes in the life course (the constant cycle of beginnings and endings) (Kellehear, 2005, p. 60).

What is possible?

In relation to people living with a life-threatening illness and carer responsibilities, the Open Society Institute (OSI) has tabled five human rights standards related to palliative care (refer to Table 10.1). These standards not only apply to individual and organizational practice in health care systems but also in the workplace.

Developing a human rights approach to workplace culture based on participation, accountability, non-discrimination, empowerment and linkages may protect the vulnerable, such as women carers. Moving in and out of work to attend to carer responsibilities, or to medical treatment if ill, requires flexibility and understanding in the workplace. Howe suggests that social policies and support practices that generate 'flexicurity – flexibility and security' are worth considering (2007, p. 48).

Table 10.1 Human rights standards related to palliative care

Item	Human rights standards related to palliative care
1	The freedom from cruel, inhuman, and degrading treatment
2	The right to life
3	The right to the highest attainable standard of health
4	The right to information
5	The right to non-discrimination and equality

Source: Open Society Institute Resource Guide (2007, p. ii).

Support, he states, 'needs to occur at the various points of transition by institutional arrangements that maintain or enhance employability, gender equality and social inclusion ... across the life course' (p. 64). To encourage this approach, he suggests that there need to be incentives that encourage people to 'take risks associated with particular transitions ... through life-long learning and a social risk management approach' (pp. 47, 77). He argues that support could be provided through 'employment bridges – by investing in people, education and training, and support, in such a way that employability is maintained and social protection safeguarded' (Howe, 2007, p. 76).

A key challenge for employers is to manage life course transitions in the workplace while finding ways to maintain and improve productivity and profits, and retain valued staff. In end-of-life workplace transitions, there is also the need to address support for vulnerable employees, including those who are grieving. The issues around vulnerability, grief, loss and fairness loom large for women – given that the majority of carers are women – who are marginalized by having to work casual hours, part time or on fixed-term contracts. According to Howe (2007, p. 27), the number of people in Australia working part time or on fixed-term contracts is among the highest in the OECD. Nine out of every ten Australians below the age of 65 years who are caring for a frail parent are women (NATSEM, 2006, p. 21).

A life course lens

Howe argues that, in order for fairness to be embedded in policy and practice, it is 'important to gain an understanding of people's contributions and entitlements not just at one point in time, but across the life course' (2007, p. 73). At the Centre for Public Policy and Risk conference in 2005, Schmid explored the notion of 'placing social policy in an ethical frame ... in relation to what kind of society we want to live in' (cited in

Howe, 2007, p. 46). Schmid argued for shared responsibility through a transitional labour market approach (TLM), as a means of anticipating and managing social risk (cited in Howe, 2007, p. 47). Howe suggests that a TLM approach, already having 'wide currency in the European community, may provide a useful framework for understanding how public policy might cope with the frequent changes and accompanying uncertainty people experience in their lives today' (2007, p. 48).

Schmid (2005) identifies five major life course transitions in relation to employment:

1. between education and employment;
2. between (unpaid) caring and employment;
3. between unemployment and employment;
4. between retirement and employment; and
5. between precarious employment and permanent employment (cited in Howe, 2007, p. 59).

As Schmid acknowledges, each of these transitions presents its own risks and opportunities. Illness, death and/or carer responsibilities can occur at any point within and between these transitions, adding another layer of vulnerability and risk. In these circumstances, the impact on individuals, communities, businesses and women carers in particular may be further compromised; workplace support needs may need to be more comprehensive to provide better support for women carers during these five major transitions in and out of employment.

Schmid (2005) outlines four elements that facilitate good transitions:

1. empower individuals by building or maintaining their employment capacity;
2. provide active support instead of passive payments;
3. establish a balance between central regulation and individual or local flexibility; and
4. stimulate networks and co-operation.

(cited in Howe, 2007, p. 59)

These elements could also facilitate gender equality in relation to employment.

Transition risks, states Howe, 'must be anticipated and turned into opportunities for employability and social inclusion ... this means investing in people' – especially women (2007, p. 104). Transitions across the life span affect neighbourhoods and communities, not just businesses; in labour market transitions, communities and individuals can feel at risk (Howe, 2007, pp. 102–3). Governments need to minimize the insecurity and uncertainties associated with life course transitions, particularly for women carers. For example, the UK government, post Thatcher, made a massive financial commitment to neighbourhood regeneration because there was a recognition that it was at the local level where these transitions were most stressed (Howe, 2007, p. 103).

As Howe (2007) points out, the TLM approach is much broader than the French policy of reduced weekly hours of work. He also points out that the education–work–retirement trajectory can no longer be seen as separate sequential blocks (pp. 112–13). He highlights that the TLM approach includes flexible arrangements for moving between paid work and other worthwhile activities advocating a more equal distribution of paid and non-paid time between the genders (p. 110). These activities could include education, skills development, carer responsibilities, volunteer work, or medical treatment for illness; all of which involve women to different degrees.

According to Howe, the benefits of addressing tensions related to use of time and facilitating labour market transitions are:

- higher rates of lifelong learning;
- higher rates of employment skills acquisition;
- higher rates of mature-aged workers extending their involvement in work with reduced work over time.

(2007, p. 113).

Howe suggests that a time bank and a skills bank may provide entitlements, through legislation, that take into account leave and absences from work (2007, pp. 124–5). With many carers, mostly female, accepting less challenging and lower paid work in order to accommodate their caring responsibilities, Howe's proposal places this approach in a social justice context. As he insightfully highlights, lifelong learning may prove to be the most powerful intervention that can be made to promote a just society (p. 132). This approach promotes a 'shared benefits-shared responsibility' framework between business, government, individuals, communities, men and women, and, most importantly, invests in those who are at risk of lacking the skills to compete in today's labour market – mostly women (Howe, 2007, p. 185).

Howe argues that: 'it is important to have a strong and vibrant economy ... but it is even more important that we build a strong and vibrant society' (2007, p. 145). Critically, the TLM approach permits people to use periods of change to their longer term advantage, with the capacity to turn risks into opportunities (p. 186). For women in particular, the TLM approach enables them to make decisions about work-education-carer responsibilities within an environment that promotes change in health-promoting ways based on flexibility and 'flexicurity' (Howe, 2007, p. 181). Importantly, policies, programmes and activities that facilitate supporting employed carers through these periods of transition may better highlight the universality of loss, and prepare individuals for their own death and dying, or the death of their loved ones. In so doing, the reality of women as carers and their carer experiences, including grief and bereavement, could gain recognition and acceptance. With this could come equality in the workplace and the broader community.

In 2007, An Integrated Approach to Evaluation for Grief Support in the Workplace was developed through La Trobe University and the Victorian Consortium for Public Health. The research, based at Creative Ministries Network, an agency of the Uniting Church, Victoria, suggests that the spiritual support needs of everyday grief for people at work may be met through:

- interventions, methods and processes such as support (individual and group);
- vital listening and storytelling (as an intervention);
- appropriate human resource/occupational health and safety policies;
- leadership through compassionate service;
- befriending; and
- connecting, humanizing actions and activities ... for example, ritual, acceptance of, and learning from, mistakes.

This approach is congruent with the OSI resource guide recommendations noted in the five human rights standards related to palliative care referred to in Item 3 in Table 10.1 (2007, OSI, p. 35).

The research project offers a model, yet to be piloted, to underpin a *Compassionate Cities* approach in the workplace (refer to Figure 10.1). As Figure 10.1 depicts, a workplace ethos that embraces leadership through compassionate service and befriending support, may provide the mechanism through which grief and loss can be authentically supported. Developing an evaluation approach also enables this practice to be embedded, monitored and improved where appropriate. Most importantly, this approach has the potential to move the debate about women-friendly workplaces beyond the female domain to embrace all people in the workplace, regardless of gender, age, industry sector or nationality.

Figure 10.1 Three domains of an integrated approach to evaluation for grief support in the workplace.
NB: This model has been adapted from Creative Ministries Network and its Work-Related Grief Support Programme.

Conclusion

New legislation and social policies are emerging within Europe, the United States, Canada, the United Kingdom and Australia as each country's workforce population changes to manage the transitions associated with the life course trajectory, including end-of-life transitions from the point of diagnosis or beginning of a carer's responsibilities through to the end of the early bereavement period. These changes have the opportunity to benefit women and their work-carer responsibilities and rights to educational achievement. Governments, the business world, employers and employees, communities and individuals have the opportunity to respond creatively through social and compassionate policy frameworks, programmes and practices which recognize vulnerable people, especially women carers. A transitional labour market approach partnered with a compassionate, befriending workplace approach, may provide the mechanisms through which just and fair workforce participation may occur for women throughout the life course. With the majority of carers being female, and since an increasing number of women need to work, women-friendly workplaces are an ethical imperative. The time is ripe to embrace the challenge in authentic education-life-work affirming ways across the life span, including through an end-of-life transition period.

Acknowledgment. I wish to express my heartfelt gratitude to Prof. Brian Howe, former Deputy Prime Minister of Australia (1991–95), Centre for Public Policy, The University of Melbourne, for the privilege of receiving his permission to use material from his book.

References

AMP.NATSEM (2006) *The Cost of Caring in Australia 2002 to 2005 – Who Cares?*, AMP.NATSEM Income and Wealth Report, Issue 13 May.

Australian Bureau of Statistics (2008) *4102.0 – Australian Social Trends*, AUSSTATS, viewed 25 October 2008, http://www.abs.gov.au/AUSSTATS/abs@rsf/Lookup/4102.0Chapter7102008.

Australian Government Equal Opportunity for Women in the Workplace Act 1999, Attorney General's Dept., Canberra. 2001, viewed 28 October 2008, http://www.eowa.gov.au/About_EOWA/Overview_of_the_Act/The_Act/EOWW_Act_1999.pdf

Briggs, H. and Fisher, D. (2000) *Warning – Caring is a Health Hazard. Results of the 1999 Survey of Carer Health and Wellbeing*, Canberra, Carers Association of Australia.

Canadian Employment Insurance Regulations (1996), viewed 8 September 2005, http://www.chpca.net/public_policy_advocacy/compassionate_care_benefit.

Carers Australia (2008) *Submission to the House of Representatives Inquiry into Better Support for Carers*, http://www.carersaustralia.com.au/uploads/20080630_%20Carers%20Australia%20Submission%20to%20Better%20Support%20Needs%20Inquiry_1.pdf

Department of Health and Ageing (2007) *Effective Caring: A Synthesis of the International Evidence on Carer Needs and Interventions – Volume 1*, 6.1.4 Carer Health and Well-Being Survey 2007, Carers Australia and Deakin University's Australian unity Well-Being Index Project, viewed 8 September 2008.

Econotech (2007) *Sick at Work: The Cost of Presenteeism to Your Business, Employees and the Economy*, Medibank Private, May.

Howe, B. (2007) *Weighing Up Australian Values: Balancing Transitions and Risks to Work and Family in Modern Australia*, Sydney, University of New South Wales Press.

James, J. W. and Friedman, R. (2003) *The Grief Index: The 'Hidden' Annual Costs of Grief in America's Workplace' 2003 Report*, compiled by The Grief Recovery Institute Educational Foundation, pp. 1–33.

Kellehear, A. (2005) *Compassionate Cities: Public Health and End-of-Life Care*, London, Routledge.

Open Society Institute (ISO) and Equitas – International Centre for Human Rights Education (2007) *Palliative Care and Human Rights – A Resource Guide*, New York and Quebec, ISO.

Productivity Commission (2008) *Trends in Aged Care Services: Some Implications*, Commission Research Paper, Canberra.

Renzenbrink, I. (2002) *Foundations of Bereavement Support in Hospice and Palliative Care, A Discussion Paper, Remembering the Past, Living the Present, Shaping the Future*, Dublin, Irish Hospice Foundation.

Rumbold, B. (2008) 'Editorial', *Social Networks: The Tri-Annual Newsletter of the Palliative Care & Public Health Network*, No. 15, July, p. 2.

Schmid, G. (2005) *Social Risk Management through Transitional Labour Markets*, Keynote address at the Transitions and Risks: New Directions in Social Policy conference, Centre for Public Policy, University of Melbourne, February, http:www.publicpolicy.unimelb.edu.au/conference2005.

State of Victoria, Department of Justice (2008) *An Equality Act for a Fairer Victoria: Equal Opportunity Review Final Report*, June 2008.

Taskforce on Care Costs (2005) *Creating Choice: Employment and the Cost of Care*, Taskforce on Care Costs Policy Paper, February 2005.

Tehan, M. (2006) *A Literature Report on Developing a Best Practice Support Model for Life-Threatening Illness in the Workplace*, Palliative Care Victoria, Department of Health and Ageing Funded Caring Communities Project, September 2005.

Tehan, M. (2007) *Leading the Way: Compassion in the Workplace*, action learning project undertaken for Master's in Public Health programme, La Trobe University, Melbourne, 2007.

UN Department of Public Information, 2008, *Goal 3: Promote Gender Equality and Empower Women*, End Poverty Millennium Development Goals 2015 Make it happen, 25 September, viewed 13 October 2008, http://www.un.org/milleniumgoals/2008highlevel/pdf/compilation.pdf.

Victorian Equal Opportunity & Human Rights Commission (2008) *Building Equality in the workplace: Family Responsibilities – Guidelines for Employers and Employees*, Industrial Relations Victoria, Department of Innovation, Industry and Regional Development; Victorian Equal Opportunity & Human Rights Commission, July 2008.

WorkSafe Victoria (2008) *WorkHealth Factsheet: A Healthier and More Productive Victorian Workforce*, Victorian Workcover Authority, viewed 16 October 2008, http://www.workcover.vic.gov.au.

World Health Organization (2001) *Table 1: Numbers and rates of registered deaths*, World Health Organization Statistical Information System, viewed 20 October 2008, http://www.who.int/whosis/database/mort/table1_process.cfm.

World Health Organization (2008) *Closing the Gap in a Generation*, the World Health Organization Commission on Social Determinants of Health. 28 August, viewed on 8 September 2008, http://www.who.int/social_determinants/final_report/ed/index.html.

11
Spirituality in the Workplace
Bernard Moss

> The idea that an organization's most valuable resource is its human resource – its people – is an idea that has been around for a long time now. It is sadly the case, however, that it often remains at a rhetorical level and does not rise above the status of an empty slogan.
>
> (Bates and Thompson, 2007, p. 283)

This chapter explores ways in which that 'empty rhetoric' could instead become a vibrant reality, whereby everyone in the organization could really feel that they are cherished, have a key role to play, and feel that they have a measure of ownership in the organization's success as well as some responsibility for its overall well-being when the going gets tough.

Setting the scene

It is worthwhile spending some time trying to clarify what the 'problem' is, or is perceived to be. Otherwise, any discussion about introducing spirituality (however this is conceived) into the workplace may simply appear to be an attempt to introduce an irrelevant 'foreign body'. And, as with unsuccessful medical transplants, the 'body' will quickly decide to reject it.

The 'workplace' means many different things to people: the experience of people working in a factory; a hospital, a theatre, a faith community project, a school or university, in the armed forces or the police, in a voluntary organization or local government department, being a manager or an employee, a solicitor or an office cleaner, stockbroker or lorry driver, will inevitably be different, and it would be naïve to assume that the 'workplace' means the same thing to everyone. For some it is a locus for self-fulfilment; for others, a place of extreme alienation; for some, it provides an opportunity to find and express themselves and come alive creatively; for others it is a 'grad-grinding' existence that helps pay the bills, and enables them 'to come to life' outside work time (Moss, 2004). The stresses and stressors will vary, and often one of the determining factors for satisfaction and enjoyment in the workplace will depend upon the unpredictable human chemistry between the people involved, irrespective of their job roles or the place they occupy within the organization's structure or hierarchy.

Nevertheless, there are some commonalities that bestride this apparent fragmented and compartmentalized workplace experience. It terms of 'stating the problem', several authors have articulated this clearly. Pava for example, draws attention to a sense of unease and incompleteness among workers, when:

> Organizations demand more time, psychic energy, loyalty, and imagination from employees than ever before, but continue to treat them as if they were interchangeable parts.
>
> (2003, p. 393)

Sheep (2006) refers to the 'quiet desperation' often experienced by people in the workplace who feel a disconnectedness between who they are and what they are required to do in the work setting, and do not know how to handle this tension. He cites Henry Ford's famous comment: 'Why is it that I always get the whole person when all I really want is a pair of hands?' (Pollard, 1996, p. 25), and continues:

> Whether or not organizations want the whole person, whole persons report for work. Mitroff and Denton (1999a) found in their study of 131 HR managers that
>
>> People do not want to compartmentalise their lives. The search for meaning, purpose, wholeness and integration is a constant, never-ending task. They especially want to be acknowledged as whole persons in the workplace where they spend the majority of their waking time.
>>
>> (Sheep, 2006, pp. xv–xvi)

This is vividly captured by Gwyther (2004) in his foreword to a UK report by Holbeche and Springett (2004) on the search for meaning in the workplace, where he invites the reader to:

Stop for a moment. Think back to this morning. Did you leap up enthusiastically eager to get to the office for another motivating day at work? Or did you shudder when the alarm clock went off, drag yourself out of bed and grimly prepare yourself for another round of what social anthropologist Studs Terkel (1974) has called, *a Monday to Friday sort of dying*?

Holbeche and Springett's (2004) report itself makes important reading, in that it explores the phenomena that underpin this chapter, and highlights the importance of enabling workers to develop and cherish a sense of meaning and purpose in the workplace. The authors argue that there is a strong *business case* for taking these issues seriously, thereby reflecting Mitroff and Denton's study, which showed that organizations that took such issues seriously also achieved a greater profitability. Their study ends with the challenging call:

> Unless organizations harness the 'whole person' and the immense spiritual energy that is at the core of everything, they will not be able to produce world-class products and services.
> (Mitroff and Denton, 1999b, p. 84)

Finally, in this brief catena of illustrative comments, there is one powerful image that manages to encapsulate the heart of the problem. In his moving reflection on an open-air sculpture of an empty raincoat by Judith Shea in Minneapolis, Handy (1995) comments:

> To me that empty raincoat is the symbol of our most pressing paradox. We were not destined to be empty raincoats, nameless numbers on a payroll, role occupants, the raw material of economics or sociology, statistics in some government report. If that is to be its price, then economic progress is an empty promise. There must be more to life than to be a cog in someone else's great machine. The challenge must be to prove that the paradox can be managed and that we, each one of us, can fill that empty raincoat.
> (p. 2, cited in Moss, 2007, p. 263)

No matter what the job, the career, or the setting in which people find themselves, the issues identified in these observations powerfully and poignantly capture the challenging nature of the workplace. And, if we add the deepening spectre of job losses and economic 'downturns', it is no wonder that people will feel worried, insecure and emotionally 'off balance', waiting for the worst to happen. It is into this complex picture that spirituality has been introduced, not as a facile 'quick fix', or an escape route from the difficulties, but as a profound way of *looking at* what is happening in the workplace, and as an invitation to explore challenges creatively and effectively. Far from being yet another 'management tool or theory' to use in an attempt to restore effectiveness and profitability to dysfunctional organizations, it suggests a more 'root and branch' approach that reflects the underlying values and aspirations.

Workplace spirituality

It perhaps still comes as a surprise to many people in the United Kingdom that both here, and especially in the United States, there has been a recent quickening of interest in workplace spirituality and in spiritual dimensions for management (for example, Beekun and Badawi, 2005; Garcia-Zamor, 2003; Howard, 2002; Jurkiewicz and Giacalone, 2004; King 2007; Krishnakumar and Neck 2002; Mitroff and Denton, 1999a,b; Pava, 2003; Sheep, 2006). Conferences now address this subject; books and articles are written exploring the theme; websites (such as www.spiritatwork.com) have been developed, all of which Howard suggests, writing from a UK perspective: 'confirm the explosion of interest in spirituality as a new dimension of management' (2002, p. 230).

For some, this may seem an unwarranted intrusion into the complex world of work. They are tempted to equate spirituality with religion, and see this as a very personal, indeed private, matter, that people who are interested 'in that sort of thing' will pursue in their own time. People have all sorts of interests, hobbies and pursuits, which may lead them to hold a wide range of outlooks and worldviews, but these should belong firmly in the 'family locker'. Furthermore, they would argue that the workplace is primarily dedicated to its chosen 'end product', and employers and employees should focus exclusively on achieving the goals and outputs for which the organization has been created and to which it needs to be committed. To introduce religious and/or spiritual matters would be an impertinence and an intrusion, and, like the ill-matched organ transplant, the organization will properly reject it.

These are important objections, and they serve two useful purposes. First, they are reminders that each organization must 'keep its eye on the ball' as far as its main objectives are concerned, and do its utmost to ensure that everyone involved in the organization stays focused on its principal objectives. The workplace is not to be seen as fertile ground for propaganda (religious or political), nor to be exploited by any of its employees for such purposes. Second, they highlight the importance of definitional clarity when terms like spirituality are introduced into the discussion. There is a real danger with a concept that can mean so many different things to so many different people, that vigorous arguments and debates, and indeed polarized antagonisms, can ensue without anyone fully understanding what the word means to the various people involved.

For those who argue strongly for the important contribution that an understanding of spirituality can make to the workplace, the meaning of the concept, although at times subtle and complex, is very clear. They argue that the very issues which together contribute to the cluster of problems that beset and haunt the workplace, as were outlined in the opening section of this chapter, are *precisely* the issues that a contemporary understanding of spirituality seeks to address.

Far from being an alien concept, spirituality needs to be understood as a way of looking at what is happening in the workplace, and as an invitation to explore the extent to which issues such as meaning, purpose and fulfilment are embedded and lived out within the organization. Krishnakumar and Neck unpack this further when they draw our attention to evidence that:

> suggests a link between workplace spirituality and enhanced individual creativity (Freshman, 1999), increased honesty and trust within the organization (Wagner-Marsh and Conely, 1999), enhanced sense of personal fulfilment of employees (Burack, 1999) and increased commitment to organizational goals (Delbecq, 1999; Leigh, 1997).
>
> (2002, p. 153)

This suggests that various strands that interweave to create the understanding of workplace spirituality include the importance of meaning and purpose; commitment; creativity and connectedness.

The search for meaning is one of the core themes that has emerged in the contemporary exploration of spirituality, whether from a religious or a secular perspective. I have argued elsewhere (Moss, 2005) that a helpful way of understanding spirituality is to regard it as what we do to give expression to our chosen worldview. And, in as much as our attitude towards work is an essential ingredient to that worldview, then our spirituality – and our attitude towards work – will necessarily be intertwined with it (for an Islamic perspective on these issues, see Beekun and Badawi, 2005).

Workplace spirituality: two important strands

It is important to distinguish between two strands here. First, each and every one of us has an individual spirituality, a 'take' on life if you like, that will inevitably influence our attitude to work. For some who hold to a specifically religious outlook on life, there will be particular requirements that managers need to ensure are firmly in place in order to meet their responsibilities to their employees under a fast-growing diversity agenda. The provision of designated places for prayer, for example; an awareness of certain religious dress codes, and a sensitivity to particular religious festivals or periods of fasting that some employees need to be observed are examples of this.

Furthermore, as some writers in the United States point out, there are some spiritual activities that *in themselves* have been shown to enhance performance at work, and therefore deserve serious consideration by employers to make time and space available for such activities at work. Tischler, Biberman and McKeage (2002) cite one example of this with Transcendental Meditation (TM). Their review of over 600 studies reveals a range of positive outcomes from TM, including enhanced creativity, concentration and intellectual functioning. Similar claims could be made for the practice of yoga and other breathing/meditation disciplines in Eastern cultures, where the picture of the workforce gathering together at the start of the working day to engage together in 'tai chi' or similar activities is well known. Employers seem to recognize that, whatever individual benefits there may be from such activities, there are also shared benefits for the organization in terms of corporate cohesion, commitment and productivity. For this reason time and space are made available, together with a degree of active encouragement to participate, for the benefit of the organization as a whole. It was not so long ago in the United Kingdom, for example, that a profession now as fully secular as the probation service used to begin its daily work with a corporate act of prayer.

These are all genuine examples of one aspect of spirituality in the workplace, in that they refer to specific activities that tap into the human spirit and inner motivation of the people who make up the workforce. In many ways they enhance the spirit of belonging and commitment without which the organization would be far less able to achieve its stated goals and objectives. Some of the activities are distinctly religious, but not all of them are: some activities can be shared by anyone and everyone irrespective of the worldviews they have chosen. It might even be argued that corporate team-building exercises and 'away days/courses' fulfil a similar 'spiritual' function, in that they seek to enhance the *spirit* of the team and develop its cohesiveness.

Another example of the sort of activity that may be classified as 'spirituality in the workplace' would be special interest groups. These too can be deliberately religious in tone. Christians, Jews, Sikhs or Muslims, for example, who work in large organizations may meet from time to time to share issues of common interest and concern, perhaps to pray together, or to debate workplace ethical dilemmas or difficulties that an adherence to their faith may create. They provide a mutual support network, the result of which will be to help them give of their best within the workplace, or to campaign for certain changes that will enhance their experience as employees. A non-religious or secular example of this would be in large organizations where perhaps a minority of employees are from minority ethnic groups, and who feel that the white majority is being institutionally racist in its outlook and behaviour. A black workers' support group would provide an opportunity for black workers to share experiences and gain mutual support, but importantly also to provide a strong representational voice to the management, perhaps through trades union channels, to address the fundamental (and, of course, illegal) inequalities they are subjected to as black workers.

Another facet of this would be the level of care that an organization takes when employees go through particularly difficult and emotionally draining times, such as serious illness or bereavement. As Gilbert, Moss, Bates and Thompson all point out, in a special issue of the journal *Illness, Crisis & Loss* (2007) dedicated to loss and grief in the workplace, for an organization to ignore these experiences and to carry on almost as if nothing has happened is to deny the fundamental spirituality both of the individuals concerned and the workplace itself, resulting in a reduction of efficiency, let alone humanity, for everyone involved.

All of these examples illustrate the first strand of what spirituality in the workplace can mean. This strand involves the organization making 'reasonable adjustments' to ensure that the various cultural and religious (and at times of crisis, personal) needs of the workforce are being met appropriately; of ensuring that injustices and inequalities are properly challenged and addressed, and in some cases providing a range of activities that can be seen to enhance the well-being of the workforce for the benefit of the organization's productivity and success. This strand is of immense importance, but as far as a discussion about workplace spirituality is concerned, it does not go far enough.

The second strand to this concept lies at a much deeper and more profound level and goes to the very heart of how an organization sees itself and its purpose. It raises questions about meaning and purpose, and affects the organization *as a whole*, not just the specific needs of some of the workforce. As Howard notes:

> Perhaps one of the most significant attributes of spirituality is that at its root it is a matter of seeing – it is all of life seen from a certain perspective (Turner, 1999) It is about 'metanoia' (Senge,1990) – a fundamental shift in mind in which individuals come to see themselves as capable of creating the world they truly want rather than reacting to circumstances beyond their control.
>
> (2002, p. 235).

This broader understanding of workplace spirituality invites us to raise some fundamental, even existential, questions about the workplace. These questions include:

- Why am I doing this work?
- What is the meaning of the work I am doing?
- Where does this lead me?
- Is there a reason for my existence and the organization's?

(Krishnakuman and Neck, 2002, p. 154).

Given that the search for meaning *within the workplace* has been identified as one major indicator of overall personal satisfaction, this role of spirituality clearly is significant. Again, as Howard comments:

> Despite the post-modern insistence that grand narratives are dead, people are still looking for some spiritual certainties in life. People need an awareness of the 'big picture' – but want it revised, updated and made relevant. That's partly why issues about spirituality are arising in the workplace where people spend so much of their lives and begin to question what it's all for.
>
> (2002, p. 234)

Spirituality or spiritual intelligence: what's in a name?

Holbeche and Springett's research, however, discovered what others have also found, that the term 'spirituality' can be as 'off putting' and misleading to some as it is encouraging and meaningful to others. One focus group participant, for example, jibbed at the use of the word 'spirituality' and exclaimed: 'Is there no part of life which managers can't get their hands on?' (2004, p. 25).

Therefore, to derive the greatest benefit from the term (if we may put it in such a way), we need to regard it less of a concrete, tightly defined concept, and more of a 'gateway' word that points us in a particular direction. We need to be clear that, although, as we have seen, the term has a particular resonance and importance to people who belong to faith communities, there is a wider application that fulfils a unifying role *for everyone* involved in the organization, including those who have chosen a secular, rather than a religious, worldview as their template for living.

It is at this point that the concept of spiritual intelligence (SQ) may be usefully introduced. Zohar and Marshall (2001) developed this concept as an enhancement and enrichment of other forms of intelligence. Building upon the well-known concept of a person's IQ, Goleman (1996, 1998) introduced the notion of emotional intelligence (EQ), which Zohar and Marshall further developed into SQ – spiritual intelligence. They argue that SQ is the innate human capacity to ask the question 'why?', and to engage with the complex longing and struggle to find and create meaning, both for ourselves as individuals and also in the organizations to which we belong, including our workplace settings. It will be our SQ that enables us to 'think outside the box', and to release the creative potential and energies latent within us, and 'to understand that the whole can be greater than the sum of its parts' (Holbeche and Springett, 2004, p. 23).

This approach takes us to the very heart of what makes an organization really successful in human terms, as well as being profitable and productive. An approach informed by SQ will actively strive to ensure that everyone in the workplace feels fulfilled, and is able to contribute effectively to its well-being as well as to its success, because:

> many employees want to work for organizations where there is a set of values that they can relate to personally, and which are put into practice. In such contexts employees are more likely to commit to the organization and want to give of their best.
>
> (Holbeche and Springett, 2004, p. 47)

Again it is important to stress that SQ should not be conceptualized rigidly, but (as with spirituality) it is to be understood as a 'gateway' or 'pointer' to a set of principles and an encouragement to look at the 'world' in a particular way. Some writers (Tischler, Biberman and McKeage, 2002, for example) have argued that a fuller understanding of EQ would remove any necessity for the development of SQ. There is a parallel here with those who find the use of the term 'spirituality' off putting. But the emphasis in SQ (and in our understanding of secular spirituality) upon 'meaning making' in particular gives it the 'edge' in this debate: it seems to be able to capture the spirit of the enterprise in a way that EQ does not.

This point is further emphasized by the work of Emmons who enriches the discussion by suggesting that another dimension of SQ includes: 'the ability to invest everyday activities, events and relationships with a sense of the sacred' (2000, p. 10). Such an approach clearly resonates with many faith communities' approaches to the workplace and their relationships with each other and with the 'created world'. But the idea of the sacred also has rich secular connotations, where all human life is regarded as precious, and where a sense of awe, mystery, wonder and transcendence is cherished. This secular idea of the sacred takes us back to the notion of spirituality being a 'special way of viewing the world' discussed earlier in this chapter. One very tangible example of this appears in Gilbert who cites the encounter between President J. F. Kennedy and a cleaner at the NASA Space Centre. Kennedy asked this man what he was doing, and revealingly he replied: 'I am helping to put men into space Mr President' (2005, p. 14). For him, his apparently menial task was an important part of a greater enterprise; he saw the 'big picture' and his place within it; and importantly he took a sacred pride in the contribution he was making to the organization's well-being and success.

It would, of course, be naïve to expect every worker in every organization to have this sense of the sacred. There is still too much exploitation of workers for this to be realistic, because whatever SQ or spirituality may stand for, it most definitely does not condone exploitation, oppression or discrimination. On the contrary, part of its agenda will necessarily involve challenging anything that undermines human value and the sense of the sacred. But, that this is an ideal to which every organization should aspire, and that an understanding of spirituality and SQ is an important journey towards achieving that aspiration, is the essential argument of this chapter.

Workplace spirituality and transformational leadership

From this position it follows that the role of the leader or manager is crucial to achieve this aspiration. Managers set the tone for an organization: they articulate and represent its values, and have a conjoint responsibility for implementing the strategies necessary for organizational success, and for ensuring the well-being of the workforce. While they may not see themselves as spiritual leaders – that nomenclature seems to be reserved for faith community leaders – nevertheless:

> leaders can transform organizations by seeking to create conditions that free organizational energy, promote positive relationships, and which encourage personal growth by liberating individual responsibility for choices and actions.
>
> (Howard, 2002, p. 237)

These are the very conditions which, if absent, contribute massively to the sense of meaninglessness and alienation among a workforce; but which, if encouraged and cultivated, can enhance the sense of satisfaction, pride and creativity that is fundamental to a successful organization and its members. These are also among the characteristics identified by those who argue for an understanding of spirituality in the workplace, and those who support the notion of SQ.

Conclusion

This chapter began by arguing that workplace spirituality would quickly be rejected as irrelevant and an impertinent intrusion if it did not relate to the real issues, problems, challenges and aspirations of the organization. The problems of workers feeling alienated in the workplace, of not feeling valued, or being able to flourish within their work settings were then discussed. In this context two strands of workplace spirituality were identified. The first strand emphasized the responsibility of any organization to make reasonable adjustments to respect and accommodate the spiritual and religious needs of the workforce as part of its diversity commitment and responsibility.

The second strand of workplace spirituality, however, goes much deeper, and involves the way in which an organization sees and understands itself. It takes us into more profound questions about vision and purpose; how an organization cherishes, values, stretches and rewards its employees; and how it provides opportunities for creativity and (at least) some sense of personal fulfilment in the workplace.

The chapter concluded with a brief discussion of the transformational role that leaders and managers need to play if these aspirations are to be fulfilled. Workplace spirituality, and the associated concept of spiritual intelligence, offer a framework or paradigm within which everyone in an organization can begin to grapple with the big questions of meaning and purpose in the workplace, and the contribution that everyone can make to its well-being and success. When taken seriously, therefore, workplace spirituality will no longer run the risk of being rejected as irrelevant, but rather will be welcomed and celebrated as a key to success.

References

Bates, J. and Thompson, N. (2007) 'Workplace Well-being: An Occupational Social Work Approach', *Illness, Crisis & Loss* 15(3), pp. 273–84.

Beekun, R. and Badawi, J. (2005) 'Balancing Ethical Responsibility among Multiple Organizational Stakeholders: The Islamic Perspective', *Journal of Business Ethics* 60, pp. 131–45.

Burack, E. H.(1999) 'Spirituality in the Workplace', *Journal of Organizational Change Management* 12(4), pp. 280–91.

Delbecq, L. (1999) 'Christian Spirituality and Contemporary Business Leadership', *Journal of Organisational Change Management* 12(4), pp. 345–9.

Emmons, R. (2000) Is Spirituality an Intelligence? Motivation, Cognition and the Psychology of Ultimate Concern', *The International Journal for the Psychology of Religion* 10(1), pp. 3–26.

Freshman, B. (1999) 'An Exploratory Analysis of Definitions and Applications of Spirituality in the Workplace', *Journal of Organisational Change Management* 12(4), pp. 318–27.

Garcia-Zamor, J.-C. (2003) 'Workplace Spirituality and Organizational Performance', *Public Administration Review* 63(3), pp. 355–63.

Gilbert, P. (2005) *Leadership: Being Effective and Remaining Human*, Lyme Regis, Russell House Publishing.

Gilbert, P. (2007) '"Nobody Noticed": Leadership and Issues of Workplace Loss and Grief', *Illness, Crisis & Loss* 15(3), pp. 219–32.

Goleman, D. (1996) *Emotional Intelligence; Why it Can Matter More than IQ*, London, Bloomsbury.

Goleman, D. (1998) *Working with Emotional Intelligence*, New York, Bantam Books.

Gwyther, M. (2004) 'Foreword', in Holbeche and Springett (2004).

Handy, C. (1995) *The Empty Raincoat: Making Sense of the Future*, London, Arrow Business Books.

Holbeche, L. and Springett, N. (2004) *In Search of Meaning in the Workplace*, Horsham, Roffey Park.

Howard, S. (2002) 'A Spiritual Perspective on Learning in the Workplace', *Journal of Management Psychology* 17(33), pp. 230–42.

Jurkiewicz, C. and Giacalone, R. (2004) 'A Values Framework for Measuring the Impact of Workplace Spirituality on Organizational Performance', *Journal of Business Ethics* 49, pp. 129–42.

King, S. (2007) 'Religion, Spirituality and the Workplace: Challenges for Public Administration', *Public Administration Review*, January/February, pp. 103–14.

Krishnakumar, S. and Neck, C. (2002) 'The "What", "Why" and "How" of Spirituality in the Workplace', *Journal of Managerial Psychology* 17(3), pp. 153–64.

Leigh, P. (1999) 'The New Spirit at Work', *Training and Development* 51(3), pp. 26–34.

Mitroff, I. I. and Denton, E. A. (1999a) *A Spiritual Audit of Corporate America: A Hard Look at Spirituality, Religion and Values in the Workplace*, San Francisco, Jossey Bass.

Mitroff, I. I. and Denton, E. A. (1999b) 'A Study of Spirituality in the Workplace', *Sloan Management Review* 40(4), pp. 83–92.
Moss, B. (2004) 'TGIM: Thank God it's Monday', *British Journal of Occupational Learning* 2(2), pp. 33–43.
Moss, B. (2005) *Religion and Spirituality*, Lyme Regis, Russell House Publishing.
Moss, B. (2007) 'Towards a Spiritually Intelligent Workplace?', *Illness, Crisis & Loss* 15(3), pp. 261–71.
Pava, M. (2003) 'Searching for Spirituality in All the Wrong Places', *Journal of Business Ethics* 48, pp. 2393–400.
Pollard, C. W. (1996) *The Soul of the Firm*, Grand Rapids, MI, Harper Business.
Senge, P. (1990) *The Fifth Discipline: The Art and Practice of the Learning Organization*, New York, Doubleday.
Sheep, M. (2006) 'Nurturing the Whole Person: The Ethics of Workplace Spirituality in a Society of Organizations', *Journal of Business Ethics* 66 Spring, pp. 357–75.
Terkel, S. (1974) *Working*, New York, Pantheon.
Tischler, L., Biberman, J. and McKeage, R. (2002) 'Linking Emotional Intelligence, Spirituality and Workplace Performance: Definitions, Models and Ideas for Research', *Journal of Managerial Psychology* 17(3), pp. 203–18.
Turner, J. (1999) 'Spirituality in the Workplace', *CA (Canadian Institute of Chartered Accountants) Magazine* 132(10), pp. 41–2.
Wagner-Marsh, F. and Conley, J. (1999) 'The Fourth Wave: The Spiritually-Based Firm', *Journal of Organisational Change Management* 12(4), pp. 292–301.
Zohar, D. and Marshall, I. (2001) *SQ: Connecting with our Spiritual Intelligence*, London, Bloomsbury.

Part 3
International Perspectives

12
The Darker Side of the American Workplace

Seth Allcorn

The American workplace defies easy explanation. The diversity of regional cultures, enterprises, economies, rural and urban locations, differing sizes, public and private orientation and value systems creates a hard to understand context that negates one's best efforts to generalize about what exactly it is like to work for any one organization or the generic organization. To be noted is also the fact that larger organizations contain many subdivisions, each of which contains their own cultures where one of these subcultures may be an outstanding, inspiring and uplifting place to work within a larger organization dominated by punishing organizational dynamics. In sum, the American workplace does defy easy description, not unlike organizations spread across the globe.

The best workplaces that promote member well-being are often cited for many employee-friendly attributes, such as competitive pay and benefits; employee development programmes; family-friendly attributes, such as child care and flexible hours; and workplace cultures that promote individual and team effectiveness, value individuals and their contributions promoting engagement; and effective management that develops trust and respect among co-workers. Worker experience of the workplace as well as self-experience is favourable if not very positive. When asked: 'What is it like to work here?', the responses invariably include enjoying one's work and others in the workplace. Work is felt to be fun, challenging, meaningful and collegial, where everyone's perspectives are heard. A workplace context that promotes this level of positive self-experience and group dynamics is to be applauded. Unfortunately many organizations do not measure up and, as a result, lose the many contributions their employees can make to improving organizational effectiveness. Organizations, including those thought to be among the best places to work for, contain along a range many forms of organizational pathology that make them less than desirable workplaces. They contain punishing personal experiences that strip one of self-efficacy, self-esteem and the ability to invest one's creativity and productivity in one's work, thereby diminishing organizational effectiveness.

The darker side of American organizational life needs to be inspected to more fully appreciate its contribution to compromising organizational performance by crushing the life out of individuals, groups and the organization as a whole. 'Going postal' is after all a phrase attached to the American workplace, where its organizational counterpart – downsizing and organizational re-engineering – just as surely eliminate workers from the workplace. In these cases and many others the nature of organizational leadership that drives these hostile workplace cultures is the root cause. The remainder of this chapter is devoted to exploring a root cause matrix that describes four dysfunctional organization types that arise from pathological leadership narcissism. The four perspectives provide views of organizational life that promotes understanding and forms a basis for organizational intervention and change that avoids turning workers into casualties who are then treated by institutional means such as employee assistance.

Organizational narcissism: a new perspective on the darker side of the American workplace

Subjective experience of one's self (self and self-esteem) is experience that begins in infancy and continues throughout life, creating who we are. We may be integrated and self-confident or to some degree along a range, less well integrated as a result of parental failures. These failures lead to the development of a myriad of individualistic psychological defences that create problems in personal adjustment and tensions in relating to others, who may be hungered after or feared. What happens to, or around, an individual is evaluated in terms of one's self. Threats to one's psychologically defensive responses to life that support narcissistic character traits must be defended against. This less than adaptive, narcissistically-based, psychologically defensive outcome creates a range of workplace behaviours on the part of leaders who contribute to the development of pathological workplace culture (Schein, 1985).

Theoretical elements of narcissism

Pathological narcissism arises from parental failings to provide a loving, accepting and secure context for development. Karen Horney notes:

> In simple words, they [parental figures] may be dominating, overprotective, intimidating, irritable, over-exacting, overindulgent, erratic, partial to other siblings, hypocritical, indifferent, etc. It is never a matter of just a single fact, but always the whole constellation that exerts the untoward influence on a child's growth.
>
> (1950, p. 18)

DSM-IV describes narcissism as 'a pervasive pattern of grandiosity (in fantasy or behavior), need for admiration, and lack of empathy' (First and Tasman, 2004, p. 1258) that can be diagnosed when any five of these nine criteria are met:

1. Grandiose sense of self-importance.
2. Preoccupied with fantasies of unlimited success, power, brilliance, beauty, or ideal love.
3. Believes he or she is special and unique.
4. Requires excessive admiration.
5. Sense of entitlement.
6. Interpersonally exploitative, taking advantage of others to achieve his or her own ends.
7. Lacks empathy.
8. Often envious of others or believes that others are envious of him or her.
9. Shows arrogant, haughty behaviours or attitudes.

Five of the nine must be present to achieve the level of a diagnosed disorder. This appreciation leads to the conclusion that there are many combinations of attributes, leading some to conjecture that the more commonly found combinations constitute types of narcissistic disorder.

Linking narcissism to the workplace: Karen Horney's solutions to anxiety

Karen Horney has, as her primary focus the real self, that is, the 'central inner force, common to all human beings and yet unique in each, which is the deep source of growth' (1950, p. 17). However, profound insecurities arising from inadequate parenting create basic anxiety that diminishes one's inner self and feelings. The outcome, depending upon individual proclivities, is to cling to parental figures, rebel and fight back, or shut out everyone. These interpersonal outcomes are movements toward, against and away, and may be recast into the expansive appeal to mastery (against) the self-effacing appeal to love (toward) and the resigned appeal to freedom (away). The expansive appeal contains three features – perfectionism, narcissism and arrogant pride that, if threatened, is defended by vindictive triumph. The following discussion suggests that mastery, self-effacing and resigned solutions to anxiety are narcissistic disorders.

Irresolvable basic anxiety results in reliance upon one of these directions of movement as the predominant response. This compulsive reliance upon a preferred defensive solution does not rule out secondary retreats to the other solutions. This outcome displaces the real or true self, creating what Masterson (1988) refers to as false self. A reaction formation arises relative to others (movement toward, against, away) that is tenaciously defended for its anxiety abatement, creating a personality dominated with interpersonally defensive character traits.

Elsa Ronningstam's typology of narcissism

This typology provides a complement to Horney that further informs the development of the four organizational diagnostic types as distinguished from other forms.

Normal narcissism

Ronningstam notes:

> In a broad sense, narcissism refers to feelings and attitudes toward one's own self and to normal development and self-regulation.... Healthy narcissistic functions, such as a sense of the right to one's own life, striving for the best in life, appreciation of health and beauty, and ability to compete as well as to protect and defend oneself, are usually first attended to when they are absent or noticed as extreme.
> (2005, p. 31)

In contrast, when people feel that they are not entitled to express what they want, they expect others to guess their wishes and become upset if their expectations are not met.

Pathological narcissism

In contrast to healthy narcissism, pathological narcissism arises when the ability to manage one's feelings of anger, shame and envy is compromised. Others find themselves used to protect or enhance this individual's self-esteem at the expense of interpersonal authenticity and intimacy (Ronningstam, 2005, p. 69). Ronningstam describes three types of pathological narcissism: arrogant, shy and psychopathic. Each has similarities to Horney's narcissistic, arrogant-vindictive and self-effacing solutions to anxiety.

Arrogant narcissism

Arrogant narcissism closely resembles the above description of a narcissistic personality disorder, including Horney's discussion of narcissism:

- Inflated, vulnerable self-esteem;
- Grandiosity;
- Strong reactions to criticism and defeats – threats to self-esteem;
- Strong feelings of anger, shame and envy;
- Hyper reactive to perceived humiliations;
- Mood variations – depression, irritability, elation;
- Interpersonal relations serve to protect and enhance self-esteem;
- Arrogant and haughty attitude;
- Entitled, controlling and hostile behaviour;
- Impaired empathy and lack of commitment to others.

In sum, grandiosity and a sense of superiority, self-importance and uniqueness permits viewing others with disdain. Related behaviour may include seeking admiration, boastfulness, pretentiousness, self-centred interactions with others, development of grand plans, and pursuing power and control. These individuals are sensitive to not receiving narcissistic supplies from others and may attack others who do not support their grandiosity.

Shy narcissism

The shy narcissist possesses many of the self-effacing properties that Horney lists for the appeal to love. This individual is in flight from arrogant narcissistic qualities, creating a sense of low self-efficacy and self-worth, and possibly morbid dependency upon others. The following attributes underscore these properties:

- Inhibitions prevent development of capabilities;
- Shame for ambitions and grandiosity;

- Compensatory fantasies of being special and perfect;
- Intolerant of criticism, hypersensitive to humiliation and criticism, hyper-vigilant, feelings easily hurt, self-denigrating, extreme self-preoccupation;
- Not deserving of entitlement, modest, humble, unassuming;
- Intense shame reactions and fear of failure;
- Low affect;
- Inhibited interpersonally and vocationally;
- Attentive, modest, humble;
- Impaired empathy;
- Strong feelings of envy.

In sum, shame, combined with a strict conscience and self-criticism, impairs functioning. Grandiose strivings and achievement are avoided. This individual is unhappy, pessimistic and lacks a sense of fulfilment. A portion of this self-minimization is associated with the application of perfection turned upon one's self, creating feelings of deficiency.

Psychopathic narcissism

Psychopathic narcissism results in behaviours consistent with Horney's arrogant and vindictive type. Arrogant pride is fragile and must be defended to avoid the return of feelings of worthlessness. Associated attributes are:

- Immoral and willing to use aggression to protect and enhance an inflated self-image;
- Hyperactive and willing to expend limitless time and energy to succeed and win out over rivals, where aggression, sadism and revenge may become the norm;
- Feelings of envy and rage fuel excessive and hyperactive responses to threats;
- Feelings of exceptional entitlement support interpersonal exploitiveness and when frustrated, irritability and rage reactions emerge;
- Strong feelings of envy for others exist.

In sum, exceptional arrogance and a willingness to vindicate excessive self-pride at almost any cost to self, others and the organization arise. These individuals are hypersensitive and rapidly interpret situations as rewarding or as threatening or humiliating (Ronningstam, 2005, p. 84). They can dish it out, but they cannot take it.

Synthesizing Horney and Ronningstam

The works of Horney and Ronningstam have similarities and differences. The significance of Horney's triad of movements (against, toward, away) is that it offers a simple but challenging perspective that is generalizable to other levels of analysis, such as group and organizational dynamics. Ronningstam's typology provides additional insights into narcissism that encourage recasting Horney's three appeals (mastery, love and freedom) and solutions to basic anxiety (expansive, self-effacing and resigned) as narcissistic disorders. It is these three directions of movement, appeals and solutions informed by Ronningstam's typology that become the framework for the discussion of four organizational disorders – narcissistic, arrogant, dependent and avoidant organizational disorder (Allcorn, 2005, 2003).

Organizational disorders

The four organizational disorders contain shared themes that include uses of material aspects of organizations. This appreciation leads to the conclusion that subjective and objective data must be used to diagnose these disorders. To be noted is that saying an organization suffers from a disorder risks reifying organization. The following organizational disorders, rather than entering into reification, are more appropriately thought of as themes and artefacts of organizational life and organizational culture. The following typology is modelled after DSM-IV diagnostic categories to promote critical thinking about what is being found in the workplace and to what degree. This modelling is not intended to imply that they have the same rigour as DSM. Workplace examples are provided to anchor each type in workplace experience.

Notes on organizational regression and contagion

The diagnoses reveal pervasive themes that contain shared unconscious content discerned by listening to what organizations' members think and feel, including recognition, and of projections, transference and countertransference (Diamond and Allcorn, 2003; Stein, 1994). The group relations perspective offers additional insight. Kernberg, in his chapter, 'Organization Regression' (1985), suggests organization is a context where subordinates may individually and collectively, consciously and unconsciously influence their leader's self-experience and awareness and, by extension, behaviour. These influences contain manipulative and controlling elements aimed at creating a leader consistent with the expectations of others. These influences contribute to psychological regression on the part of the leader, who may become dysfunctional as a result of this rich and hard to know milieu of individual, group and operating variables. There is, then, a bi-directional interactive leader and follower dynamic context that yields the view that one can speak of a sense of organizational regression and pathology, and of a notion such as a narcissistic organizational disorder (Bion, 1961). A social contagion perspective amplifies unconscious shared interpersonal and group dynamics. The four disorders create self-sealing and self-perpetuating systems of thought, feeling and intersubjectivity throughout an organizational structure. A CEO who suffers from a narcissistic deficit may seek narcissistic supplies from subordinates who are, figuratively speaking, sucked dry of positive self-experience. These individuals subsequently turn to their subordinates for narcissistic supplies, creating another instance of narcissistic deficit that may in turn be passed downward throughout the organizational structure. A related example is the elation of a winning athletic team or the disarray, despair and disorganization of a losing team (Mandell, 1976). I now turn to a description of the disorders.

The narcissistic organizational disorder

Six of the following should be present:

- The organization and some of its members are 'larger than life' caricatures.
- The organization is often in the spotlight and its leaders seek opportunities to show off themselves and their organization to receive attention and recognition.
- The organization, its mission and accomplishments are described in grandiose terms, accompanied by grand thoughts and ideas for the future. Denigrating comparisons are offered regarding other organizations, regulators and competitors.
- There is an inattention to the details required to implement the grand ideas, creating marginal outcomes and failures that are covered up, forgotten, dismissed or pre-empted by more grand plans.
- Scapegoats are often sacrificed.
- Splits are present in the form of those who are loyal supporters (in-group) and those who are neutral or not supporters (out-group).
- Paternalism (maternalism) are present along with idealization of the organization and its leaders.
- Organizational resources are used to reward supporters and withheld from the out-group.

- Leaders are overly responsive to criticism, as are many employees.
- There is a history of killing the messenger or ignoring and marginalizing others who call into question what is going on (not a team player).
- There is evidence of insensitivity to customers/clients/patients and their needs, as well as a disregard for laws and ethics.

These diagnostic criteria are easy to identify in organizations, as the following example illustrates.

Practice Focus 12.1

Northeast Supply is led by a well-known turnaround executive, Al. He has an intimidating and threatening presence. He has to save the organization both from itself and past leadership, implying failure on the part of many. Al is good at handling the media, board and stockholders and often mentions popular management buzzwords. He is also seen by others as generating ideas that he is unable to follow through on because they lack enabling details and an understanding of financial and production management. Al has elevated those who like and admire him and support his ideas to higher positions, in return they provide unquestioning loyalty. Those who question the new directions or offer information in support of other directions are marginalized or eliminated. Performance expectations are sky high, but there is a growing appreciation there is not all that much action. Al is great at selling the 'sizzle'. Many underlying problems are not being addressed and shortfalls are papered over. Al often seems to be a front man who has an enabling group of supporters. An organization that appears to have had many of the qualities of World Com where an inability to manage its grand vision led to failure. The emerging failure was papered over by one merger or acquisition after another.

The arrogant organizational disorder

Seven of the following should be present:

- Exceptional pride is held for the organization and its future successes.
- Leaders see few limitations to what may be accomplished and are not inhibited as to how to fulfil their vision.

- Feelings of entitlement support exploitiveness of others, customers and the public interest.
- Envy and rage arise when excessive pride is threatened and the pursuit of goals frustrated. The leader and management group become hyperactive and willing to expend limitless time and energy to succeed and win out over rivals, including aggression tinged with sadism and revenge.
- Firings and demotions are common. Non-supporters and resistors have been banished to internal organizational Siberias. Resistance is a threat that is not tolerated.
- Management by intimidation is common.
- Fear suppresses accurate reality testing and creativity.
- Filtered information flows alter organizational reality. Magical thinking leads to a belief that operating problems will pass without taking action. It is dangerous to confront management behaviour that contributes to problem generation.
- Others are blamed and scapegoated.
- The sense of mood within the organization is unpredictable where, one day, a great success is celebrated and, a week later, there exists despair over not achieving a small goal.
- Many are alienated from the organization and its leadership group preferring to hide out in their foxholes (offices and cubicles).
- In- and out-group dynamics are polarized and there is considerable evidence of distressing and destructive internal competition.

These diagnostic criteria share attributes in common with the Narcissistic Organization Diagnostic. The difference is that the leader does not care what other people think of her or the organization. Organization members see themselves as better than competitors. Practice Focus 12.2 exemplifies this.

Practice Focus 12.2

The CEO, senior management team of Superior, Inc., and the company as a whole are thought to be better than their competitors. Competition is cut throat with few limits on behaviour. There are colourful stories of overcoming competitors, and government interests demonstrate that they take a lot of pride in defeating any organization that gets in their way. Superior out-thinks, out-competes and out-aggresses other organizations. The organizational culture also contains many of these dynamics. Individuals and divisions are often involved in unyielding internal competition that exhausts organizational resources, making it less responsive to threats and opportunities. Divisions that have leaders who have doubts about the direction and culture remain silent for personal and career survival.

An organization that contained many of these attributes was Enron that had 'Smartest Guys in the Room' (2005 documentary directed by Alex Gibney, based on a book by the same title by Bethany McLean and Peter Elkind, 2003). Enron management saw very few limitations as to what it could do, including manipulations of the energy market in California. Their arrogance was enabled by others, such as defunct Arthur Anderson.

The dependent organizational disorder

Five of the following should be present:

- Effective leadership is largely absent. No one seems to be in charge much of the time. There is a sense of organizational suffering from the lack of leadership. It is hoped that a leader will emerge who will save the organization.
- The organization is indifferent to its future. There is no drive to succeed.
- Accepting the status quo and mediocrity is the norm. Everyone is aware of problems, but no one assumes responsibility for them. There are stories of the best people leaving.
- There are examples of failures to respond to crises, opportunities and threats. There is a sense of lack of direction.
- Fantasies exist of being special and that recognition will soon be received. It may be thought that a great success is nearing without expending effort to accomplish the work necessary to achieve it.
- The focus is on being team players and togetherness. This discourages self-differentiation and individual and group achievement to which shame and shaming may attach.
- There exists an accumulation of organizational dead wood, stories about double standards and an unwillingness to address performance issues.
- Perfectionism is turned inward upon the organization, creating a self-fulfilling prophecy of not being good enough. This creates a sense of being dependent upon others who are envied.

In such organizations there exists a near absence of direction, leadership and organizational energy.

> **Practice Focus 12.3**
>
> The Division director of Child Protective Services has been changed on average every 18 months for a decade either due to scandals or changes in governors. The varying levels of management skills plus changes in direction, combined with chronic underfunding have led to the employees feeling neglected and demoralized. Social workers receive low compensation, making retention and recruitment a problem. Many positions are unfilled. Those who remain have caseloads that are higher than recommended. Home and in office visits are held to a minimum. The completion of forms and other paper work has been streamlined to the point that only essential information is completed. Deficient records lead to errors and the occasional inability to locate distressed families and children. Clerical staff are underpaid and believe they would be better off on benefits. The best employees leave, creating an accumulation of lower-performing employees.

Organizations such as this are representative of this disorder where the positive aspects of organizational life are largely extinguished. There may exist an irrational hope that things will spontaneously change (a new administration). The organizational theme is one of being at the mercy of forces beyond control.

The avoidant organizational disorder

Seven of the following should be present:

- The organization and its leaders are isolated from the world.
- The organization has developed its own peculiar self-reliant philosophy that is sustained at all costs, even when there are indications that it threatens organizational survival.
- There are elements of fear, anxiety and paranoia about internal and external events that fuel hypersensitivity and feelings of being set-upon, used and abused, and coerced.
- Individual achievement is emphasized along with imagery of great people working alone to accomplish great feats.
- External influences are viewed with distaste since they are felt to contain implicit coercive qualities requiring change to adapt.

- There exists a sense that doing nothing is an option. Planning, goal setting and achievement are largely absent.
- There exists a lack of zest for work and an absence of striving to achieve.
- The status quo is preferred over change. There is a pervasive denial of organizational abilities and assets that could be used to create change.
- Employees and divisions are distanced from each other. Getting together is not thought to be constructive and may actually be seen as a threat to personal autonomy.
- There exists a belief that someone will save the organization from itself.

Practice Focus 12.4

Innovation was a company founded on a much-needed solution to an unmet niche market. Near complete market dominance made profitability and growth an effortless affair. Little consideration was given to improving the quality of its leadership team or to improving product design and marketing. Success eventually created competitors that have eroded Innovation's market share. Top management, however, is indifferent, since the company is profitable. Competitors are held in contempt since Innovation is the 'original'. Many in middle management are frustrated with the indifference to competitors and diminished sales. Production is down and few adjustments in staffing levels have been implemented. Unresolved interdivisional conflict as to who should receive additional resources exists. At the same time, the CEO and senior management team play the blame game when problems occur. Employees share the view that Innovation has become a deer in the headlights. The company is drifting without effective direction. Paradoxically, anyone who steps up to offer direction is limited or forced out. Change is not an option, it seems.

Organizations may act as though they are independent of their larger operating environment and pursue autonomy from societal influences. Examples are sects, horribly illustrated by Jones Town and on a larger scale North Korea where, in both cases, death of citizens is a prerequisite to maintaining isolation. Many industries and organizations seek regulatory and legal shelter from competitors while fending off the imposition of regulations preferring deregulation.

Notes on intervention

Organizational culture is an enduring system of thinking, feeling and acting that abates anxiety (Schein, 1985). It promotes good self-experience by avoiding anxiety ridden out of control experience that may range from distressing to disabling. Changing these cultures is a challenge that required developing a holding and transitional organizational culture that contains playful, reflective and creative spaces and times, and promotes personal integrity, interpersonal authenticity, true self-minimizing destructive, narcissistic qualities.

Consulting intervention examples

The above Practice Focus vignettes are informed by first-hand experience as a consultant and executive. After organizational data are collected and interpreted the remaining question is: What can be done? (Levinson, 1972).

I now return to the four vignettes and what might be considered for intervention. These are framed from the perspective of a consultation. However, recently promoted or transferred executives can assume a comparable role of leading change. The discussion focuses on the elements of the respective diagnoses that must be addressed to create change. Also to be appreciated is that change in personnel may be advisable.

Northeast Supply

Al sees himself as a great leader. He acts powerfully and has a cadre of sycophants to insulate him from adverse outcomes. The challenge is how to engage Al and his colleagues in a reflective process that will lead to greater insight into operations and direction. The key is contracting for this feedback as a part of the consulting engagement. Al must be recruited to the proposition that remediating operating problems will make him look good. Al and the leadership group must believe creating a better organization is to everyone's advantage. The outcome is improved by consultants who encourage data informed decision making, accurate reality testing and a sense of pride in ownership of the change. To be noted the consultant (or executive) must be prepared to contain anxiety created by change to avoid the CEO and leadership team retreating from the task.

Superior

Members of the leadership group know they are brighter than everyone else, including the consultant. In order to maintain this belief they create an alternative reality that flows seamlessly into organizational life. The organizational diagnosis may be dismissed, or only a convenient portion addressed. The diagnosis should contain quantitative findings, such as employee survey data and documentation of operating problems. Concrete examples of problems that need to be attended to are provided. Recruiting Superior's leadership into a reflective stance is problematic. The ability to contain anxiety is a key factor. In this case anxiety arises where performance is not satisfactory, illegal or unethical and acknowledging it is avoided. The facilitator must guide the group to a satisfactory response thereby paradoxically reinforcing their belief that they are better than everyone else – something that, if necessary, can be used to advantage.

Child Protective Services

Organizations that are demoralized, de-energized and disempowered have leaders and members who know this is true. Interventions will not change the level of funding, but they can promote reflection about the organization's response to this reality. Reflection may lead to awareness that there exists too much lethargy, and the lack of resources is used as an excuse. Engaging the group in locating their contribution to this state of affairs may lead to a more proactive stance. Facilitation should focus on empowering the group to solve some of its problems, including drilling the solutions down to who is going to do what by when. Containing anxiety associated with shame and rage arising from not taking action is important.

Innovation

The leadership group has an anxiety-abating strategy of being indifferent to events that threaten the company. It may seem as though there is no one in charge. Those in charge do not effectively lead the company, thereby creating avoidable threat. There may be resistance to acknowledging that Innovation is no longer dominating its niche market. The intervention challenge is to promote reflection and critical thinking without creating a sense of being set upon by the consultant's expectations and those of the employees. The leadership team may be recruited to the proposition of creating task groups to solve problems and develop proactive planning. Containing the anxiety of the leadership group becomes a central element in allowing others to perform needed work. Will comforting control be lost? Can we be creative without creating chaos?

The four intervention examples have touched briefly upon the central psychosocial elements that have to be addressed by a consultant. Much the same can be said for executives taking new roles. Successful change creates a context where the organization's culture creates many fewer organizational casualties, while also improving organizational effectiveness.

Notes on limitations

Every schema has limitations. In this, case organizational diagnosis and intervention in pursuit of an organization context that embraces transitional space and time are a challenging undertaking (Amado and Ambrose, 2001). The presence of a keen sense of true self and interpersonal and organizational awareness is the challenge, especially when stressful, unanticipated organizational problems and resistance to change are encountered. These contain anxiety that promotes individual and organizational regression (Diamond and Allcorn, 1990). Herein lie the challenge and inherent limitation.

In conclusion

This chapter has contributed to the development of systematic thinking that applies psychoanalytic theory to the workplace (Gould, 1991). It has provided four organizational disorders based on teasing apart narcissism into a sub-typology. The resulting descriptions of organizational disorders provide a way of sensing and knowing organizations. These disorders provide a point of departure for diagnosing and treating organizational disorders where the quality of organizational narcissism must be understood in order to locate a response to promote organizational effectiveness by creating a safe enough holding environment to permit the re-emergence of transitional space and time.

References

Allcorn, S. (2003) *The Dynamic Workplace: Present Structure and Future Redesign*, Westport, CT, Praeger.
Allcorn, S. (2005) *Organizational Dynamics and Intervention: Tools for Changing the Workplace*, Armonk, NY, M. E. Sharpe.
Amado, G. and Ambrose, A. (2001) *The Transitional Approach to Change*, London, Karnac.
Bion, W. (1961) *Experience in Groups*, London, Tavistock.
Diamond, M. and Allcorn, S. (1990) 'The Freudian Factor', *Personnel Journal* 69(3), pp. 52–65.
Diamond, M. and Allcorn, S. (2003) 'The Cornerstone of Psychoanalytic Organizational Analysis: Psychological Reality, Transference and Counter-Transference in the Workplace', *Human Relations* 56(4), pp. 1–23.
First, M. and Tasman, A. (2004) *DSM-IV-TR*, Chichester, Wiley.
Gould, L. (1991) 'Using Psychoanalytic Frameworks for Organizational Analysis', in Kets de Vries and Associates (1991).
Horney, K. (1950) *Neurosis and Human Growth*, New York, W. W. Norton.
Kernberg, O. (1985) *Internal World and External Reality*, Northvale, NJ, Jason Aronson.
Kets de Vries, M. and Associates (eds) (1991) *Organizations on the Couch*, San Francisco, Jossey-Bass.
Levinson, H. (1972) *Organizational Diagnosis*, Cambridge, MA, Harvard University Press.
Mandell, A. (1976) *The Nightmare Season*, New York, Random House.
Masterson, J. (1988) *The Search for the Real Self*, New York, The Free Press.
McLean, B. and Elkind, P. (2003) *Smartest Guys in the Room*, New York, Penguin Group.
Ronningstam, E. (2005) *Identifying and Understanding the Narcissistic Personality*, Oxford, Oxford University Press.
Schein, E. (1985) *Organizational Culture and Leadership*, San Francisco, Jossey-Bass.
Stein, H. (1994) *Listening Deeply*, Boulder, CO, Westview Press.

13
A Hong Kong Perspective

Siu-man Ng, Ted C. T. Fong and Xiao-lu Wang

Introduction

Hong Kong is a highly significant place when it comes to workplace issues, as it reflects a mixture of traditional Chinese values and modern Western practices. This chapter examines the work–life imbalance that has arisen in such a context and the culturally appropriate strategies needed to restore balance.

Located in south-east China with an unexploited natural harbour, Hong Kong was historically considered by the Western oceanic powers as an ideal base for entering the ancient country. Hong Kong was ceded to the British from the late nineteenth century until the end of the twentieth century. While China has been in political turmoil much of the time over the past century, Hong Kong provided a haven for many businesses and served as the most important gateway between the East and West. With a well-implemented British-like legal, administrative and education system, many international corporations set up their Far East offices in Hong Kong and hired many Chinese employees (Cheung and Chow, 1999). Local companies also flourished, especially after the Second World War, and some of them emerged as regional and even international corporations.

However, the 'window role' of Hong Kong gradually diminished after the rapid modernization of China since the late 1970s. The handover of sovereignty of Hong Kong from London to Beijing in 1997 signified further socio-economic integration of the 'city-state' into the mainland, as well as the dilution of its uniqueness among its peer cities in China. Over the past few decades pessimists have repeatedly predicted that 'Hong Kong will die'. Amazingly, Hong Kong managed to get through successive (painful) economic transformations, most notably

A Hong Kong Perspective 175

a rapid post-war industrialization, followed by an equally rapid de-industrialization. Nowadays, Hong Kong is a cosmopolitan city of seven million people with a GDP per capita comparable to that of many developed countries. She is unanimously praised for her efficiency and business-friendly environment.

A market-oriented culture and traditional Confucian values of self-reliance and self-sacrifice have so far helped Hong Kong's economic success – but not without cost. The sustainability and desirability of such a relentless pursuit of competitiveness has recently been much deliberated within Hong Kong. There is a growing concern for the negative consequences of extreme work–life imbalance on individuals, families and society as a whole. The critical issue is how to strike a balance for such a small, open economy which has little or no control over its ecological environment. It is also important to address cultural issues, especially the Confucian values which have played a pivotal role in shaping many traditional Chinese work practices.

Traditional Chinese Confucian values and work–life balance

Confucianism, founded by Confucius and Mencius, originated in the Zhou dynasty (1045–256 BC). It is the most well known traditional Chinese philosophy and ideology in the West. During the Han dynasty (206–220 AD), China became an official Confucian nation by decision of the influential Emperor Wu. Since then, Confucianism has become the major school of thought in the Chinese government, as well as businesses and families, and has played a pivotal role in shaping practices in the workplace.

The core concept of Confucianism is its fundamental belief in human goodness. This school of thought places significant emphasis on the cultivation of virtuous and benevolent human characteristics which extend love and care to other human beings. Confucianism is a representative form of relationalism which views people as members of their social communities, rather than independent individuals (Hwang, 2000). Instead of focusing on individual rights or personal interests, relationalism highlights the fulfilment of one's responsibilities and obligations to other individuals and to society at large. The focus, then, is on the overall betterment of the collective body.

Confucianism advocates five principal relationships and the regulation of reciprocity. The five principal relationships are: the clement ruler with the faithful minister; the gentle father with the filial son; the virtuous husband with the submissive wife; the lenient elder brother with the compliant younger brother; and the kind elder with the deferent junior. One of the most important features of Confucianism is hierarchy. Confucianism advocates an explicit social hierarchy which focuses on status and class in social affairs and the allocation of resources (Siu, 2003). The essential criterion of granting social distinction is based on the benevolent morality of a person, with greater emphasis on moral character than talent or achievement (Chen and Lee, 2008). This ensures that social differentiation is just and functional. Hierarchy in Confucian leadership philosophy carries a symbiotic relationship to order, stability, morality and authority.

Confucian values in the Hong Kong workplace

Despite rapid modernization and westernization, Confucian values remain at the core of Chinese life in many domains, but especially the workplace (Von Glinow and Teagarden, 1988). Workplace practices in Hong Kong have been deeply influenced by this traditional philosophy. Work-related Confucian values, including collectivism, loyalty, endurance and hierarchy are still common in contemporary Chinese society. This set of Confucian values forms a core part of values in the workplace throughout China, including Hong Kong (Hui, 1992). These values have been emphasized and regarded as the foundation of social norms and conventional reference for Chinese management.

Hong Kong is often regarded as the place where the East converges with the West. The contrast of Chinese traditional culture and British bureaucracy has made Hong Kong one of the most unusual cities in the world. On the one hand, modern Western culture has profoundly affected the lifestyle and attitudes of the Hong Kong Chinese population. The impact of modernization and individualization has altered some of the traditional values of the population. For example, compared to mainland China or Taiwan, the Hong Kong Chinese have a greater sense of ambition and competitiveness and they are more eager to strive for material wealth (Yang, 1998). In addition, there have been major structural changes to the economy over the last two decades involving a shift from an industrial economy to a service-oriented economy. The worldwide globalization trend and rapid modernization of mainland China further challenged traditional Chinese workplace values in Hong Kong.

On the other hand, despite being an international metropolitan city, over 98 per cent of the population of Hong Kong is ethnic Chinese who are very conscious of their ethnic and cultural identity. Despite the massive influence of foreign Western culture, there is no sign of a sense of loss or cultural identify breakdown among them (King, 1996). Since the transfer of sovereignty of Hong Kong from the British to the Chinese government in 1997, Hong Kong is now an official part of China and the national identity of the Chinese population is more deeply recognized nowadays. The population still puts significant emphasis on Chinese traditional values or traits, such as filial piety, responsibility and respect for hierarchy. These traditional Confucian values remain well preserved in contemporary Chinese society.

For the Hong Kong Chinese, family is the primary concern at both normative and behavioural levels, with the family often considered as more important than society. Family is undoubtedly an essential part of the life of Hong Kong Chinese. The majority of Hong Kong Chinese are willing to provide financial support and care for their parents after they have grown to adulthood. It is typical for Chinese people in Hong Kong to spend their spare time with their family members. Given the importance of the familistic ethos in Hong Kong, the issue of work–life balance becomes more critical as the imbalance between work and life interferes greatly with familial relationships, thus creating further stress to individuals.

Alongside the surging economy of China, research on leadership in Chinese workplaces has become more popular. Previous studies took an indigenous approach in exploring the pattern of leadership in Chinese organizations and results revealed distinct and unique features of leadership in Chinese workplaces. Westwood and Chan (1992) labelled the leadership style as paternalistic, reflecting traditional Confucian ideas.

Paternalistic leadership

Paternalistic leadership is defined as a leadership approach that merges strict discipline and power with paternal benevolence and moral integrity (Farh and Cheng, 2000). Paternalistic leadership comprises three key factors: authoritarianism, benevolence and moral leadership.

Authoritarianism refers to a leader's pursuit of total control and authority over subordinates and demands indisputable compliance from subordinates. Examples of authoritarian leadership include rigorousness, authority and suppression with the intention of hiding, which aims at prompting awe or fear among subordinates. Farh and Cheng (2000) proposed that authoritarian leadership originates from traditional Confucianism culture. In the aforementioned paternalistic father–son relationship, under Confucian beliefs the father has absolute authority over his children and all other family members, and has ultimate control and legitimacy in all family issues (Cheng, Chou and Farh, 2000). The same phenomenon occurs in a leader–subordinate relationship in the traditional Chinese workplace, with the employer maintaining control and strong authority, while subordinates are obliged to be submissive. Authoritarian management practices are not uncommon, even among modern Chinese business organizations.

Benevolence refers to the leader's manifestation of individualized, holistic concern for the personal or familial well-being of subordinates through, for example, favour-granting behaviors, such as showing understanding, individualized care, empathy and forgiveness. It is suggested that benevolent leadership stems from the Confucian paragon of the five cardinal relationships and the norm of reciprocity. In theory, a father should treat his children well and the children should show respect and filial piety to the father. Benevolence from the superior creates indebtedness in inferiors and then inferiors attempt to reciprocate cordially. The reciprocity may result in loyalty, greater compliance at work or genuine gratitude (Yang, 1957).

Moral leadership is described as a leader's behaviour that illustrates superior personal virtues, self-discipline and selflessness. Examples of moral leadership might be selfless behaviors such as not abusing power for one's own good, maintaining integrity and fulfilling one's responsibilities, and not taking any personal benefit in the name of public interest. These behaviours intend to set a moral example for subordinates to follow.

Empirical research shows that corresponding psycho-behavioural responses have been observed in the subordinates under the three types of paternalistic leadership (Farh and Cheng, 2000). Authoritarian leadership prompts a stronger sense of compliance and dependence; benevolent leadership evokes gratefulness and repayment from subordinates; and moral leadership induces higher levels of respect and identification among subordinates. These responses are associated with greater organizational loyalty and commitment and, to a certain extent, they have facilitated success in many corporations and enhanced the development and prosperity of the economy.

Nevertheless, the style of authoritarian leadership may have brought about enormous stress to the individuals, with corresponding burdens to the society at large. This leadership style often denies any interaction or communication between leaders and their subordinates, resulting in poor interpersonal relationships in the workplace. Although authoritarian leadership can raise loyalty and work productivity in the short term, it has been associated with detrimental factors such as lowered work efficiency, declining job satisfaction and worsening body health. These more unfavourable factors linked to Confucianism may ultimately become an obstacle to modern development, leading to adverse effects on individuals' health and the overall well-being of society. Indeed, some of these traditional cultures and behavioural norms are no longer so respected or abided by as in the past.

On the other hand, benevolent leadership and moral leadership do contribute to a higher level of job satisfaction by the encouragement of interpersonal interaction between leader and subordinates. These two types of leadership are far more acceptable than the authoritarian leadership to employees in Hong Kong, especially the younger or better-educated employees. In addition, moral leadership comprises useful qualities, such as setting a good example with one's own conduct and virtue, being scrupulous in differentiating public and private interests which then better evoke a sense of organizational commitment and job satisfaction among employees.

Workplace issues in Hong Kong

One apparent phenomenon in Hong Kong is the long working hours that employees are expected to put in at their places of work. According to recent surveys (Mahtani, 2006; Mahtani and Leo, 2007), the average contractual working hours per week were 46.5 in 2006 and 47.3 in 2007. These mandated working hours alone already exceed the standard set by the International Labour Organization (2005) which suggests a maximum of 40 hours per week. The picture is even more unhealthy if overtime work is taken into account.

In Hong Kong, overtime is the norm, rather than the exception. About two-thirds of respondents in the above surveys reported working overtime at least once a week, with over one-fifth working overtime nearly every day. A survey conducted by researchers at the Chinese University of Hong Kong (*Hong Kong Economic Journal*, 2005) revealed the average overtime of Hong Kong employees to be around 6 hours per week. While blue-collar workers usually have compensation pay or leave, it is an unspoken rule in offices in Hong Kong that overtime work is 'normal' and not compensated for. It is uncommon for employees to leave earlier than their supervisors, mainly because, traditionally, positive meanings are attached to overtime work. For example, working overtime is associated with being hardworking, productive, loyal and even with one's personal importance in the organizational structure.

Work and life balance

Sufficient rest and occasional leave from the job are crucial for employees to maintain their productivity and well-being. Nevertheless, in addition to long working hours, inadequate rest is another common problem at workplaces in Hong Kong. The survey conducted by Mahtani and Leo (2007) found that the average paid leave of employees was only 15.3 days in 2006. The figure was further reduced to 13.9 days in 2007. Around 36 per cent of employees did not take all of their annual leave entitlement. Worse still, nearly 10 per cent were not even entitled to any annual leave.

The same surveys suggested that only 42 per cent of those surveyed felt that their work and life were balanced. The most significant problems revealed were:

- 70 per cent of the employees spent less than two hours per day on their personal activities;
- 60 per cent reported prolonged exhaustion and fatigue after work;
- 43 per cent could not devote sufficient time to their partner and family;
- 41 per cent felt that the intense pressure from work caused them to suffer from somatic symptoms such as insomnia and poor appetite;
- 36 per cent felt that they could hardly allocate any extra time for recreational or physical activities;
- 33 per cent became sick more easily and frequently because of heavy workloads;
- 32 per cent felt that long working hours had greatly weakened their productivity and quality of work;
- 31 per cent believed that their intense work had impaired their relationship with their friends and family members; and
- 30 per cent felt strained, depressed and worn out after work.

These findings reflect the simple fact that many employees in Hong Kong are prone to various kinds of health and family problems, and these problems could pose severe burdens and hindrance at individual, familial and organizational levels.

Advances in information technology (IT) have triggered another wave of revolution in human civilization. The trend of globalization has accelerated and expanded beyond imagination since the introduction of the first personal computer in the 1970s. In a globalized market, the 'winner-gets-all' phenomenon is common in many sectors. In order to survive and ultimately become the winner in their respective market niche, companies have to keep reinventing themselves. Shortened product cycles make even the market leaders anxious about losing their edge quickly to emerging competitors. In many organizations, waves of 'downsizing', 'de-layering', 'process re-engineering' and 'global outsourcing' followed one after another. In the case of Hong Kong, these changes have been even more abrupt because of the rapid modernization of China. A nonstop sense of crisis among Hong Kong corporations resulted in higher demands of work and thus greater job stress for the workers (WHO and ILO, 2000).

Employees are also aware of the crisis in the IT era and appreciate the importance of continuing education so as to maintain their 'employability'. Nevertheless, many employees found it hard to devote sufficient time for professional development. For those who persist in doing so, they have to do it very late in the evenings. Most continuing education classes in local universities go beyond nine or even ten o'clock at night.

More recently, the 'overtime culture' has been critically challenged. Prolonged working hours can be counterproductive with possible harmful effects like reduced quality and quantity of work, frequent sickness absences and burnout. An observational study in Hong Kong revealed an association between prolonged working hours and reduced sleeping hours (Ko et al., 2007) and these two factors are predictive of obesity in the Hong Kong Chinese. Obesity is a strong risk factor of metabolic syndrome, diabetes and cardiovascular diseases.

The psychosocial stress due to work–life imbalance has been found to be harmful to employees' physical and mental health. Physically, higher levels of work stress were found to be associated with hypertension, cardiovascular diseases, and gastrointestinal disorders (Pollard, 2001). When exposed to higher levels of work stress, workers are prone to various mental health problems (Iacovides et al., 2003). Depression is one of the most prevalent mental disorders in the workplace. A recent local survey suggested a prevalence of depression at 8.3 per cent (*Sing Pao Daily News*, 2005), which is more than four times higher than 20 years ago. The costs of this mental disorder, including reduced productivity and staff turnover, are estimated to be up to 4 billion Hong Kong dollars per year (1 US\$ = 7.8 HK\$) (Lerner et al., 2004). In addition, prolonged exposure to work stress could result in job burnout, which refers to a state of physical, emotional and mental exhaustion resulting from long-term involvement in work situations that are emotionally demanding (Maslach, Schaufeli and Leiter, 2001). Job burnout is associated with reduced professional efficacy, lowered job satisfaction, frequent sickness absence and higher staff turnover.

It is an indisputable fact that work–life imbalance has been a significant issue in Hong Kong over the past decade (Thompson, Yau and Nig, 2008). Imbalance between work and life has been associated with lower productivity and work quality. More alarming is the finding that 27 per cent of employees even considered moving out of Hong Kong in order to take up work positions with less stress. As there is always stiff competition around the world for talent, improving work–life balance is essential for Hong Kong to retain and attract the best people.

Incorporating traditional Chinese values and practices in modern workplaces

The previous discussion clearly suggests that Hong Kong is one of the worst places in terms of work–life balance with its extreme emphasis on work. On the other hand, being the most advanced and westernized among Chinese societies, Hong Kong has much valuable experience in applying both Chinese and Western work practices and is in a good position to pioneer work–life balance policies that are appropriate to modern Chinese corporations. Smith (1962) proposed that work is essentially a crucial part of our lives. Work itself deserves sufficient respect, support and security, as it is so important to one's sense of being. Hong Kong is paying a heavy price for such an imbalance which it now needs to deal with squarely.

Traditional Confucian values underpin much of Chinese workers' diligence, discipline, obedience and even submissiveness. There are a number of significant downsides of such collective values in the modern world. Excessive work not only leads to negative effects on the wellbeing of individuals and their families, but it will also lead to burnout which eventually harms productivity and quality of work. Moreover, indiscriminate obedience runs the risk of nurturing flattered, inflated leaders.

In a post-industrialized economy like Hong Kong, creativity and innovation are sometimes more important than simply working hard. To achieve this it requires a certain level of assertion of the individualistic self, which was a near taboo in ancient Confucian China. Realizing the 'small self' (that is, the personal self) and balancing it with the 'big self' (the work team, company and even the society at large) is an important paradigm shift observed in many post-war Chinese ideas, especially arising from those thinkers with a Western education. Chinese corporations should not simplistically label the new generations as non-conforming. Instead, it is essential for them to nurture a new corporate culture that values different perspectives and the enthusiastic sharing of views. Better realization of the 'small self' goes beyond the work domain. It is also about better quality of life. Employees can and should have 'no guilt feelings' for not working overtime or for making use of entitled annual leave for personal and family enjoyment. While keeping the traditional Confucian virtue of responsibility, employees should also be comfortable in enjoying or exercising their rights as stipulated in terms of employment or labour laws. Not only will the employees benefit from such practice, but crucially their families may benefit as well.

Traditionally, Confucianism emphasizes leaders more than systems. While there is no doubt about the importance of good leaders, they are no substitute for good systems. Chinese employees are not only looking for good leaders, but also expect good systems. Good systems here refer to an appropriate organizational structure and reasonable organizational policies, rules and procedures. These systematic or structural characteristics of organizations not only keep organizations running well, but also determine power relationships and give opportunities for voice (Ambrose and Schminke, 2003). As such, the structure of some organizations makes them systematically fair, allowing participation, providing due process and so on, whereas the structure of other organizations makes them systematically unfair (Sheppard, Lewicki and Minton,1993). Therefore, the system or structure of an organization plays an important role in determining fairness. In other words, organizational justice can also be achieved through constructing organizational systems in certain ways (Greenberg, 1993). For example, Schminke, Ambrose and Cropanzano (2000) found that more decentralized organizations were perceived as more procedurally fair than centralized organizations, and that smaller organizations were perceived as more interactionally fair in leader–member exchange than large organizations. Procedural justice and interactional justice are two dimensions of organizational justice (the third dimension is distributive justice – McFarlin and Sweeney, 1992). Procedural justice represents the degree to which a decision is based on formal rules and regulations. Accordingly, procedures which determine a certain decision result are even more important than the result *per se* to the emotional, cognitive and behavioural reactions to the result and the decision maker (Aryee and Chay, 2001; Fields, Pang and Chiu, 2000). Interactional justice pertains to the human side of organizational practices and relates to aspects of the communication process between the source and the recipient of justice, such as politeness, honesty and respect (Tyler and Bies, 1990). Interactional justice results in trust in supervisors, perceived organizational support and so on (Albrecht and Travaglione, 2003; Cropanzano and Prehar, 1999; Fischer and Smith, 2006; Wong, Ngo and Wong, 2002; Wong et al., 2005). Procedural justice and interactional justice have been identified as important protective factors of the psychological well-being of employees (Brockner, Tyler, and Cooper-Schneider, 1992; Cohen-Charash and Spector, 2001; Lind and Tyler, 1988; McFarlin and Sweeney, 1992). Recent studies have shown that procedural justice is equally important to Chinese employees in terms of outcome in job satisfaction and organizational commitment (Lee, Bobko and Chen, 2006; Wong et al., 2005).

However, to achieve organizational justice in the workplace against a background of Chinese culture is not a simple task. On the one hand, organizations have adapted to be more organic in order to upgrade their efficiency and survive the fast-changing, uncertain and highly competitive economic environment. Organic organizations are characterized by flexible, loose, decentralized structures. Formal lines of authority are less clear, power is decentralized, communication channels are open and more flexible, and formal rules and regulations take a back seat to adaptability in helping employees accomplish goals (Ambrose and Schminke, 2003; Burns and Stalker, 1961; Slevin and Covin, 1997; Stopford and Baden-Fuller, 1994). Instead of relying on formal rules and strict regulations to eliminate the human element from decision making, organic organizations tend to depend on face-to-face communication (Lengel and Daft, 1988), discussion and elaboration (Courtright, Fairhurst, and Rogers, 1989), informal control systems (Ouchi, 1980) and interpersonal interactions and transactions (Nadler and Tushman, 1997). The significance of these interpersonal influences in organic organizations should decrease the relevance of procedural justice in decision making. On the other hand, the management of organizations in Hong Kong is under the influence of Confucian management philosophy such as 'Renzhi'. 'Renzhi', the literal meaning of which is 'ruling by man', still plays an important role in today's management of Chinese enterprises, no matter whether they are private or state owned. This philosophy emphasizes human factors or social-interpersonal relationship factors, rather than laws or rules in the decision-making process.

Organizations in Hong Kong and mainland China will encounter the dilemma between making systems organic or the structuring and loss of procedural justice. How to solve this dilemma and establish a balance between these two will largely depend on nurturing work ethics and integrating advanced management experiences from Western companies.

With a long history under British rule, Hong Kong has adopted many sophisticated British systems in both the public and private sectors. The Hong Kong experience has clearly shown that good systems can be set up and run well in Chinese organizations. For instance, the Hong Kong government is known for its efficiency and freedom from corruption.

In conclusion, perhaps 'balance' is the key word in realizing work–life balance in modern Chinese corporations. Most notably, it is about the balance between the 'small and big self', and 'leader and system'. Hong Kong has already gone a long way in institutionalizing systems in both the public and private sectors, and these systems could well balance the significance of good leaders. Currently, the major imbalance lies in an over-restraint of the 'small self'. The source of this restraint is both personal/internal and systemic/cultural. Although this imbalance has been well known since Hong Kong entered the post-industrialized era, real improvements in the work–life imbalance have been rather limited so far. The small scale of the Hong Kong economy and the lack of control over its macro-economy account for much of the slow progress. Because of a constant sense of crisis, it is understandable that the government and business managements tend to be conservative in introducing new initiatives.

Nowadays, the problem of work–life imbalance is unanimously recognized by employees, employers and the government in Hong Kong. They share common interests that balance must be restored, though special consideration is needed concerning traditional Chinese culture and the specific situation of Hong Kong, both internally and externally. Though changes have been incremental, the people of Hong Kong acknowledge that a serious move forward is needed to create a better quality of life for all.

References

Albrecht, S. and Travaglione, A. (2003) 'Trust in Public-Sector Senior Management, *International Journal of Human Resource Management* 14, pp. 76–92.

Ambrose, M. L. and Schminke, M. (2001) 'Are Flexible Organizations the Death Knell for the Future of Procedural Justice?, in Cropranzano (2001).

Ambrose, M. L., and Schminke, M. (2003) 'Organization Structure as a Moderator of the Relationship between Procedural Justice, Interactional Justice, Perceived Organizational Support, and Supervisory Trust', *Journal of Applied Psychology* 88(2) pp. 295–305.

Aryee, S. and Chay, Y. W. (2001) 'Workplace Justice, Citizenship Behavior and Turnover Intentions in a Union Context: Examining the Mediating Role of Perceived Union Support and Union Instrumentality', *Journal of Applied Psychology* 86, pp. 154–60.

Brockner, J., Tyler, T. R. and Cooper-Schneider, R. (1992) 'The Influence of Prior Commitment to an Institution on Reactions to Perceived Unfairness: The Higher They Are, the Harder They Fall', *Administrative Science Quarterly* 37, pp. 241–61.
Burns, T. and Stalker, G. M. (1961) *The Management of Innovation*, London, Tavistock.
Carroll, J. S. (ed.) (1990) *Applied Social Psychology and Organizational Settings*, Hillsdale, NJ, Erlbaum.
Chen, C. C. and Lee, Y. T. (2008) *Leadership and Management in China: Philosophies, Theories, and Practices*, Cambridge, Cambridge University Press.
Cheng, B. S., Chou, L. F. and Farh, J. L. (2000) 'A Triad Model of Paternalistic Leadership: The Constructs and Measurement', *Indigenous Psychological Research in Chinese Societies* 14, pp. 3–64 (in Chinese).
Cheng, B. S., Chou, L. F., Wu, T. Y., Huang, M. P. and Farh, J. L. (2004) 'Paternalistic Leadership and Subordinate Responses: Establishing a Leadership Model in Chinese Organizations', *Asian Journal of Social Psychology* 7, pp. 89–117.
Cheung, G. W. and Chow, I. H. S. (1999) 'Subcultures in Greater China: A Comparison of Managerial Values in the People's Republic of China, Hong Kong, and Taiwan', *Asia Pacific Journal of Management* 16, pp. 369–87.
Cohen-Charash, Y. and Spector, P. E. (2001) 'The Role of Justice in Organizations: A Meta-analysis', *Organizational Behavior and Human Decision Processes* 86, pp. 278–321.
Courtright, J. A., Fairhurst, G. T. and Rogers, I. E. (1989) 'Interaction Patterns in Organic and Mechanistic Systems', *Academy of Management Journal* 32, pp. 773–802.
Cropanzano, R. (ed.) (1993) *Justice in the Workplace: Approaching Fairness in Human Resource Management*, Hillsdale, NJ, Erlbaum.
Cropanzano, R. (ed.) (2001) *Justice in the Workplace II: From Theory to Practice*, Hillsdale, NJ, Erlbaum.
Cropanzano, R. and Prehar, C. A. (1999) 'Using Social Exchange Theory to Distinguish Procedural from Interactional Justice', paper presented at the meeting of the Society for Industrial/Organizational Psychology, Atlanta, Georgia, USA.
Fairbank, J. K. (ed) (1957) *Chinese Thought and Institutions*, Chicago, University of Chicago Press.
Farh, J. L. and Cheng, B. S. (2000) 'A Cultural Analysis of Paternalistic Leadership in Chinese Organizations', in Li, Tsui and Weldon (2000).
Fields, D., Pang, M. and Chiu, C. (2000) 'Distributive and Procedural Justice as Predictors of Employee Outcomes in Hong Kong', *Journal of Organizational Behavior* 21(5), pp. 547–62.
Fischer, R. and Smith, P. B. (2006) 'Who Cares about Justice? The Moderating Effect of Values on the Link between Organizational Justice and Work Behaviour, *Applied Psychology: An International Review* 55, pp. 541–62.
Greenberg, J. (1993) 'The Social Side of Fairness: Interpersonal and Informational Classes of Organizational Justice', in Croprazano (1993).
Hui, C. H. (1992) 'Values and Attitudes', in Westwood (1992).
Hong Kong Economic Journal. (2005) 'Working Overtime is Prevalent in Hong Kong', *Hong Kong Economic Journal*, 5 November, p. P02 (in Chinese).
Hwang, K. K. (2000) 'Chinese Relationalism: Theoretical Construction and Methodological Considerations', *Journal for the Theory of Social Behavior* 30, pp. 155–78.

Iacovides, A., Fountoulakis, K. N., Kaprinis, S. and Kaprinis, G. (2003) 'The Relationship between Job Stress, Burnout and Clinical Depression', *Journal of Affect Disorder* 75, pp. 209–21.
ILO (2005) *Key Indicators of the Labour Markets (KILM)*, 3rd edn, Geneva, International Labour Organization.
King, A. Y. (1996) 'The Transformation of Confucianism in the Post-Confucian Era: The Emergence of Rationalistic Traditional in Hong Kong', in Tu (1996).
Ko, G. T. C., Chan, J. C. N., Chan, A. W. Y., Wong, P. T. S., Hui, S. S. C., Tong, S. D. Y. et al. (2007) 'Association between Sleeping Hours, Working Hours and Obesity in Hong Kong Chinese: The "Better Health for Better Hong Kong" Health Promotion Campaign', *International Journal of Obesity* 31, pp. 254–60.
Lee, C., Bobko, P. and Chen, Z. X. (2006) 'Investigation of the Multidimensional Model of Job Insecurity in China and the USA', *Applied Psychology: An International Review* 55, pp. 512–40.
Lengel, R. H. and Daft, R. L. (1988) 'The Selection of Communication Media as an Executive Skill', *Academy of Management Executive* 2, pp. 225–32.
Lerner, D., Adler, D. A., Chang, H., Berndt, E. R., Irish, J. T., Lapitsky, L. et al. (2004) 'The Clinical and Occupational Correlates of Work Productivity Loss among Employed Patients with Depression', *Journal of Occupational and Environmental Medicine* 46, pp. 46–55.
Li, J. T., Tsui, A. S. and Weldon, E. (eds) (2000) *Management and Organizations in the Chinese Context*, Basingstoke, Palgrave Macmillan.
Lind, E. A. and Tyler, T. R. (1988) *The Social Psychology of Procedural Justice*, New York, Plenum.
Mahtani, S. (2006) *The State of Work Life Balance in Hong Kong Survey 2006: A Summary of Research Findings*, Hong Kong, Community Business.
Mahtani, S. and Leo, K. (2007) *The State of Work Life Balance in Hong Kong Survey 2007: A Summary of Research Findings*, Hong Kong, Community Business.
Maslach, C., Schaufeli, W. B. and Leiter, M. P. (2001) 'Job Burnout', *Annual Review of Psychology* 52, pp. 397–422.
McFarlin, D. B. and Sweeney, P. D. (1992) 'Distributive and Procedural Justice as Predictors of Satisfaction with Personal and Organizational Outcomes', *Academy of Management Journal* 35, pp. 626–37.
Nadler, D. A. and Tushman, M. L. (1997) *Competing by Design*, New York, Oxford University Press.
Ouchi, W. G. (1980) 'Markets, Bureaucracies, and Clans', *Administrative Science Quarterly* 25, pp. 129–41.
Pollard, T. M. (2001) 'Changes in Mental Well-Being, Blood Pressure and Total Cholesterol Levels during Workplace Reorganization: The Impact of Uncertainty', *Work and Stress* 51, pp. 14–28.
Schminke, M., Ambrose, M. L. and Cropanzano, R. (2000) 'The Effect of Organizational Structure on Perceptions of Procedural Fairness', *Journal of Applied Psychology* 85, pp. 294–304.
Sheppard, B. H., Lewicki, R. J. and Minton, J. W. (1993) *Organizational Justice: The Search for Fairness in the Workplace*, New York, Lexington Books.
Sing Pao Daily News. (2005) 'In Hong Kong, the Morbidity of Depression is up to 8.3%, which is Four Times Higher than 20 Years Before', *Sing Pao Daily News*, 28 April (in Chinese).

Siu, O. L. (2003) 'Job Stress and Job Performance among Employees in Hong Kong: The Role of Chinese Work Values and Organizational Commitment', *International Journal of Psychology* 38, pp. 337–47.

Slevin, D. P. and Covin, J. G. (1997) 'Strategy Formation Patterns, Performance, and the Significance of Context', *Journal of Management* 23, pp. 189–209.

Smith, K. U. (1962) *Behavior Organization and Work*, Madison, WI, College Press.

Stopford, J. M. and Baden-Fuller, C. W. F. (1994) 'Creating Corporate Entrepreneurship', *Strategic Management Journal* 15, pp. 521–36.

Thibaut, J. W. and Walker, W. L. (1975) *Procedural Justice: A Psychological Analysis*, Hillsdale, NJ, Erlbaum.

Thompson, N. G., Yau, J. and Siu-Man Ng (2008) 'Work-Life Balance: Lessons from the United Kingdom and Hong Kong', *Journal Of Psychology in Chinese Societies* 9(1).

Tu, W. M. (ed.) (1996) *Confucian Traditions in East Asian Modernity: Moral Education and Economic Culture in Japan and the Other Four Mini-Dragons*, Cambridge, MA, Harvard University Press.

Tyler, T. R. and Bies, R. J. (1990) 'Beyond Formal Procedures: The Interactional Context of Procedural Justice', in Carroll (1990).

Von Glinow, M. A. V. and Teagarden, M. B. (1988) 'The Transfer of Human Resource Management Technology in Sino-U.S. Cooperative Venture: Problems and Solutions', *Human Resource Management* 27, pp. 201–29.

Westwood, R. I. (ed.) (1992) *Organizational Behaviour: Southeast Asian Perspectives*, Hong Kong, Longman.

Westwood, R. I. and Chan, A. (1992) 'Headship and Leadership', in Westwood (1992).

WHO and ILO (2000) *Mental Health and Work: Impact, Issues and Good Practices*, Geneva, World Health Organization and International Labour Organization.

Wong, Y. T., Ngo, H. Y. and Wong, C. S. (2002) 'Affective Organizational Commitment of Workers in Chinese Joint Ventures', *Journal of Managerial Psychology* 17, pp. 580–98.

Wong, Y. T., Wong, C. S., Ngo, H. Y. and Lui, H. K. (2005) 'Different Responses to Job Insecurity of Chinese Workers in Joint Ventures and State-owned Enterprises', *Human Relations* 58, pp. 1391–418.

Yang, L. S. (1957) 'The Concept of Pao as a Basis for Social Relations in China', in Fairbank (1957).

Yang, K. S. (1998) 'Chinese Responses to Modernization: A Psychological Analysis', *Asian Journal of Social Psychology* 1, pp. 75–97.

14
Death, Illness and Grief: Foundational Mysteries for Transforming and Humanizing Work

John Bottomley

Introduction

This chapter on promoting workplace well-being in the Australian context is bracketed by two reflections on the relationship between the ideology of work in Australian industrialized society and Indigenous Australians' experience. If the opening bracket into Indigenous experience helps us see how work in Australian industrialized society is captive to denial about the realities of death, illness and grief in Australian work organizations, the closing bracket discloses a path to well-being.

Between the brackets, the chapter identifies ways in which Australian society's master narrative of economic progress driven by a rational and autonomous humanity is fragmenting. Awareness of this change is both personal and political. I offer two personal narratives, one to highlight how workplace well-being is contested ground, and the other to reveal the spiritual power vital to humanizing work. The chapter also draws upon two research projects. One was a study of work-related suicide, and the other a study of support for staff with a life-threatening illness. These two studies are used to identify a range of barriers to well-being deeply embedded in the taken-for-granted violence of work relations, and the impact of these factors on being human.

Integrating insights through narrative, listening and openness to the mysteries of life is critical to the development of workplace well-being that seeks for human wholeness.

Opening bracket: an industrialized world founded on denial of death

Australian workplaces are built on land acquired by the British Crown through its dispossession of the country's Indigenous people. The colonial invasion was driven by the emerging industrialized world's belief in human progress and its need for resources for increased agricultural and industrial production to feed growing markets.

The Crown's legal fiction of 'terra nullius' maintained that the continent was empty. The nation has for the most part lived in denial of the death, illness and grief of Indigenous Australians on which the nation's economic, social and political life was founded. From their beginning, Australian industry and commerce were shaped by an ideology of work infused with the prevailing culture's denial of this profound injustice.

Australia's history has profound implications for the promotion of workplace well-being because the ideology of work and the prevailing culture fundamentally deny the injustice on which the nation's industrial life is founded. Burying the reality of Aboriginal people's experience of death, illness and grief in the name of economic progress has contributed to the denial of these same truths in the working lives of all Australians.

Narrative one

A redundancy programme in the early 1990s at Melbourne's Water Board resulted in employee numbers falling by over 6000 people in ten years, with a 31 per cent decline during one year (Melbourne Water Corporation, *Annual Report, 1993–94*, p. 2). The County Court awarded compensation to the widow of one man who committed suicide, finding that 'Melbourne Water contributed to her husband's death' (*The Sunday Age*, 14/11/1993, p. 6)

In response to news that three Melbourne Water employees had committed suicide during this redundancy programme, the Uniting Church commissioned my organization to research the impact of the corporatization of the Water Board. While visiting a human resource manager of one of the newly corporatized water utilities, I noticed the sign on his wall: 'Our employees are our most valued resource.' The finding that the corporation contributed to an employee's suicide places a question mark against their claim to value their employees above all else, making the claim look like empty rhetoric. Work is contested ground, where workplace well-being programmes must take account of how economic and political forces endeavour to shape the lives of working people to function in an increasingly globalized economy.

Work is an arena shaped by conflicting forces embedded in competing ideologies and philosophies about what it means to be human. On what foundation should our understanding of what it means to be human be based?

A meditation on death

Something is profoundly wrong when work contributes to a working person's suicide. Yet the arguments for corporatization and privatization of Victoria's public sector utilities were presented as best practice for promoting workplace well-being. In summary, the State government's public sector workplace reform agenda espoused the following principles:

- A commercialized state enterprise offers staff self-fulfilment and self-realization compared with public service bureaucracies that stifle staff involvement and ideals.
- Employees are empowered to become self-regulating, and self-fulfilling, with an entrepreneurial productive spirit.
- Clients are redefined as customers who are offered competitive choices through market, rather than bureaucratic, mechanisms.

These changes were intended to reduce government debt and free the State to provide incentives for private enterprise investment and hence economic growth for Victoria (Bottomley, 1996, pp. 3–4). From 1995 to 2007 this was also the ideological approach to working life that underpinned the employment relations and privatization policies of the Federal government.

But did the reality of the reformed workplace match the beliefs espoused by governments?

Soul-destroying work

Behind the rhetoric of self-fulfilment and empowerment, the suicide deaths of three workers expose an ideology that coerces those captured in its grip to participate in soul-destroying work. This conflict between the demands of a free market economy and the dignity due to human beings at work is not new. In 1891, Pope Leo XIII condemned the practice where workers were captive to degraded conditions, declaring that workers are not to be coerced into violating their human dignity by delivering their souls into economic slavery (Leo XIII, 1991, pp. 22–3). Providers of programmes for workplace well-being need to have a well-grounded sensibility for justice to ensure their efforts are not complicit in covering over the injustice of dehumanizing work.

Fearful silences

An impetus for the corporatization of the water industry was established by Australian 'studies of the water cycle (that) focused on the *economics* of water and the desire to improve *economic efficiency*' (Johnson and Rix, 1993, p. 2, emphasis added). These studies showed little concern for the *people* working in the industry. This neglect of 'the human' had inevitable consequences. The deaths of water industry workers exposes the way economic imperatives became ideology, imposing a narrow view of life that does violence to those who are disempowered by these imperatives.

Enhancement of well-being in workplaces may begin with listening for the silence in work organizations. This is the silence of voices stifled by fear of losing what little of their humanity they believe they have left to cling to. For water industry workers, the fear of losing touch with their humanity was a source of stress. The fear of being exposed as 'not coping' exacerbated the breakdown of previous networks of solidarity across the corporation. Workers then felt isolated and further silenced. Such silence conveys the message that organizational violence against the human spirit is part of the natural order.

Workplace well-being programmes are limited when the workplace is toxic due to a dehumanizing economics rooted in centres of government or corporate power often far removed from the particular workplace.

Work as violence

There is increasing and overdue attention today in workplace well-being programmes on bullying prevention. But work-related suicides expose a more pernicious truth – the structure and culture of work in free-market economies such as Australia have within them a deep-rooted violence.

In his study of redemptive violence, Wink argued: 'violence tends to turn something into the very thing it opposes' (Wink, 1992, p. 91). Redemptive violence is violence done under the promise of benefits to all. This is the violence that occurred when the lofty goal of empowering workers' lives resulted in tragic death. Union respondents to our survey also reported other manifestations of dehumanized work and family conditions, including:

- Widespread dissatisfaction with their training, occupational health and safety, and salaries.

- Increased work pressure from the loss of their most experienced workmates through redundancy, the constant change of restructuring, and the increased complexity of their work tasks because of 'having to do more with less'.
- Dissatisfaction with becoming dependent upon external contractors.
- Increased initiative at work, but divided opinion as to whether they had more freedom.
- Increased stress, lower morale and less job security than three years ago.
- Less time with families, reduced quality of life with their families, and increased family conflict.

(Bottomley, 1996, pp. i, ii)

Promoting workplace well-being may be stifled due to government or corporation policies and programmes that seek to bend employment relations to the State's economic needs by 'creating' workers who are efficient, autonomous and detached from notions of tradition and community.

When an ideology narrowly defines what is human, it undermines the promotion of workplace well-being. Programmes accommodated to our society's prevailing ideology, which bends 'the human' to the ideology's absolute value on productivity and efficiency, will, sadly, contribute to workers remaining trapped in unsafe work. The task of journeying with a workforce burdened by injustice to a state of well-being is therefore intensely political!

Work-related suicide highlights the importance of the cultural meaning of work itself. It is not enough to tailor workplace well-being programmes to the needs of individual work organizations. An exclusive focus on the needs of work organizations in planning for workplace well-being risks being blind to the nature of work itself and the needs it fills for the efficient functioning of our industrialized free market economy.

Our work as research consultants for a Palliative Care Victoria (PCV) project in 2005–05 may help examine this challenge further.

A meditation on illness

My agency provided research support and advice to PCV for an Australian government-funded project to develop a model for support in the workplace for people with a life-threatening illness and employed carers of people with a life-threatening illness.

Facing a 'life-threatening' illness means facing life and illness under the shadow of death. When death is a possible outcome for a disease, the question of what it is to be human looms large. How a person with a life-threatening illness can then be supported in their workplace brings sharp focus to what it means to be human in relation to the person's work.

The medical world diagnoses and treats diseases. A person is diagnosed with a particular disease, then offered treatment aimed at curing the sickness. How the person and those around them live with the disease is the 'illness experience'. The illness experience is shaped by cultural factors governing perception, labelling, explanation and valuation of the experience of being sick. The culture of work and work factors are a significant part of the complex interactions that define how the disease is experienced by the sick person and others around them.

The PCV project involved interviews with 30 people. Ten were people diagnosed with a life-threatening illness, six were managers of the ill person and five were work colleagues. Five respondents were carers of a person with a life-threatening illness, three were their manager/employer, and one was a work colleague. Those interviewed worked in industries such as hospitality and service, freight and packaging, education, agricultural science, medical transport, legal services, construction and health care.

Work and illness: conflicting views on self identity and life's meaning

Work in Australian society is an important source of people's self-identity. It provided two aspects to the identity of the ill people interviewed: First, they believed work enables people to be independent and self-reliant, overcoming all that binds and inhibits them. One person said: 'It means security, both financially and with relationships.' They also believed work enables people to be self-centring and self-integrating, determining for themselves whom they will be. As one person said: 'Work keeps me sane. It is very physical, and keeps my mind and body healthy.'

If work is valued as an important foundation for personal identity and worth, then the experience of illness is feared as the opposite – that is, people fear their illness will cause their loss of identity and worth. Those interviewed feared four things about being ill. First, life would be restricted. One person said: 'Once you are diagnosed, you lose control of your life. You are told what you need to do.'

Second, ill people may fear they will become socially isolated as their social networks break down. The owner of a franchise small business said her relationship with head office had been detrimental to her mental and emotional health, saying: 'They are scared of my illness. The number of people who have dropped off contact because they are scared of the illness has really rocked me.'

The third fear was they would suffer loss of identity when their view of themselves was discredited, either in interactions with others or from unmet expectations of their own. One ill person said one of the least helpful things that happened to him at work was his boss saying: 'don't tell people about your illness.'

Fourth, many feared becoming a burden and being more dependent. They worried their illness would become the major source of their identity. One person said: 'Eventually it will get me. My worrying days are ahead of me. It does get to you. It's hard.'

Once a working person is diagnosed with a life-threatening illness, they begin to live with two competing views about their identity and worth. One view is grounded in the widely held beliefs about the positive place of work for shaping and valuing human identity in Australian society. The competing view represents a negative view about human identity because illness puts at risk all that work says is of value in human identity. The ideology of work ties people's identity positively to their work by conferring meaning about their worth as a human person. At the same time, the ideology of work ties ill people's identity negatively to their work by ascribing to them a diminishing worth due to their illness.

A working person's life-threatening illness may therefore be a profoundly confusing and disturbing experience for them. In addition to the physical impact of the disease on their body, the Australian ideology of work interprets their illness to say their identity is becoming restrictive, isolating, discrediting and burdensome.

Australian work culture also interprets the ill person's identity to their workplace, often leading to distancing and marginalizing behaviours by supervisors and work colleagues that fulfil the fears and beliefs about life-threatening illnesses embedded in the culture. The diagnosis of a life-threatening disease for a working person often unfolds a workplace illness experience shaped by a work culture inadequate to hold in a safe way the profound emotional distress for the ill person, as well as for their supervisors and work colleagues.

Talking it through: the importance of listening for developing support

Several ill people spoke again to members of the research team some time after their interview about how the interview changed their experience of being ill at work. One said he was pleased the interview was conducted in a safe environment for such personal disclosure. He said: 'I was often asked how I was in the corridor. I am glad we didn't do this interview in the corridor.' It appears work often has little space or time for dealing with the deeply personal nature of life-threatening illness.

One manager of a staff member with a life-threatening illness wondered why he was telling the interviewer 'all these things'. The interview helped him realize he had not paid attention to all that was happening due to his staff member's illness, 'and this has prompted me to do something about it.'

Many of those interviewed said the research interview provided a rare opportunity to explore their feelings – both managers and work colleagues, as well as the ill person. They were able to speak about the whole experience they were facing and began to articulate and construct the story of their experience through the way the interview was conducted. This process enabled them to tell their story in a way that organized the fragments and pieces of their experience and made sense of the fragments as a narrative of what life means.

Three points emerged that can assist in facilitating workplace well-being from listening to people tell their story. When people create meaning in the midst of their confusion and uncertainty, they find a new foundation for a deeper awareness of their humanity.

Assessing what support is on hand, and what is needed

Listening without criticism to both the movement and the 'dead ends' in an employee's narrative established a framework for assessing what support is needed. Careful listening to the different workplace narratives provided insight into what support had already been marshalled, how effective it was proving, and what other support may be needed.

One manager made a comprehensive assessment of his workplace's well-being needs when one of his staff was diagnosed with a terminal illness. He assessed the need in areas such as human resource management, and occupational health and safety. He then marshalled appropriate support, such as payment of leave entitlements, availability of resources for staff training and support services for his section, agreement with the ill person on a communication strategy for communicating the ill person's needs, and a protocol for negotiating any required changes in work roles and tasks.

The manager also researched the illness with a specialist support organization, ensured the privacy of the ill employee was protected, relaxed the dress code to relieve pain and stress caused by wearing a tie, and replaced and modified equipment as required to support the ill person's work capacity.

Reflecting together on the manager's narrative also helped him identify areas of support he needed to address – his uncertainty about responding to the emotional stress of a staff member who was very close to the ill person, how to meet his own needs, work's responsibility to the ill person's family, succession planning, and relations with the organization's clients.

Meeting the real needs

Accepting and noting down all the painful or distressing experiences when they are narrated can create trust for the person telling the story that their feelings – even those they may discount – are being valued. These feelings may be the ones that disclose important needs and real issues to be addressed.

One manager said he wanted to remain positive with his ill staff person, so he avoided discussing the person's illness at work. However, the manager's decision to be 'positive' meant his employee's dying was ignored until after the man died. The manager reported two unintended consequences. After the man's death, a number of staff became openly unsettled about their own mortality, and quite unproductive at work. Some staff also felt the company's refusal to acknowledge their colleague's illness raised questions for them about what they wanted from their work, and particularly, whether they wanted to continue to work with this company.

Four types of well-being support: key elements

A narrative approach to people's sense of well-being reveals the unique nature of each person's experience and the shared experiences of people. The shared experiences suggest matters that can be framed into policy and procedures, while the individual experiences can remind well-being providers that implementing programmes needs to be exercised with continuous listening, clarifying, collaboration and evaluation with all participants to provide effective well-being support.

The project identified four types of support may be needed for those at work with a life-threatening illness. These are likely to be equally relevant for effective programmes of well-being support. The types of support are:

1. *Economic support.* This is instrumental behaviour that directly helps the person or organization. It may include helping financially, examining workload issues, and taking care of them.

2. *Emotional support.* The person or organization is provided with empathy, caring, love and trust.
3. *Information support.* This involves the provision of information to the person or organization that helps them to cope with the situation. It helps them to help themselves.
4. *Appraisal support.* The person or organization is given information or feedback to facilitate self-evaluation.

Narratives reveal how one pattern of support does not fit every situation. How support was provided differed from one workplace to another according to industry, size of the organization and the pressures in the production cycle, the nature and stage of the person's illness, their family circumstances, and the previous experience of all parties with illness, disability and death.

Promoting workplace well-being depends upon dealing with the humanity that is disclosed by close listening to the narratives of those who will be programme participants, rather than a 'one size fits all' approach.

A meditation on 'what it is to be human'

These meditations on death and illness bring to the fore the extent to which work and the workplace are at the heart of contested ground in Australian society for what it means to be 'human'. For the view of 'the human' disclosed by these meditations is in radical opposition to the view of 'the human' that is required to meet the needs of an industrialized world.

The modern world's accepted view of death is that the biological finality of death is the end of human life. In this view, grief is characterized by a process that is only resolved when the grieving individual successfully detaches from their relationship with the dead person. This assumes the grieving person is alone in their grief, and that they are the centre of their grief experience. Our society believes grief, like illness, is a temporary abnormality from which 'normal' people recover to again become rational, independent people with a normal relationship to the 'real' world.

Remaining attached to the dead person through thinking about them, talking with them, and being in continuous spiritual relationship with them is often regarded as abnormal or deviant behaviour. Yet, this is the character of behaviour we see in the grief of countless people supported through our Work-Related Grief Support programme. After a work-related death, the path of support and healing for grieving people often needs to address their fear of stigma and madness as they constantly remember their loved-one, talk with them through music, journaling, art making and dreams, and discover the place of their loved-one's spirit in their hearts.

The reality of work-related death and grief exposes the emptiness of society's claim that people can fulfil their humanity through relations of production and consumption. The number of work-related deaths and injuries stands in silent judgment on the belief that our modern industrialized world has progressed through its productive capacity to master nature and fate through the power of reason and reason's technical creations.

The prevailing worldview that defines human beings as rational, autonomous and secular beings also has little to say to people whose loved one has died due to the failure of work to fulfil its promised mastery of nature (death) and fate. All it can offer is a 'grief industry' that turns grieving people back on themselves to 'work through' their feelings with a therapist whose aim is to help them accept 'reality', find 'closure' and 'move on' so that they can again be productive and responsible citizens.

This is the terrible state to which our society's ideology of work leads for understanding 'the human'. The need of our industrialized world and its free-market economy is for human beings who see their worth or value in their productive effort and consumerist lifestyle. From our meditation on death, illness and grief, it may be seen that many contemporary work organizations have little space for working peoples' emotional life, their needs for community, or their experiences of religious faith or spirituality.

A number of Australian workplace well-being consultants have targeted these missing elements in contemporary workplaces. While these emerging businesses may be signs that all is not well with the prevailing beliefs about work and its contribution to human progress, many of them appear to do little to challenge the underlying assumptions about 'the human'. If work is empty of emotion, spirit and community, these well-being programmes have emerged as a consumable commodity to fill the void. They are carefully designed illusions by which workers can be re-energised for a renewed commitment to the political economy.

Too many of these providers do not appear to have entered deeply enough into the mystery at the heart of death, grief and illness. When the ideology of work is emptied of its claims through an encounter with work-related death, or a life-threatening illness, the emptiness may only then be filled by a far more transforming truth and power.

Attending to life and death as mystery is at the heart of being human, and the yearning for pathways at work by which people may be authentically human is the need creative workplace well-being programmes will seek to meet.

Narrative two

For many years I worked to the pattern of an autonomous and independent man. However, a congenital heart defect brought a personal crisis and illness, resulting in open-heart surgery. The generous care of the intensive care nurses was a gift to my recovery. It led me to reflect upon my heart in a new way. I learned that my heart was not simply a functional organ, but a metaphor for that place within my being that stored memories, hurts and most importantly, the treasure of being loved and cared for.

Because of that reflection, I sought out a spiritual director to guide me in understanding the murmuring of my heart. Later, I began professional supervision to support the integration of my professional skills with the heartfelt wisdom that had taken root in my being. This journey of the heart has changed the way I see myself in my work, and the way I see work itself.

In particular, I learned how much the ideal of being an autonomous and independent man was detrimental to my well-being and sense of wholeness. From my childhood, the story of my life interpreted every pain and hurt as *my* loss. For long years my focus was on *my* hurt and pain – it always seemed to be about the loss of *my* identity as an independent young boy who could stand on his own two feet. Being so preoccupied with *my* loss and *my* struggle to be accepted in the mould of 'a real man' who was autonomous, strong and rational perpetuated a lived experience of never quite measuring up. To focus on my experience of loss had for decades constructed me as a victim in an unjust world.

Scarcity is a fundamental assumption for how the free-market economy works, and its use in constructing our understanding of grief as loss not only domesticates our interior world of feelings to the workings of the economy, it disempowers grieving people by constructing our lives as victims. Yet people may be liberated from such constructs through the gift of a heart open to the spiritual power of unconditional love.

Closing bracket: Dadirri (Deep Listening)

Deep Listening is a concept that appears in many Australian Aboriginal languages. In the Ngungikurungkurr language of the Daly River in the

Northern Territory, the word for Deep Listening is 'Dadirri' (Ungunmerr, 1999). It can be translated as deep and respectful listening which builds community.

Workplace well-being programmes need to cultivate Deep Listening into the mysteries of death, illness and grief. These human experiences are not problems to be fixed or behaviours to 'get over'. Rather, they are embedded in the fabric of life, and their mystery may disclose something new and vital to us about what it means to be human.

For the Koori Cohort of Researchers at Monash University: 'Deep Listening is based on stories, silences and the spaces that lie between' (Monash University seminar notice, 'Deep Listening in Research Practice,' 6/11/2008). The practice of Dadirri gives voice to my conviction that our yearning for transformed and humanizing work must embrace the wholeness of our experience of this land. Nothing needs remain buried, and this restoration is the work of forgiveness, justice and love.

The work of forgiveness, justice and love is facilitated by the deep listening available through meditating on the mysteries of death, illness and grief, through listening to narratives of struggle, and disclosing personal stories of the heart. Workplace well-being programmes may fruitfully attend to the gifts of Indigenous culture that integrate work with rest, celebration, community and nature in a holistic reverence for the mystery of creation.

The story of forgiveness, justice and love as a spiritual power at the heart of creation is a counter-narrative to the soulless and utilitarian ideology of work in modernity and postmodernity. This is a narrative that is disclosed by Deep Listening to working people's experiences of death, grief and illness. It is a narrative that invites attention to a foundation for authentic workforce well-being programmes which promotes activities that:

- Draw upon notions of abundant love in contrast to scarcity;
- Encourage awareness of the human need for forgiveness rather than the fear-based risk management of 'mistakes';
- Are open to the mystery of spirituality and spirit rather than evidence-based rationality; and
- Facilitate healing narratives that enable participants to connect the fragments of their individual lives, and interconnect with the narratives of others, in a holistic movement that connects people with their emotional and spiritual truths both individually and collectively.

At its heart, the promotion of workplace well-being calls forth not only a judgment on the dehumanizing character of the prevailing ideology of work, but also invites a healing of the wounded social, economic, political and ecological environment that will transform work to activity that is creative and life giving. Perhaps only then will Australia grasp what it means to be a reconciled nation.

References

Bottomley, J. (1996) *The Pressure is Enormous: The Hidden Costs of Corporatisation*, Melbourne, Union Research Centre on Organisation and Technology, Working Paper No.12.
Bottomley, J. and Tehan, M. (2005) *They Don't Know What to Say or Do!* Palliative Care Victoria, Melbourne.
Johnson, M. and Rix, S. (1993) *Water in Australia: Managing Economic, Environmental and Community Reform*, Sydney, Pluto Press and Public Sector Research Centre.
Leo XIII (1991) *Rerum Novarum*, London, Catholic Truth Society.
Melbourne Water Corporation, *Annual Report, 1993–94*.
The Sunday Age (1993) 14 November.
Ungunmerr, M. R. (1999) in Isaacs, J., *Spirit Country: Contemporary Australian Aboriginal Art*, San Francisco, CA, Hardie Grant Books.
Wink, W. (1992) *Engaging the Powers: Discernment and Resistance in a World of Domination*, Minneapolis, MN, Fortress Press.

15
Promoting 'Labour Well-Being in a Classless Society': An Initial Examination of the Unfulfilled Prophecy

Vassilis Ioakimidis and Georgios Bithymitris

Issuing the death certificate of the Greek working class

The European Union employment strategy, as it was defined by the Lisbon Agenda, has brought the issue of 'better jobs' and 'workers' well-being' to the centre of discussion in Greece (as in most of the member states). However, such a debate was not in conflict with the Organization's fundamental commitment to the advancement of regional capitalist economies. Thus the recent vague debate on 'better jobs and working conditions' was combined, in a rather contradictory way, with the grim reality of labour deregulation. The indistinguishable word 'flexicurity' dominated the Greek government's rhetoric, in line with the Commission's objective to: 'promote flexibility combined with employment security and reduce labour market segmentation, having due regard to the role of the social partners' (EC, 2005, p. 2).

It is quite apparent that the EU's concept of labour well-being within a free market context presumes a long-desired environment of 'social partnerships' between employers and workers, away from 'parochial' class confrontations. Therefore, along with the Lisbon Agenda, academic justifications which support the idea of a classless society re-emerged. Since the early seventies we have witnessed a plethora of analyses rushing to celebrate the 'end of the working class' (see below). Even though such claims follow different methodological, ideological and analytical directions, from conservative to neo-Marxist (see Giddens, 1990; Gorz, 1982), the focus appears to remain on the 'obvious changing nature of labour' and the 'disappearance of the traditional working class'. Early interpretations of the – admittedly complex – labour transformations seemingly gained more credibility after the collapse of the Soviet Union. It was then, when the discussion over the 'end of work' (Rifkin: 1995) became a triumphal celebration of 'the end of history' (Fukuyama, 1992).

Indeed, the visible – and to some extent natural – transformations in the nature of labour, the unprecedented geopolitical changes and the ineptness of the Left to respond to these challenges, offered fertile soil for the growth of the aforementioned approaches. Therefore, it comes as little surprise that class politics and trade unionism experienced a period of retreat, if not demonization. It was within this context that employers and employees, the state, trade unions and – last but not least – the infamous 'civil society' were baptized as 'equal partners', who share the same interests and ought to take joint decisions. After all, it is a classless and peaceful society we live in. It is not a coincidence that one of the strongest advocates of this idea is the Association of Greek Employers who believes that:

> Through long-term dialogue, social partners have managed to restore trust, grow mature.... The realisation of a large number of agreements between social partners on education, training and employability issues are signs of the social partners' new role.
>
> (Association of Greek Employers)

It is worth noting that the new ethos of 'social dialogue' has even brought about changes in terminology, as the universal right for full employment has been reduced to an 'issue of employability'. In particular, in the case of Greece, under the guidance and supervision of big international organizations (IMF, EU, World Bank), the major Greek parties were soon transformed into caricatures of their big Western ideological allies, unconditionally using exactly the same terminology and phraseology (Ioakimidis, 2008). It was roughly the same period, as in the countries of the capitalist centre, when the Greek working class was also declared dead and any discussions pointing otherwise were referred to the official death certificate (namely the EU Maastricht Treaty).

On an academic level, the 'post-Fordist' literature which informs the aforementioned agenda puts a special emphasis on the 'doomed trinity' of tertiarization–feminization–individualization (see Frege and Kelly, 2003, p. 8). The 'end of the working class' prophets outlined the main aspects of the 'doomed trinity' as follows (see Seferiades, 1999, for a critique of these assertions).

Tertiarization. This appears to be the most popular argument in favour of working class 'fragmentation'. According to this approach, the analogy between industry and services has been overbalanced in favour of the latter, due to technological breakthroughs. What has emerged is the 'New Production Paradigm' (flexible specialization), which challenges the rules of the 'Fordist reality' and completely redefines the production sphere (functions of enterprises, productive procedures, institutional frames, competitiveness frames, international environment and so on – Freeman and Perez, 1988, p. 34). Employees in the tertiary sector are generally considered to be better educated, more flexible, and are thus expected to enjoy more promising prospects, better wages, less monotonous tasks and less exausting conditions than blue-collar workers. Even if there is a section within the service sector that experiences bad working conditions (for example, waiters, drivers, shop assistants or, as Gorz, 2003, put it: the 'service class'), this further supports the theory of a 'fragmented working class' (Clark, Lipset and Rembel, 1993). If we also take into account the contingent workers (part-timers, people on fixed contracts, subcontractors and so on), a new division seems to threaten workers' unity: the core-periphery division of wage labour (Harvey, 2006). To summarize, the tertiarization theory is credited for undermining the old-fashioned, confrontational style of collective action used to characterize industrial workers with full employment.

Feminization. Apologists of 'post-Fordism' tend to believe that the alteration of contemporary working-class composition and attitude is usually attributed to the mass entrance of women into the labour market. The post-war stereotype of male 'breadwinner', within the context of rapid growth and Keynesian arrangements, was undoubtedly to be eroded after the economic crises of the seventies. Empowered by the new tecnological premises and the expansion of a knowledge-based economy, female employment (mostly part time) became a declared priority for European Community policy makers. As in the case of tertiarization, 'post-Fordist' abstract generalizations claim that feminization will result in a further decomposition of working-class identity (see Burrows and Loader, 1994).

Individualization. The third 'post-Fordist' tendency underpins the idea that new technologies enhance productivity, save capital (due to flexible, 'just-in-time' methods that substitute post-war mass production), and thus lead to positive-sum games between employers and employees (Cohen-Rosenthal and Barton, 1993). Deliberative practices undermine traditional collective bargaining. Employees, working in the 'powerful' and modernized tertiary sector, prefer to represent themselves, rather than resort to unions or other means of collective action (political parties, professional associations and so on). They are considered as sufficiently qualified and independent to protect themselves from the threats of a 'risk society' (Beck, 1993).

Although not always coherent and well connected, the above arguments appear to act as the vanguard of postmodern narratives. Interestingly, they all seem to agree on the assumption that the dramatic labour developments and transformations have resulted in individual labour needs and conflicts unable to be expressed uniformly and, thus, unable to represent the majority of wage labour. Beyond the traditional class analyses based on exploitation, new divisions based on professions, skills, gender and race have been theoretically advanced as better explanations concerning income inequalities and workplace adversities. The last, but not the least, postmodern assertion indicates that unionization is destined to die, unless the movemement commits itself to the adoption of a non-militant, more flexible and individual-oriented strategy.

Modern rhetoric, old-fashioned practices and the quest for labour well-being

Despite well-orchestrated efforts to mask the existent class inequalities and signal the end of class wars, the bleak reality of poverty and unemployment tells a different story. As the official statistical macro-economic data indicate, the Greek economy has experienced significant development and generation of profit. None the less, the actual number of people living under the poverty line and those who face long-term unemployment was never reduced and it is still one of Europe's highest (see BBC, 2004; Rizospastis, 2000). As research indicates, 27 per cent of Greeks live below the poverty line and: 'slowly but steadily a "third world" is being created inside Greece, an EU member state with a population of 11 million' (LSE, cited in Fotiadis, 2007).

Moreover, as we demonstrate below, even employed people (especially in the service sector) face the grim reality of 'modern proletarianization', which includes job insecurity and dissatisfaction, severe financial pressures, alienation and stress.

It is this paradox that forces us to argue that, even though the nature of employment has seemingly changed, the class structure of labour has in fact been strengthened. The creation of a gigantic service sector has done nothing to ease class divisions. In reality, the evidence we provide indicates that even professionals who, in the past, were clearly considered as middle class, now face working and social conditions that could classify them as the new white-collar working class. In this chapter we offer an initial analysis of mainly quantitative data that indicates not only a continuation of the class structure of employment in Greece, but also a rapid increase in the number of employees who could be identified as belonging to the working class. Given that the present contribution to the debate is rather preliminary, we do not claim to offer an exhaustive analysis of the issue. However, in a period when mainstream academic and political approaches have rushed to issue the death certificate of the Greek working class, our aim is to highlight current evidence that might indicate otherwise.

In order, to validate our assumptions we processed and analysed primary statistical data from the 2002/3 and 2004/5 European Social Survey (see data sources), a biennial multi-country survey that covers over 30 nations. In addition, we processed a statistical analysis of the variables that concern Greece. We have also filtered out those respondents who are not currently waged employees and those whose economic activity does not seem to belong to the tertiary sector. Statistical documentation is based on cross-tabulations which were tested by using the chi square criterion (x^2). Moreover, in terms of working conditions in Greece, we have utilized secondary data obtained from the 2007 European Working Conditions Survey conducted by the European Foundation for the Improvement of Living and Working Conditions (Parent-Thirion et al., 2007).

As we demonstrate below, analysis and presentation of evidence from the data challenge the dominant post-Fordist assumptions reviewed in the previous section. In particualar, in this analysis we attempt to address the following issues:

1. Supposing that the 'New Production Paradigm' is a good fit in the case of the Greek economy (service sector explosion in 1990s, industrial restructuring, agricultural declining), what has really happened to the working conditions of the tertiary sector? Has there been an improvement or a deterioration, and for whom?
2. Are third-sector employees conciously refraining from collective action and celebrating 'flexibility' and 'individualism', or is there another reason that keeps them away from unionization?

There are quite different paths in calculating employment growth in the tertiary sector. For example, Leiulsfrud, Bison and Jensberg (2005) have drawn data from the European Social Survey (Round I) through three different patterns of class stratification, relying on Erikson,

Goldthorpe and Portocarrero's (EGP) neo-Weberian model, Wright's Marxist model and Esping-Andersen's post-industrial model.

An EGP model can be identified easily if we look at the classification that the National Statistical Service of Greece (ESYE) makes by its one-digit system to identify individual occupation groups: legislators, senior officials, and managers (I), professionals (II), technicians and associate professionals (III), clerks (IV), service workers and shop/market sale workers (V), skilled agricultural and fishery workers (VI), craft and related trade workers (VII), plant and machine operators and assemblers (VIII) and, finally, elementary occupations (IX). Although it is obvious that group IV should belong to what we call tertiary workers, it is not clear what part of tertiary employment concerns other groups as professional staff, clerks, managers and so on. Thus, it is better to use a classification based on economic activity. Accordingly, the tertiary sector includes: trade (G), hotels and restaurants (H), transport and communications (I), banking, insurance and finance (J), other services (K, M, N, O). As we can see in Table 15.1, employment in the tertiary sector has definitely increased during the last decade by a rate of 7.3 per cent, while employment in the secondary sector has remained relatively stable as a percentage of total employment, and primary sector employment has diminished by a rate of 6.6 per cent.

However, the statistical data available at the national database does not tell us a lot about the origins, mobility, working relationships or labour well-being of all these service sector newcomers. In our attempt to comprehend the effects of tertiarization of employment (in terms of the mobilization potential), we gathered further evidence concerning Greece from available databases and especially the raw data provided from the European Social Survey Round I (2002/3) and Round II (2003/4). What we ultimately tried to do is an inter-occupational comparison of working conditions within the tertiary sector. Then we compared the findings with the national and EU average in the above categories, provided by

Table 15.1 Classification by occupation

Year	Sector		
	Primary	Secondary	Tertiary
1998	18.4%	23.1%	58.4%
2007	11.8%	22.5%	65.7%
1998–2007	−6.6%	−0.6%	7.3%

Source: ESYE (1998, 2007).

the 2005 survey of the European Foundation of Working Conditions (EFWC, see Parent-Thirion et al., 2007).

Using this approach we initially estimated the occupational composition of the tertiary sector in Greece and its contribution to working-class decomposition. After the exclusion of the primary and secondary sector, we came up with the following occupational distribution within the waged population (that is, where the current main activity is paid work) of the service sector (Table 15.2).

Lack of data for the following years does not allow us to speak about trends in inter-occupational composition. However, it is clear that tertiary employment is not growing evenly: service workers and clerks have the lion's share of this growth. How do they experience exogenous factors that affect mobilization potential (for example, quality of working conditions)? Can we speak about improvements that cut them off from the large body of the working class and fragment their collective identity, which then leads to a more individualistic and anti-unionist stance? Starting with the latter, in relation to our research objectives (labour well-being and trade unionism commitment), we observed that, despite wider occupational restructuring, inter-occupational approval of need for trade unions is still strong (Figure 15.1). Such commitment does not show significant variation from a gender perspective either, suggesting that arguments for the erosion of working-class consciousness through tertiarization and the feminization of labour may be groundless.

This should not lead to misunderstandings about rates of unionization, but is not devoid of obstacles and difficulties. In fact, despite the acknowledgment of union necessity, mainstream trade union practices are percieved with scepticism by the majority of tertiary employees (Figure 15.2). Moreover, service workers' potential to act collectively is reduced due to the low union coverage, regardless of their approaches on union activities.

Table 15.2 Proportion of employees against total employed within the Tertiary Sector by one-digit groups of individual occupations

	I (Managers & senior officials)	II (Professionals)	III (Technicians & assoc. professionals)	IV (Clerks)	V (Service workers)
2002/3	9.9%	23.1%	13.9%	20.5%	32.7%
2004/5	6.2%	16.1%	8.9%	29.1%	39.7%

Source: ESS Round 1 and 2, see Data sources.

210 *International Perspectives*

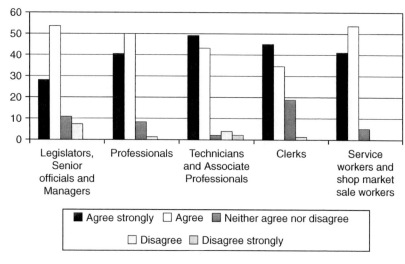

Figure 15.1 Employees need strong trade unions

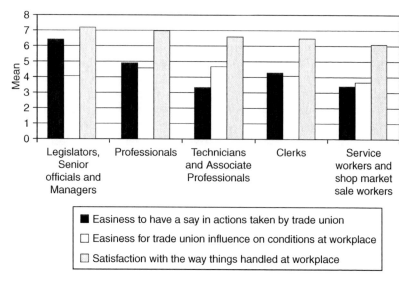

Figure 15.2 Perceptions about unions

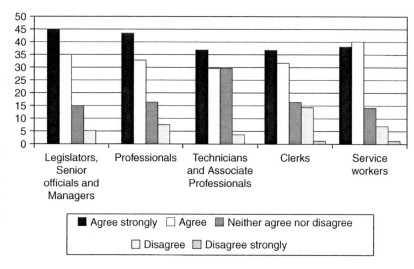

Figure 15.3 Belief that businesses are only interested in profits

Although exponents of the 'end-of-class politics' suggest that low interest in politics is a basic indicator of individualization of the feminized/tertiarized working class, other indicators of individualization are excluded from their analyses. Interestingly, according to ESS1, workers from both sexes uniformly approve of solidarity-based voluntary action that aims to help other people. They also reject the idea that social welfare is an issue for the individual. Even though workers' approval of voluntary action can be misinterpreted at the expense of the public welfare state and offer a base for soft privatization policies, one cannot ignore the strong element of solidarity that transcends tertiary employees' perceptions. Such a commitment to voluntary activities based on solidarity, combined with their acknowledgment of trade unions, clearly challenges the belief that collectivism has been eroded in the sector. This idea is also supported by the convergence of the perception of what is broadly termed 'business ethics'. As Figure 15.3 indicates, the vast majority of employees agree that businesses are only interested in profits, and also that large firms work together in order to keep prices high.

In relation to our second hypothesis, that is, that there is a correlation between working conditions and the formation of collective identities within the workplace, we make use of data provided by ESS1 and ESS2 (see Data sources) under the following thematic clusters: incomes, working time, work organization, job content, job satisfaction, work and family life. Finally, we have juxtaposed our findings with EFWC's results referring to EU and national averages.

ESS 1 and 2 offer data for total household income, which is categorized in 12 groupings. We recoded this variable into three broad categories: lower incomes, medium incomes and higher incomes. Working on the basis that individuals who live on their own have different needs compared to a couple or a family, we distinguished between total individual and total family incomes. Lower individual incomes account for less than 1000 euros per month. Medium individual incomes account for 1000 to 3000 euros, and higher individual incomes over 3000 euros. The respective amounts for those who live with husband/wife or partner are 0–2000 euros, 2000–5000 and over 5000 euros. Finally, we posed the question: 'How do you feel about your household's income nowadays?'

As one can see from Figure 15.4 (ESS1), service workers' distributions by family income – and, to a greater extent, by individual income – seem to be a little different when compared with the other tertiary professions' distribution. Their feeling about their household's income follows the same pattern. As becomes evident, clerks, service workers and one-third of associate professionals believe that they cope with difficulties on their present income. In fact, high incomes and those with comfortable living incomes (up to 5000) appear to be a minority among tertiary employees.

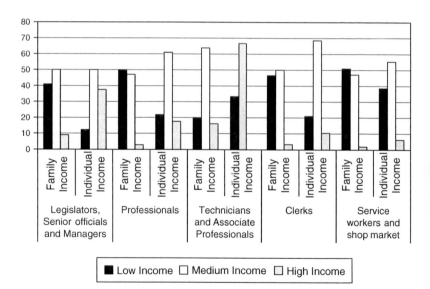

Figure 15.4 Family and individual incomes

Promoting Labour Well-Being in a Classless Society 213

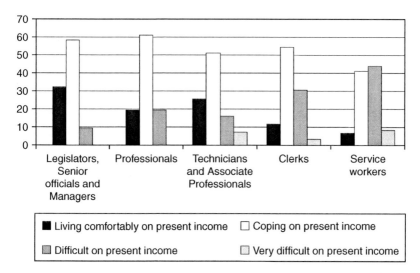

Figure 15.5 Perceptions of household current income

Even among senior officials and managers, those who earn more than 5000 euros (family income) account for less than 10 per cent of the total population of this professional category. On the other hand, the vast majority of service workers who live with a spouse/partner appear to be low-income employees.

Evidence from ESS2 (Figure 15.5) does not alter the above picture in a significant way. Interestingly though, 20.4 per cent of professionals just cope with their present income, while about half of the service workers (47 per cent) find coping with living costs difficult or very difficult. To sum up, the evidence we gathered from clerical and professional wage distribution (ESS1 and 2, see Data sources) indicates that: (a) tertiary workers cannot be considered as a homogenous occupational category, and (b) the hypothesis that tertiary workers do not belong to the working class due to their higher income appears invalid.

In addition, according to EFWC's classification, labour well-being is also connected with the employee's autonomy in the workplace and the organization/structure of employment. Observing the ESS1 (Figures 15.6 and 15.7) we establish that flexibility in working hours and daily work structures, as well as interprofessional differences, seem to be more important than gender differences. Service workers and clerks have substantially less job autonomy. This situation supports our expectations about the self-understanding of the majority of tertiary workers.

Additionally, only a very small proportion of them aspire to have their own business in the near future.

ESS2 further supports the above picture (Figures 15.8, 15.9 and Table 15.3), as service workers and clerks appear to be excluded and alienated from work organization, working schedule (start/finish), the pace of work and, to a much greater extent, policy decisions. These findings confirm our general assumption that not all tertiary employees enjoy the high levels of job autonomy some post-Fordist writers would suggest. In addition, they experience increased levels of control, monitoring and, on many occasions, intimidation and bullying. Interestingly, such labour intensification includes one-third of professionals who report extreme time pressure and hard working conditions. In a series of interviews, Ioakimidis (2008) has captured social care workers' frustration concerning their deregulated labour conditions. One of the interviewees clearly described this sense of alienation:

> I am really tired, and I felt this way even from the first few months. This is not what I expected when I chose social work.... I feel trapped. I have a huge workload and most of the cases do not have positive results. I only stay in this job because I add my small salary to my husband's one in order to cope as a family. Even this small contribution is important in our family wage. Additionally, I work close to my house and I can look after my children. But this is not what I dreamt of.
>
> (Ioakimidis, 2008, p. 299)

Job role/satisfaction is highlighted through data extracted from ESS2 solely. Service workers and clerks are reported as having less variety in their daily tasks; they learn new things at significantly lower rates than any other occupational category, while a significantly smaller proportion of service workers consider their job as secure. Associate professionals (30.8 per cent) and service workers (27.7 per cent) appear to consider their job as a threat to their own health and well-being. Finally, although, according to the chi-square test, there are no significant differences in considering intensity of work, service workers consider their job as more demanding in even higher rates than other tertiary employees. As the EFWC survey indicates, service workers experience far more job intensity (Figures 15.8 and 15.9) and less job control (Figures 15.6 and 15.7).

Concerning job satisfaction, service workers are second to professionals in overall pessimism (32.3 per cent). Prospects for the majority of tertiary workers do not seem to be much better compared with the national average (37.4 per cent and 27 per cent respectively).

Promoting Labour Well-Being in a Classless Society 215

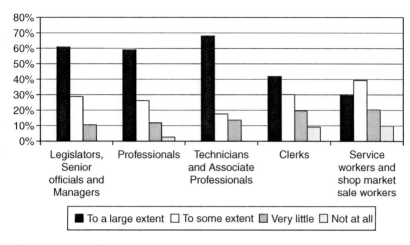

Figure 15.6 To what extent they control their own work

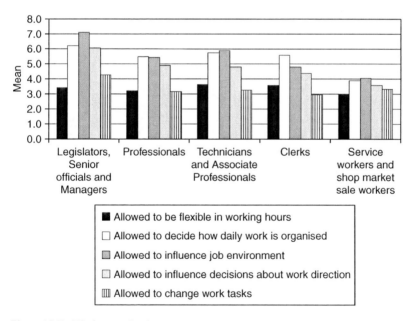

Figure 15.7 Work organization

216 *International Perspectives*

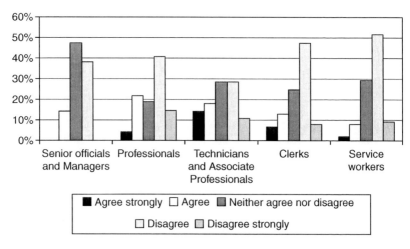

Figure 15.8 Lack of time to cope with workload

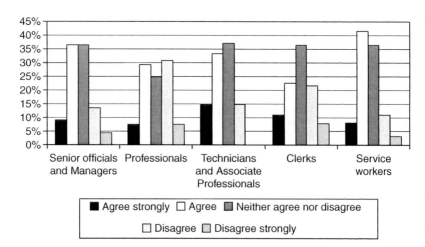

Figure 15.9 Job requires very intensive work

Finally, we gathered evidence related to working time, as it appears to be a crucial indicator of workplace well-being. It is worth noting that part-timers (employees whose total contracted hours are less than 30 hours per week) are excluded from our statistical tests. As Table 15.3 indicates, service workers (both male and female) appear to work significantly more hours than other tertiary employees. These categories exceed the average of the total of the Greek working class (45.4). Working hours for male service workers and senior officials are even worse (50.76 per cent and 47 per cent). ESS2 also provides indicators of work impacts on family life. With the exception of male professionals, all the other professional categories (service workers of both sexes in particular) find their job is an obstacle to their family life: 56.6 per cent and 66.6 per cent of male and female service workers respectively consider their job prevents them from spending adequate time with their partner/family. Moreover, about two-thirds of tertiary employees of both sexes appear to feel too tired after work to enjoy their time at home. Half of the target population report worrying about job issues, even when not working. Interprofessional differences emerge when one examines weekend working. The lion's share belongs to service workers: 79 per cent of male service workers and 66.7 per cent of female service workers work on weekends. Male service workers reported that flexibility in working schedules also affects their family life: about half of them work several times a month or more frequently during evenings/nights, while 47.7 per cent of them work several times a month or more frequently overtime at short notice. Respective rates for female service workers are about 30 per cent. Schabracq and Cooper (1997) have clearly demonstrated the devastating consequences that flexible working time might have on a worker's well-being.

To sum up, there is significant evidence to suggest that the majority of tertiary workers would not agree that their working hours (Table 15.3) fit family commitments well or very well.

Table 15.3 Working hours per employment category

Employment category/ working hours	Total contracted hours per week in main job overtime excluded		Total hours normally worked per week in main job overtime included	
	ESS1	ESS2	ESS1	ESS2
Professionals	36.3	36.5	39.4	42.2
Technicians and Associate Professionals	40.0	39.5	45.6	43.1
Clerks	38.4	38.4	42.0	39.7
Service workers and retail workers	42.1	40.0	47.2	43.3

Conclusion: the promotion of well-being

Throughout the earlier discussion we have tried to offer an initial exploration of workplace well-being within the Greek tertiary service sector. Our intention was to present service workers' labour experiences and conditions, while testing them against dominant 'post-Fordist' arguments concerning the end of the working class. Moreover, service workers and clerks tend to differentiate themselves from other tertiary employees in the way they perceive their well-being in the workplace. The most explicit evidence is that, although tertiary employees constitute a heterogeneous category, the majority (namely service workers and clerks) experience extremely bad working conditions that are far from being considered as the triumph of a classless society. Economic restraints, lack of job autonomy, alienation, low job satisfaction, long working hours and negative impacts on family time are no longer an exclusive 'privilege' of the shrinking blue-collar sector. In fact, the tertiarization and feminization of employment have not resulted in the decomposition of the working class, either in terms of labour conditions or in relation to collective action.

With the increase in third-sector jobs came the gradual and undeniable proletarization of service workers. The great expansion of the third sector in Greece resulted in the production of unprecedented profits which, far from benefiting the development of Greek society as a whole, generated sharper inequalities. During the last decade, business profits proliferated at an extraordinary pace, mainly in the form of concentrated bank capital, as well as the accumulation of wealth in insurance companies and in fields such as private health, private education, commerce and legal services (INE GSEE, 2008, p. 177). At the same time, a constellation of clerical, low-skilled service employees formed new sections of the proletariat; even professionals who were previously considered the traditional 'middle classes' have started losing their status (lawyers, teachers, doctors, social workers, journalists). The transference of this labour force from manual jobs to service positions is far from being a class shift. Callinicos (1983), who has studied similar trends in the British context observed that:

> The decline in the proportion of productive workers has been accompanied by the expansion of other forms of employment. Effectively, women in particular have been transferred from manual jobs (especially in the textile and clothing industries) to white-collar

clerical jobs, and to public-sector manual work. That does not mean they have ceased to be part of the working class. In terms of their relation to the means of production, they are still compelled regularly to sell their labour-power. At work, they have little or no control over the work they do. They are very low-paid. In all these respects, the shorthand typist, or checkout girl, or school cleaner is as much part of the proletariat as the horny-handed male engineer or miner.

Contrary to the post-Fordist prophesies, tertiarization and feminization have led to an inter-occupational downward convergence of working conditions and diminished the gap between 'manual' and 'non-manual' employees. Moreover, as we argued earlier, the concept of inevitable individualization and detachment from collective action does not appear to be valid, as the great majority of employees insist on the necessity and importance of trade unions. This argument is further supported by the reappearance or creation of new grass-roots militant unions in sectors of the 'New Production Paradigm', including the financial and banking sectors, information and telecommunications and energy (Rizospastis, 2004; 2008). The most interesting examples of this development include the reactivation of horizontal unions in hotels and restaurants, which, during 2008, accomplished significant successes in working conditions, which included the alteration of short-term contracts to full-time contracts. Another significant development has been the unionization and activation of social care workers who work in local government (see Ioakimidis, 2008). Such a tangible radicalization of service workers further enforces the argument that working-class expansion does not appear only on paper, but also constitutes a complex trend that deserves further exploration. Within this context of a macro-level deterioration of labour conditions in Greece (especially in the third sector), we believe that the discussion concerning labour well-being should be reconnected to the examination of the class nature of employment. Despite the importance of individual demands for labour well-being, this cannot be achieved permanently, unless labour issues are analysed within the political context from which they emerge. As the Greek case indicates, the beautification of the free market's consequences cannot ultimately hide the structural inequalities and conflicts that the system produces. Hence, the discussion of labour well-being needs to be redirected to the fundamental issue of the nature and function of the free market.

References

Allen, J. (1992) 'Post-Industrialism and Post-Fordism', in Hall, Held and McGrew (1992).
BBC (2004) 'Greece First in Economic Growth', http://www.bbc.co.uk/greek/business/story/2004/03/040305_economy.shtml.
Beck, U. (1993) *Risk Society: A New Modernity*, London, Sage.
Bell, D. (1973) *The Coming of Post-Industrial Society*, New York, Basic Books.
Burrows, R and Loader, B. (eds) (1994) 'Towards a Post Fordist Welfare State?', London, Routledge.
Callinicos, A. (1983) 'The "New Middle Class" and Socialists', *International Socialism Journal* 2(20).
Clark, T., Lipset, S. and Rempel, M. (1993) 'The Declining Political Significance of Social Class', *International Sociology* 8, pp. 397–410.
Cohen-Rosenthal, E. and Barton, C. E. (1993) *Mutual Gains: A Guide to Union Management Co-operation*, 2nd edn, Ithaka ,NY, ILR Press.
Dosi, G. et al. (eds) (1988) *Technical Change and Economic Theory*, London, Pinter.
EC (European Commission) (2005) *Working Together for Growth and Jobs. Integrated Guidelines for Growth and Jobs (2005–2008)*, Luxembourg, Office for Official Publication of the European Communities.
ESYE (1998) *Labor Force Survey* (Erevna Ergatikou Dynamikou), Athens, ESYE.
ESYE (2007) *Labor Force Survey* (Erevna Ergatikoou Dynamikou), Athens, ESYE.
Giddens, A. (1990) *Consequences of Modernity*, Cambridge, Polity Press
Goldthorpe, J. H. (2002) 'Globalisation and Social Class', *West European Politics* 25(3), pp. 1–28.
Gorz, A. (1982) *Farewell to the Working Class: An Essay on Post-Industrial Socialism*, London, Pluto Press.
Gorz, A. (2003) 'Labor and Post-Industrial Society', in Hall, Held and McGrew (2003).
Freeman, C. and Perez, C. (1988) 'Structural Crises of Adjustment, Business Cycles and Investment Behaviour', in Dosi et al. (1988).
Frege, C. and Kelly, J. (2003) 'Union Revitalization Strategies in Comparative Perspective', *European Journal of Industrial Relations* 9(1), pp. 7–24.
Fotiadis, A. (2007) 'GREECE: More Poverty Than Meets the Eye', in *IPS News*, http://www.ipsnews.net/news.asp?idnews=40033.
Fukuyama, F. (1992) *The End of History and the Last Man*, New York, Free Press.
Hall, S., Held, D. and McGrew, A. (eds) (1992), *Modernity and its Futures: Understanding Modern Society*, Cambridge, Polity Press.
Hall, S., Held, D. and McGrew, A. (eds) (2003) *Modernity and its Futures: Understanding Modern Society*, Cambridge, Polity Press.
Harvey (2006) *A Short History of Neoliberalism*. New York: Oxford University Press.
INE GSEE (2008) *Greek Economy and Employment* [Labour Institute of General Confederation of Greek Unions, *Ellinikh Oikonomia kai Apasxolhsh*], Athens, GSEE publication.
INE GSEE-ADEDY [Labour Institute GSEE-ADEDY] (2008) *Annual Report 2008: Greek Economy and Employment*, Athens, INE GSEE-ADEDY.
Ioakimidis V. (2008) 'A Critical Examination of the Political Construction of Greek Social Work', unpublished PhD thesis, Liverpool, University of Liverpool.

Lazonick, W. (1990) *Competitive Advantage on the Shop-Floor*, Cambridge, MA, Harvard University Press.
Leiusfrud, H., Bison, I. and Jensberg, H. (2005) 'Social Class in Europe: European Social Survey 2002/3', NTNU Social Research in http://ess.nsd.uib.no/files/2003/ESS1SocialClassReport.pdf, accessed 25/12/2008
Parent-Thirion, A., Macias, E. F., Hurley, J. and Vermeylen, G. (2007) *Fourth European Working Conditions Survey*, Luxembourg, Office for Official Publications of the European Communities.
Rifkin, J. (1995) *The End of Work: The Decline of the Global Labor Force and the Dawn of the Post-Market Era*, New York, G. P. Putnam and Sons.
Rizospastis (2000) 'Profit increase over 3,770%', *Riszospastis* Daily Newspaper, 4 June 2000, p. 23.
Riszospastis (2004) 'Trade union activities annoys Hyat', *Rizospastis* Daily Newspaper, 14 October 2004, p. 15
Riszospastis (2008) 'Trade unionism and the banking sector: The first powerful intervention', *Rizospastis* Daily Newspaper 31 July 2008, p. 14
Schabracq M. and Cooper C. (1997) 'Flexibility of Labor, Well-Being, and Stress', *International Journal of Stress Management* 4(4), pp. 259–74.
Seferiades, S. (1999) 'Low Union Density Amidst a Conflictive Contentious Repertoire: Flexible Labour Markets, Unemployment, and Trade Union Decline in Contemporary Greece', EUI Working Paper SPS No. 99/6, pp. 1–45.

Data Sources

European Social Survey Round 1(2002/3): http://ess.nsd.uib.no/index.jsp?year=2003&country=&module=download.
European Social Survey Round 2 (2004/5): http://ess.nsd.uib.no/index.jsp?year=2005&module=download&country=.

Index

Aboriginal people, 190, 200, 202
Abuse, 23, 25, 34, 40, 41, 64, 78, 168
Academic, 87, 100, 203, 204, 207
Accident, 3, 31, 32, 33, 37, 128
Accountability, 133
Adair, 106, 107, 115
Adults, 15, 28, 41, 42, 88, 94, 100, 101
Afro-Caribbean, 59
Alban-Metcalf, 112, 115
Albrecht and Travaglione, 184
Alimo-Metcalf, 107, 112, 115
Allcorn, 157, 162, 172, 173
Amado and Ambrose, 172
Ambrose and Schminke, 183, 184
American Black Power Movement, 59
Amphetamines, 29, 31
Andrea Adams Trust, 23, 25, 26
Anger, 64, 116, 118, 119, 161
Anthony, 47
Anxiety, 3, 42, 43, 45, 51, 71, 78, 119, 122, 129, 159, 160, 161, 163
Arguments, 145, 191, 206, 209, 218
Aryee and Chay, 183
Asian communities, 59
Asylums, 43, 44, 45
Australia, 31, 41, 128, 129, 130, 132, 133, 134, 138, 139, 192, 202
Authoritarian, 177, 178, 179
Autonomy, 10, 25, 64, 103, 169, 213, 214, 218
Awareness, 12, 14, 36, 51, 52, 90, 93, 146, 148, 163, 171, 172, 189, 196, 201

Baker et al., 4
Barber, 24, 26
Barrier, 56
Bates, 13, 15, 85, 87, 91, 100, 102, 110, 113, 115, 125, 126, 141, 147, 152
Bauman, 103, 115
Beck, 206, 220
Belief system, 57

Belonging, 85, 146, 207
Bereavement, 42, 75, 76, 129, 131, 132, 133, 137, 138, 139, 147
Berridge, 37, 38
Berry et al., 29
Billen, 1054, 115
Binge drinking, 28, 32
Biomedical, 117, 118, 119
Bion, 164, 173
Bipolar affective disorder, 45
Blackburn, 32, 39
Blame, 7, 21, 24, 122, 169
Block and Ghoneim, 31
Body language, 18
Bolton, 24, 26, 124, 126
Bonnett, 58, 69
Bono, 101
Booker, 4, 15, 21, 26
Boundaries, 4, 15, 21, 26
Boyce et al., 50
Bracken, 78, 79, 81, 129
Bradford council, 28
Brah, 51, 59, 69
Breakdown, 17, 42, 62, 72, 177, 192
Brewin, 79, 80, 81
Brimfield-Edwards, 22, 26
Brockner, Tyler and Cooper-Schneider, 184
Browne Jacobson, 34
Buckley, 112, 115
Bunting, 104, 112, 115
Burrows and Loader, 205

Callinicos, 218, 220
Campbell and Cairns, 86
Canada, 31, 41, 132, 138
Canadian Centre for Management Capitalism, 94, 100
Capitalism, 43, 44, 104, 116
Career progression, 65
Career, 4, 41, 62, 63, 64, 65, 90, 106, 143, 167
Chaos, 74, 172

Chen and Lee, 176
Cheung and Chow, 174
Children, 33, 44, 55, 60, 76, 122, 132, 168, 178, 214
China, 174, 175, 176, 177, 181, 182, 184, 186, 187, 188
Chinese University of Hong Kong, 179
Chinese values, 174, 182
CIPD, 34, 37, 38, 39, 86, 100, 120, 123, 127
Citizenship, 113, 185
Clark, Lipset and Rembel, 205
Claxton, 90, 98, 100
Client, 73, 97
Cockerham, 43, 49, 52
Cognitive, 31, 39, 68, 75, 183
Cohen-Charash and Spector, 184
Cohen-Rosenthal and Barton, 205
Collaboration, 25, 197
Collectivism, 176, 211
Collins, 29, 39, 116
Community, 35, 37, 57, 58, 69, 74, 80, 103, 106, 108, 113, 114, 115, 129, 130, 132, 135, 137, 141, 151, 187, 199, 201, 202, 205
Compartmentalize, 75
Compassion, 68, 75, 81, 140
Compliance, 177, 178
Confidentiality, 38
Conflict, 4, 8, 10, 16, 17, 18, 19, 20, 21, 23, 25, 64, 68, 98, 99, 121, 124, 126, 169, 191, 193, 203
Confucian, 175, 176, 177, 178, 182, 183, 184, 187, 188
Consensus, 17
Conway and Briner, 36
Corporate Manslaughter and Corporate Homicide Act 2007, 33
Counselling, 12, 13, 20, 48, 125
Court, 32, 33, 190
Cranwell-Ward and Abbey, 6
Crime, 29, 32, 40, 41, 72, 78
Crisis, 15, 48, 52, 61, 76, 78, 104, 116, 126, 130, 147, 152, 153, 181, 185, 200
Critical thinking, 67, 163, 172
Cropanzano and Prehar, 184
Crouch et al., 31
Cunardi et al., 32

Cunningham et al., 32
Cure, 46, 47
Curran, 31, 39, 42, 52

Dadirri, 200, 201
Dale, 86, 100
Daloz, 95, 100
David Cameron, 85
Dehumanizing, 192, 202
Delusions, 48, 49
Demographic change, 56, 60
Demotivating, 6
Department of Health, 42, 50, 51, 52, 53, 70, 115, 129, 139, 140
Department of Trade and Industry, 22, 26
Dependence, 28, 39, 41, 178
Depression, 3, 42, 45, 51, 121, 129, 130, 161, 181, 187, 195
Diagnosis, 43, 45, 48, 138, 171, 172, 173
Diagnostic Statistical Manual (DSM), 45
Dignity, 10, 24, 25, 26, 51, 75, 124, 126, 191
Disability Discrimination Act 1995, 51
Disability, 50, 51, 52, 132, 198
Discipline, 44, 45, 53, 88, 102, 152, 177, 178, 182
Discrimination, 4, 7, 26, 51, 54, 58, 62, 63, 69, 70, 127, 129, 131, 133, 134, 150
Distress, 5, 15, 23, 48, 51, 52, 120, 121, 195
Diversity, 54, 55, 56, 60, 61, 62, 63, 64, 65, 69, 146, 151, 157
Divorce, 8, 72, 76
Domestic violence, 32
Dominelli, 60, 69
Drink, 21, 28, 30, 31, 35
Duty of care, 33, 37, 38

Eating disorder, 45
Econotech, 130, 139
Educational attainment, 57
Embodiment of distress, 120, 121
Emmons, 150, 152
Empathy, 72, 74, 112, 159, 161, 162, 178, 198

Emperor Wu, 175
Empowerment, 10, 15, 49, 133, 191
Encouragement, 10, 64, 65, 146, 149, 179
Enron, 104, 167
Enterprises, 157, 184, 188, 205
Equality, 14, 25, 54, 55, 58, 60, 62, 63, 65, 67, 70, 127, 131, 133, 134, 135, 137, 140
Erikson, 207
Ethical, 36, 85, 104, 113, 134, 138, 147, 152
Ethnicity, 56, 57, 58, 60, 61, 70, 118
EU Maastricht Treaty, 204
Europe, 28, 43, 52, 100, 128, 130, 131, 138, 221
Eustress, 5
Evidence based, 47, 92, 127
Exercise, 8, 13, 91, 95, 96, 106, 118
Existential, 76, 78, 148
Expertise, 13, 21, 42, 45, 64, 74, 81, 92, 99, 101, 106
Exploit, 10, 122
External facilitator, 20

Facilities, 10
Faith, 115, 141, 147, 149, 150, 151, 199
Family friendly, 157
Farh and Cheng, 177, 178
Faubion, 117, 127
Feedback, 93, 109, 170, 198
Feminist, 61
Fields, Pang and Chiu, 183
Fighting, 18
Financial, 22, 76, 77, 108, 120, 132, 136, 165, 177, 206, 219
Fineman, 75, 119
Fischer and Smith, 184
Flexibility, 129, 133, 135, 137, 203, 207, 213, 221
Flexicurity, 133, 137, 203
France, 44
Freeman and Perez, 205
Free-market, 191, 192, 193, 199, 200, 203, 219
Friends, 28, 33, 47, 48, 131, 180
Frost, 75

Fukuyama, 204
Functionalist, 98
Furnham and Taylor, 122, 123

Gabe et al., 62
Gender, 30, 69, 80, 115, 118, 131, 134, 135, 140, 206, 209, 213
George, 29, 36
Ghodse, 28, 29, 37, 39
Gibbs, 96
Giddens, 203, 220
Glass ceiling, 64
Global terrorism, 57
Goal, 86, 89, 105, 131, 140, 166, 169, 192
Godfrey and Parrott, 33
Goldberg, 56
Golding, 31
Goldthorpe, 208
Goleman, 149
Golightly, 45
Gorz, 203, 205
Gossop, 29, 35
Gould, 86, 89, 92, 172
Government, 49, 50, 54, 108, 129, 130, 132, 136, 139, 141, 143, 166, 177, 185, 191, 192, 193, 219
Grainger and Fitzner, 23
Greece, 203, 204, 206, 207, 208, 209, 218, 219, 220, 221
Greenberg, 183
Grey, 86, 89
Grievance, 67
Grieving, 71, 72, 76, 77, 130, 132, 134, 198, 199, 200
Groups, 5, 18, 29, 30, 57, 58, 62, 67, 70, 99, 103, 105, 113, 147, 158, 172, 208, 209
Gwyther, 142

Haidt, 103
Hall, 60
Handy, 143
Harassment, 4, 7, 14, 16, 17, 19, 22, 23, 24, 25, 26, 62, 63, 110, 121, 124, 131
Harm, 5, 6, 19, 21, 23, 25, 31
Harvey, 205

Hayton, 42
Head et al., 38
Healing, 199, 201, 202
Health and Safety at Work Act 1974, 37
Heir, 44
Hewitt, 45
Heyman, 45
Hierarchy, 33, 60, 106, 142, 176, 177
Holbeche, 110, 113, 142, 143, 148, 149
Holistic, 7, 11, 37, 101, 123, 126, 178, 201
Holt, 86
Home Office, 29
Home pressures, 8
Homosexuality, 48
Hooper and Potter, 4
Hospitals, 73, 105, 112
Hostility, 18, 63, 64
Housing, 42, 57, 111
Howard, 144, 148, 151
Howe, 130, 132, 133, 134, 135, 136, 137, 139
Hui, 176
Human resource, 11, 12, 17, 24, 25, 71, 80, 81, 88, 123, 137, 141, 185, 186, 188, 190, 196
Human rights, 58, 60. 131, 133, 134, 137
Humane, 23, 24

Iacovides et al., 181
Ideology, 175, 189, 190, 191, 192, 193, 195, 199, 201, 202
Ignorance, 62
Inadequacy, 14
Incapacity, 120
Inclusion, 60, 81, 133, 134, 135
Indigenous, 177, 186, 189, 190, 201
Indirect racism, 63
Industrialization, 175
Inequality, 49
Injury, 21, 28, 118, 120, 130
Injustice, 66, 190, 192, 193
Institute of Alcohol Studies, 32
Institutional racism, 54, 62, 63, 64
Integrity, 108, 112, 170, 177, 178

Interaction, 20, 26, 36, 178, 179
International Labour Organization, 40
Interpersonal relationships, 129
Intimidation, 24, 166, 214

Jarrold, 110
Jeffs and Smith, 88
Job satisfaction, 74, 125, 179, 182, 184, 211, 214, 218
Johnson and Rix, 192
Johnson, 122, 126
Jones and Moore, 87
Justice, 14, 58, 70, 80, 81, 133, 136, 183, 184, 185, 186, 187, 192, 201

Karen Horney, 159
Karl Marx, 43
Kellehear, 133
Kelly, 112, 204
Kemp and Neale, 28
Kernberg, 163
King, 113, 144, 177
Knowles, 94
Ko et al., 181
Kolb, 92
Kotter, 107
Krishnakumar and Neck, 144, 145
Kunda, 89
Kundnani, 57
Kutchins and Kirk, 45, 48

Labour Force Survey, 3, 15, 60, 70
Labour market, 35, 135, 136, 138, 203, 205
Language, 18, 57, 60, 61, 66, 98, 118, 130, 200
Law, 34, 119
Lee, Bobko and Chen, 184
Legal issues, 36
Leiulsfrud, Bison and Jensberg, 207
Leontaridi, 203
Lerner et al., 181
Levinson, 170
Lister, 124

MacDonald, 24, 71
Macro level, 4, 219
Mahtani and Leo, 179, 180

Mahtani, 179, 180
Malingering, 117, 118, 120
Mangham, 104
Manic depression, 45
March and Weil, 113
Marginalized, 60, 134, 165
Maslach, Schaufeli and Leiter, 181
Maslow, 103
Masterson, 160
McFarlin and Sweeney, 183, 184
Meaning reconstruction, 73, 82
Mediation, 19, 20
Medical model, 47
Melbourne Water Corporation, 190, 202
Men, 29, 30, 40, 44, 136, 150
Mental disorder, 21, 46, 47, 48, 181
Mental Health Act 2007, 46
Mentor, 74, 94, 95, 96
Metropolitan Black Police Association, 63
Mezirow, 88
Micro-level, 4
Migrants, 57
Miller and Rollnick, 30
Minority groups, 7, 55, 59
Mischler, 36
Misuse of Drugs Act 1971, 33
Mitroff and Denton, 142, 143, 144
Modern proletarianization, 206
Modernization, 174, 176, 181, 188
Modood, 59
Moon, 91
Moore, 29, 30, 34, 87, 101, 105
Moss, 41, 73, 104, 141, 142, 143, 145, 147
Motivation, 23, 94, 103, 118, 146
Mourning, 72
Mullaly, 66
Muslim, 57, 59

National Centre for Social and Economic Monitoring, 129
National Health Service, 100, 105, 110, 111, 113, 115
National Vocational Qualifications, 86, 88
Neglect, 8, 32, 79,80, 123, 192

Neimeyer and Anderson, 73
Neimeyer, 73
Neoliberalism, 57
New Labour, 60, 110
New Production Paradigm, 205, 219
Normality, 39, 44, 77
Norwich Union Healthcare, 32, 37
Nurses, 29, 34, 40, 41 200
Nursing homes, 73

Obama, Barack, 56
Obsessive compulsive disorder, 45, 51
Occupational health, 13, 20, 48, 125, 137, 192, 195
Older people, 111
Open Society Institute, 133
Openness, 95, 189
Operacy, 98, 99
Oppression, 59, 64, 65, 66, 68, 150
Ostrich approach, 11
Ozga, 91

Palliative care, 130, 133, 134, 137
Panic attacks, 45
Panopticon, 44
Parker and Williams, 28, 32
Participation, 30, 53, 132, 133, 138, 183
Partnership, 110
Paternalism, 164
Pathology, 7, 9, 34, 158, 164
Pava, 142, 144
Pearlman and Saakvitne, 78
Performance management, 110
Performance targets, 90
Perkins, 47
Personnel Today 6/20/08, 63
Peters and Austin, 108
Peters and Waterman, 111
Peters, 92
Phobias, 45
Physical injury, 21
Platt, 60
Police, 20, 37, 44, 54, 63, 73, 105, 141
Pollard, 142, 181
Pope Leo XIII, 191
Positive contribution, 58
Positive outcomes, 11, 50, 52, 146

Positive support, 10
Post-Fordism, 205
Post-traumatic anxiety, 78
Post-traumatic stress disorder, 79
Potter, 4, 89
Poverty, 57, 206
Practitioners, 47, 106
Pratt and Tucker, 31, 33
Prayer, 146
Prejudice, 57, 62
Presenteeism, 32, 130, 133
President J. F. Kennedy, 150
Prevention, 12, 13, 20, 21, 33, 192
Prison, 44
Privatization, 90, 191, 211
Problem solving, 13, 19, 91, 92, 94, 98, 125
Procedures, 21, 22, 35, 48, 54, 58, 62, 92, 183, 188, 197, 205,
Productivity, 6, 28, 33, 34, 125, 128, 129, 130, 131, 134, 139, 146, 147158, 178, 180, 181, 182, 187, 193, 205
Professional development, 100, 181
Profitable, 149, 169
Prosecution, 33
Psychological, 7, 8, 11, 21, 22, 31, 32, 39, 56, 66, 78, 79, 82, 116, 118, 119, 120, 158, 164, 173, 184, 186, 188
Psychotic, 19, 21, 45
Public health, 130, 133, 137, 139
Public policy, 134, 135, 139
Public sector, 90, 105, 111, 191, 219
Punitive, 35, 49, 124

Qualitative, 4, 120
Quantitative, 120, 171, 210

Race Relations Act 1976, 54
Race Relations Amendment Act 2000, 54
Ramaekers, 31
Ratcliffe, 61, 70
Recovery, 37, 43, 46, 47, 48, 52, 200
Recruitment, 6, 22, 23, 24, 62, 63, 120, 168
Redfearn, Arthur, 28
Reflective learning, 92, 93, 94, 95, 96, 97, 98, 100

Reforms, 105, 110
Regeneration, 136
Regulations, 33, 37, 169, 183, 184
Rehabilitative programme, 35
Relaxation, 8, 9
Religion, 57, 58, 61, 89, 118, 144
Remedy, 13
Renzenbrink, 132, 139
Repress, 48
Reputation, 24, 74, 120
Resilience, 52, 133
Retention, 6, 22, 23, 120, 128, 129, 168
Retirement, 43, 130, 135, 136
Reynolds and Ablett, 86
Rifkin, 204
Rizospastis, 206, 219
Romeri, 29
Ronningstam, 160, 161, 162, 163
Roth, 93
Routine, 35, 36, 80, 104, 107
Russell, 34
Ryan, 21

Safework programme, 22
Sainsbury et al., 50
Santry, 110
Schabracq and Cooper, 217
Schein, 158, 170
Schizophrenia, 45, 48, 51
Schmid, 134, 135
Schon, 92, 94
School of thought, 175
School, 31, 72, 74, 107, 108, 114, 141, 219
Schultz, 96, 103
Scraton, 80
Sechehaye, 49
Secker and Membrey, 42, 51
Secondary trauma, 21
Seebohm and Secker, 50
Self respect, 46, 94
Senge, 88, 148
Sennett, 104
Service workers, 208, 209, 210, 211, 212, 213, 214, 215, 216, 217, 218, 219
Sheep, 142, 144

Sing Pao Daily News, 181, 187
Single parent, 56
Single, 31
Siu, 176
Sivanandan, 59
Skills, 6, 12, 13, 18, 19, 20, 47, 63, 74, 86, 90, 91, 92, 97, 98, 107, 108, 136, 168, 200, 206
Smith et al., 31
Smith, 28, 29
Smoking, 31, 36, 118
Social Exclusion Unit 2004, 42, 47
Social exclusion, 42, 47
Social inclusion, 60, 134, 135
Social policy, 124, 128, 132, 134
Socially constructed, 61, 87
Sociology, 52, 101, 118, 143, 220
Solidarity, 192, 211
Solutions, 13, 26, 42, 48, 117, 123, 159, 160, 161, 163, 171
Soviet Union, 204
Stability, 75, 77, 129, 176
Status, 30, 59, 65, 75, 77, 115, 118, 176, 218
Stein, 73, 163
Stephen Lawrence, 54, 62, 67
Stephens and Hallas, 4
Stereotyping, 57, 62
Stigma, 37, 38, 50, 51, 129, 199
Substance misuse, 28
Suicide, 189, 190, 191, 193
Summerfield, 79
Sunday Times, 30, 41
Supervision, 13, 20, 48, 87, 95, 113, 200, 204
Support networks, 50, 52
Suppression, 177
Surveillance, 44, 46, 53, 65, 68
Sympathy, 73
Symptom, 43

Taskforce, 70, 129, 132, 133, 140
Teacher, 91, 102, 107, 108, 114
Team development, 20
Teamwork, 13, 23, 25
Technology, 43, 88, 91, 101, 180
Tehrani, 78
Tensions, 10, 18, 19, 20, 21, 120, 124, 125, 136, 158

Terrorism, 57, 71, 72, 80
Thatcher, Margaret, 109
Thompson, 4, 10, 12, 13, 23, 24, 66, 73, 78, 86, 87, 99, 119, 125
Thompson, Ng and Yau, 182
Time management, 6
Trade unions, 204, 209, 210, 211, 219
Training, 9, 12, 13, 19, 20, 22, 35, 38, 50, 51, 52, 53, 79, 81, 87, 88, 94, 96, 98, 99, 104, 125, 134, 192, 196, 204
Transcendental meditation, 146
Transference, 82, 163, 173, 218
Transformational leadership, 107, 112, 150
Trotter, 35
Turner, 118, 148
Tyler and Bies, 184

Undervalued, 30 118
Unemployment, 28, 135, 206, 221
Uniformed organizations, 106
United Nations Millennium Development Goal Number Three, 131
United States, 31, 36, 38, 41, 42, 48, 56, 128, 138, 144, 146

Veazie and Smith, 31
Vicarious traumatization, 78, 82
Victimization, 24
Victorian Work Cover Authority, 131, 140
Vigoda, 123
Voluntary action, 211
Von Glinow and Teagarden, 176
Vulnerable, 8, 73, 76, 111, 113, 134, 138, 161

War on Terror, 57
Weak, 6, 96
Welfare, 8, 53, 101, 220
Wenger and Snyder, 99
Western practices, 174
Westwood and Chan, 177
Wink, 192
Work performance, 35
Work pressures, 5, 6, 8

Working class, 203, 204, 205, 207, 209, 211, 213, 217, 218, 219
Working environment, 5, 9, 10
Work-life balance, 122, 132, 175, 182, 185, 188
Worksafe, 130, 131
World Health Organization, 128, 131
www.statistics.gov.uk, 76

Yang, 176, 178
Yelloly and Henkel, 97
Young, 66

Zero tolerance, 34, 40
Zhou dynasty, 175
Zinkiewicz, 32, 33, 35, 38
Zohar and Marshall, 149